DELHI
PAST AND PRESENT

DELHI
PAST AND PRESENT

By

H. C. FANSHAWE, C.S.I.

GYAN

Published by

Gyan Publishing House
5, Ansari Road
Daryaganj, New Delhi-110002
Phone: 011-47034999, 9811692060
E-mail: books@gyanbooks.com

Distribution Network
gyanbooks.com
India, USA, Canada, UK, Australia, France

ISBN : 978-81-212-6673-4 (PB)
First Published, 1902

2nd Impression 2022

Printed at: Gyan Press, Delhi.

DELHI PAST AND PRESENT
Author: H. C. FANSHAWE

DELHI
PAST AND PRESENT

By H. C. FANSHAWE, C.S.I.

BENGAL CIVIL SERVICE, RETIRED
LATE CHIEF SECRETARY TO THE PUNJAB GOVERNMENT,
AND COMMISSIONER OF THE DELHI DIVISION

WITH MAPS AND ILLUSTRATIONS

1902

TO THE PEOPLE OF THE

OLD UNITED PROVINCE OF THE PUNJAB

I DEDICATE THIS BOOK

IN MEMORY OF THE MANY PLEASANT,

IF LABORIOUS, DAYS SPENT AMONG ALL CLASSES OF THEM

FROM THE NORTH-WEST FRONTIER

TO THE SOUTH-EAST DELHI TERRITORY,

AND WITH EVERY GOOD WISH FOR THEIR

FUTURE WELFARE.

PREFACE

It has long been my wish to attempt to write an adequate Guide to Delhi, containing a brief General History of the city. The commencement of my notes on the subject dates from more than fifteen years back, and I had hoped to complete the material at leisure while in charge of the office of Commissioner of the Delhi Division. Distress and famine, however, in 1899 and 1900, and unforeseen events in the spring of 1901, seriously hampered my efforts in this direction; and the work which I can now offer to the public is consequently not so complete as I could have wished it to be.

The first Guides to Delhi, by Mr Beresford and Mr Cooper, were both sadly incomplete and sadly incorrect; Captain Harcourt's more useful Guide has long been out of print; the little Handbook by Mr H. G. Keene, which must have been appreciated by many hundreds of visitors to the place, must also, I think, have seemed to many of them too slight a work for so large a subject. Mr Fergusson's remarks upon the architecture of Delhi, and especially upon the old Pathan architecture, are of the highest value; and the information contained in Mr Thomas' "Pathan Kings of Delhi," is, with the "Selections from Muhammadan Historians," commenced by Sir Henry Elliott and completed by Professor Dowson, and with the Ain Akbari, edited by Mr Blochman, the most valuable of all works relating to Delhi. But these are not, of course, available to the ordinary traveller, nor, if they were, could they in all cases be used by him with advantage. Mr Keene's works upon the Moghal Rulers and the Decline of their Empire, also contain much interesting information. The contributions to archæology contained in the Reports of the Archæological Survey, issued by Major-General Sir Alexander Cunningham, R.E., are also of great value, but will be found, perhaps, by many to be somewhat dry reading. Mr Carr Stephens' "Archæology of Delhi," which is mainly a translation of the well-known work by Sir Syad Ahmad, the "Asar-i-Sanadid," was unfortunately issued without being either duly corrected or brought up to date. In the present volume, I have attempted to combine with my own knowledge of the subject and of the place all that is of chief interest in the above works, together with a good deal of material taken from elsewhere, and I trust the matter so collected will be found instructive and interesting. I have included historical and archæological information in the text so far as this could be done without overloading it. The brief Chapters VI. and VII. on the History of Delhi and on the architecture of its buildings, will be found to contain supplementary details, and to present a short conspectus of these subjects as a whole, and may perhaps be perused with advantage before the places of interest at Delhi are actually visited.

The Delhi series of the papers of the Mutiny of 1857, published under the editorship of Mr E. Forrest, from which I have taken, and to which I owe, much, has allowed of the preparation of a narrative of these events which, I think, will be found in some respects more correct than any hitherto published. As will be seen from the text, I have left the Narrative of Lieutenant Norman (now Field-Marshal Sir Henry Norman, G.C.B., G.C.M.G.) to speak for itself regarding the Siege and Assault of Delhi; but additional information has been added from Lord Roberts' "Forty-One Years in India"; Captain J. G. Medley's "A Year's Campaigning in India"; Colonel Vibart's "Sepoy Mutiny"; and from other original works, including the "Diary of Jiwan Lal," edited by the late Mr C. Metcalfe, C.S.I., relating to Delhi in 1857, and certain original reports and other papers from the above series have been added to the Narrative. One of the most interesting of these reports is the record of the "Proceedings of the Trial of the ex-King of Delhi."

I would venture to hope that the present volume will afford to visitors to Delhi not only a clear guide to all that is to be seen there, but also an intelligent record of the history of the place in all its various phases, and will help to secure a permanent place in the memories of such and of many others, for the great and gallant feat of arms performed before Delhi in the summer of 1857, by a very small force under the most arduous and trying conditions. I cannot but think that the recollection of this feat, not yet fifty years ago, has become somewhat unduly dimmed; and I would fain hope that, in view of the later heroic exertions of our Army in South Africa, the re-perusal of Lieutenant Norman's Narrative will now permit it to resume its due place in the estimation of the British nation. I have sought to recover, both as regards it and as regards all matters of interest connected with Delhi, various points of interest which were, I believe, being gradually lost—*ὧς μήτε τὰ γενόμενα ἐξ ἀνθρώπων τῷ χρόνῳ ἐξίτηλα γένηται μήτε ἔργα μεγάλα τε καὶ θαυμαστὰ ἀκλεᾶ γένηται.*

In conclusion, I will venture to say a word regarding the protection of the buildings and sites of interest round Delhi. Something, indeed a great deal, has been done in this connection by the British Government—(I have been fortunate enough to be myself the means of this on several occasions in the last fifteen years)—but much more remains to be accomplished, and it may be hoped that under the *régime* of the present Viceroy, Lord Curzon of Kedlestone, and in view of the special interest which is certain to be taken in these memorials of ancientry by the large numbers who will be gathered at Delhi for the Coronation Darbar, this will be achieved. Matters have improved considerably since the Diwan-i-Khas in the Delhi Palace was used as a museum and the Diwan-i-'Am as a canteen—(the beautiful little red sandstone building at the back of the Moti Masjid of the Agra Fort, believed to represent a fragment of the palace of Salim Shah, was still occupied by a canteen when I was last there, less than a year ago); but the Music Gallery and Rang Mahal, and the Mumtaz Mahal are still utilised as military quarters, though they could easily be vacated, and the whole of the remaining Moghal buildings of the palace could then be connected by a suitable garden, which would be as much appreciated by the garrison as by visitors to the fort.

Since I took this work seriously in hand, a recommendation that a worthy monument should be erected to General Nicholson and the brave men who fought with him, has met with general favour, and I trust this will be raised in front of the Kashmir Gate. Another honour which is due to the men who fought and fell at Delhi is the proper conservation of the old military cemetery near Rajpur. It would be out of place to specify in this Preface the various buildings round Delhi which need the immediate attention of Government, and I will only urge, therefore, that money should be spent to make the gardens at the Mausoleum of the Emperor Humayun and of Nawab Safdar Jang at least as pleasing as those of the Khusru Bagh at Allahabad, and the Sikandara Tomb near Agra.

The photographs of Delhi in 1857 are published by permission of Messrs Bourne & Shepherd, the well-known Indian photographers; the other photographs are by Messrs Sultan Ahmad Khan of Delhi. The maps of Delhi and the Kutab, and of the sites of the Siege of 1857 are included, by kind permission of Mr Murray and of the Government of India in the Military Department. The plans of the Dargahs, or Shrines, at Nizam-ud-din and Mahrauli were specially prepared on the spot under my supervision.

The extracts from Bernier's record are taken from the edition published by Messrs Constable, and the references to Tavernier are made to the volume edited by Mr V. Ball.

H. C. FANSHAWE.

LONDON, *September* 1902.

TABLE OF CONTENTS.

CHAPTER I

GENERAL INTRODUCTION, WITH A BRIEF ACCOUNT OF DELHI IN 1902

CHAPTER II

THE CITY OF MODERN DELHI OR SHAHJAHANABAD

PART I.—*The City inside the walls, and, in particular, the Moghal Fort and Palace, and the Jama Masjid.*

CHAPTER VII

LIST OF THE OBJECTS OF ARCHÆOLOGICAL INTEREST IN AND AROUND DELHI, WITH A BRIEF NOTE ON THE GENERAL CHARACTERISTICS OF THEIR ARCHITECTURE

LIST OF ILLUSTRATIONS

LIST OF MAPS AND PLANS

THE EMPEROR SHAH JAHAN. (FOUNDER OF MODERN DELHI.) REIGNED 1628-1658 A.D.

[*To face p.* 1.

DELHI—PAST AND PRESENT

CHAPTER I

GENERAL INTRODUCTION

WITH A BRIEF ACCOUNT OF DELHI IN 1902 A.D.

THE city of Delhi[1] is situated in lat. 28·38 N., and long. 77·13 E., very nearly due north of Cape Comorin, and very nearly in a line with the more ancient cities of Cairo and Canton. It lies in the south-east corner of the Province of the Punjab, to which it was added after 1857, and is placed in a narrow plain between the river Jumna and the northernmost spur of the Aravalli Mountains, which rise here 80 to 110 feet above the country, and finally disappear from the surface of India at Wazirabad, three miles north of Delhi. The north-east trend of the ridge and the outlying rocky spurs under the Salimgarh Fort and the Jama Masjid[2] have secured the plain from erosion by the river; and the natural advantages of the situation, protected by a broad stream on the one side and by a mountain ridge on

[1] The original name was Dilli, of which the Muhammadan version was Dehli. The accepted spelling is Delhi.

[2] Many small outcrops of rock may be seen in the clear space between the Moghal Palace of the Jama Masjid.

the other, must have been apparent from a very early date, and particularly to the various invaders of India, who were compelled to follow the lines of the rivers.

The present Moghal city of Delhi, which should properly be known as Shahjahanabad, is the most northern and most modern of a number of capitals and fortresses constructed on the above plain between 700 and 1550 of the Christian era, from the Lal Kila of Rai Pithora at the Kutab Minar eleven miles south-west of Shahjahanabad to the Jahannuma palace and quarter, built by Firoz Shah Tughlak on the ridge, slightly in advance of the Moghal capital. These old cities from north to south were:—

1. Firozabad of Firoz Shah Tughlak (c. 1360 A.D.), adjoining modern Delhi on the south.

2. Indrapat of Humayun and Sher Shah (on the site of a still older, but doubtless small, city), two miles south of modern Delhi (c. 1540 A.D.).

3. Siri (now Shahpur), four miles south-west of Indrapat (c. 1300 A.D.)

4. Jahanpanah, or the space between Siri and Old Delhi, which became gradually occupied, and was ultimately connected by walls with the cities north and south of it (c. 1330 A.D.).

5. Old Delhi, or the Fort of Rai Pithora, the original Delhi of the Pathan invaders in the twelfth century, and containing the Kutab Minar, three miles to the south-east of Siri (1150-1350 A.D.).

6. Tughlakabad, four miles south-east of Siri, and five miles east of Old Delhi, built by Muhammad Tughlak Shah (c. 1320 A.D.).

Besides these were some unimportant and still more short-lived capitals at Kilokhri, one mile south of the tomb of the Emperor Humayun, and Mubarikabad, a little further south again, of which there are no remains at the present day.

Modern Delhi or Shahjahanabad dates only from 1650 A.D., and is thus just 250 years old. Its title to be termed the Imperial City of India rests upon a very brief pedigree, and Milton was perfectly correct in placing in his list of the great capitals of the East

"Agra and Lahor of Great Mogul,"[1]

as the principal cities of the descendants of Baber.

The royal palace was built first, between 1638 and 1648, then the city walls and the Jama Masjid, and with them various public buildings erected by members of the family of the Emperor Shahjahan, and, no doubt, many palaces of the nobles. The founder can hardly have spent more than five or six

[1] The whole passage deserves to be quoted :—

"City of old or modern fame, the seat
Of mightiest empire, from the destined walls
Of Cambalu, seat of Cathaian Can,
And Samarchand by Oxus, Temir's throne,
To Paquin, of Sinæan kings, and thence
To Agra and Lahor of Great Mogul,
Down to the golden Chersonese, or where
The Persian in Ecbatan sat, or since
In Hispahan. . . ." —*Paradise Lost*, xi. 386.

Milton very possibly based his reference upon the memoir of Mr William Finch, Merchant, who alone of all early travellers in India visited both Agra and Lahore (1609-11 A.D.), and recorded an intelligible account of these places. Regarding the Agra Palace, Finch wrote: "The gates, courts, and buildings

years in his new capital after it was fairly established (see p. 303); and his usurping son and successor, the Emperor Aurangzeb, left it in 1680, after twenty years' residence, and never returned. Till thirty years afterwards the place saw but little of the Moghal Emperor of the day; and from then to the sack of Delhi by Nadir Shah in 1739 only thirty years more intervened. Oudh and Hydrabad were practically independent by that time. Malwa was ceded to the Mahrattas four years later; in less than twenty years Ahmad Shah the Pathan sacked Delhi for a second time; and when, after the defeat of the Mahrattas at Panipat in 1761, he placed Shah Alam II. on the throne, that Emperor was absent from Delhi, and did not come back till ten years later. From his return he reigned for over thirty years wholly as the puppet of various ministers and of the Mahrattas; and the popular distich—

> "Badshah Shah Alam
> Az Delhi ta Palam."
>
> "King Shah Alam" (meaning monarch of the world)
> "From Delhi to Pálam."

(Palam is scarcely ten miles distant from Delhi to the south-west)—overstates the extent of the

belonging to it are too many for a transient description. The mighty castle of Agra is a subject sufficient for an almost entire volume of itself," and regarding Lahore, that the Castle was very fine, that the mohols (mahals, or private apartments), the courts, the galleries, and rooms of state were almost endless; that the king's apartments were overlaid with gold, and that the picture gallery contained portraits of all the descendants of Baber. Of the city of Lahore he added: "This certainly is one of the greatest cities in the East, and perhaps when all is done to it that this king (the Emperor Jahangir) designs, it may be one of the finest."

effective imperial authority of the time rather than understates it. From 1803, or at least 1806, there was no pretence of Delhi being any longer the imperial city of India, though the imperial dignity of the Moghal dynasty was humanely, but unfortunately, kept up in certain respects.

Delhi really ceased to be an imperial city with the death of Muhammad Shah in 1748, or just 100 years after the completion of the Palace by his grandfather's grandfather, and at the most liberal computation its imperial existence cannot be reckoned at more than 150 years; but the glamour of the great cities which bore that name for four and a half centuries previously has clung round and clings round it still.

The present city of Shahjahanabad extends for nearly two and a quarter miles along the right bank of the Jumna from the Water Bastion[1] to the Wellesley Bastion in the south-east corner, nearly one-third of the frontage being occupied by the river wall of the Palace. The northern wall, so famous in the history of 1857, extends just three-quarters of a mile from the Water Bastion to the Shah, commonly known as the Mori, Bastion; the length of the west wall from this Bastion to the Ajmir Gate is one and a quarter mile, and of the south wall to the Wellesley Bastion again almost exactly the same distance, the whole land circuit being thus three and a quarter miles. In the north

[1] The Water Bastion is known popularly as the Badar Rao Burj, and was known officially as the Moira Bastion; the Kashmir Bastion bore the name of the Ali Burj.

wall are situated the famous Kashmir Gate and the Mori or Drain Gate, the latter built by a Mahratta Governor and now removed; in the west wall are the Kabul, Lahore, Farash Khana, and Ajmir Gates —the first two removed—and in the south wall the Turkman and Delhi. The gates on the river side of the city were the Khairati and Rajghat, the Calcutta and Nigambod—both removed; the Kela Gate, and the Badar Rao Gate, now closed.[1]

The city is divided into two somewhat unequal portions by the Chandni Chauk, which, with the Lahore Bazar, runs for just over a mile from the Lahore Gate of the city to the Lahore Gate of the Fort. This gate is very nearly equidistant from it and from the Kashmir, Delhi, and Ajmir Gates.

The east side of the city is opened up by a road from the Kashmir to the Delhi Gate, passing in front of the Old Magazine and the Fort and Palace, and having the Jama Masjid on its right, while the western portion has a main artery in the Lal Kua and Sirkiwalla Bazar, which at the Hauz Kazi divides into three branches leading to the Ajmir Gate on the west, the Turkman Gate on the south, and by the Chauri Bazar to the Jama Masjid on the east. Two well-known streets, Egerton Road, starting from opposite the clock tower, and Billimaran, further west, connect this main western artery with the Chandni Chauk. In the south-east corner of the city, between

[1] The old gates of the city form a serious obstruction to traffic, and several more of them are about to be presently relieved by side openings through the walls. The Kashmir Gate will of course be retained untouched.

the walls and the Feiz Bazar, is the small cantonment of Daryaganj, in which a native regiment is quartered, the rest of the Delhi garrison, consisting of a battery of garrison artillery and two companies from the British regiment stationed at Meerut, being cantoned in the Fort.

Beyond the Lahore Gate and the northern portion of the west wall of the city lies the Sadar Bazar, with the Kadam Sharif and Idgah below it, and the Kishanganj and Paharipur quarters, the western Jumna canal and the south end of the Ridge above it. About half a mile west of the south end of the Ridge are the Sabzi Mandi and Roshanara Gardens, which complete the principal objects of interest on this side.

Beyond the north wall of the city, and approached by the Kashmir and Mori Gates, lies the Civil Station, skirted on its south side by the sites of the siege batteries of 1857, and the cemetery, and by the Nicholson and Kudsia Gardens, and bounded on the west by the Ridge, and on the east by the Jumna. Beyond the Ridge is the Old Cantonment, which was destroyed in May 1857, and was occupied by the force besieging Delhi from June to September in that year. This is bounded to the west by the drainage canal from the Najafgarh Jhil, upon which the military cemetery of 1857 abuts. Across the canal, to the north of the high road, is the Bawari Plain, the site of the Imperial Assemblage of 1877, and of the scene of the greater Coronation Darbar of 1st January 1903. This site lies three and a half miles from the Kashmir Gate of the city, from which all places to the north are measured, and one and a half mile from the Ridge. Two and a half miles further up the Grand Trunk road, from the point where the route to the Bawari Plain diverges, is the site of the battle of Badli ki Serai, fought on 8th June 1857, and west of the field of battle are the scanty remains of the once famous Shalimar Gardens.

Half a mile beyond the Delhi Gate, in the south-east corner of the Daryaganj Cantonment, are the ruins of the citadel of Firozabad, above which the Buddhist Lat, placed there by Firoz Shah, still rises, and a mile further south is the Purana Kila, or Indrapat. Two miles south again is the tomb of the Emperor Humayun, with the group of buildings round it described in Chapter IV., which terminates the objects of interest south of Delhi and adjoining the river.

Turning west from here, the Dargah of the great Shekh Nizam-ud-din-Aulia is first seen on the left, and after two and a half miles, Mubarikpur to the south, and the tombs of the Lodi Kings to the north, are passed; and half a mile further on, the tomb of Nawab Safdar Jang is reached. This is situated six miles from Delhi by the road from the Ajmir Gate, and from it the distance to the Kutab Minar and Old Delhi, to the south, is five miles, the road passing the tomb of Firoz Shah, one and a half mile to the west, and the Begampur Mosque one mile to the east, besides many other buildings described in Chapter V. At the original Delhi are situated the Kutab Minar, the Kuwat-ul-Islam Mosque, the Alai Darwazah, the tomb of Altamsh, and the Dargah, or shrine of Khwaja Kutab-ud-din, all of which are of great interest, besides the walls of the old Fort, and several other structures. Five miles east of the Kutab are the remains of the gigantic fortress and city walls of Tughlakabad and the tomb of Tughlak Shah. Alone of all notable places in the neighbourhood, the field of the battle of Delhi, fought by Lord Lake on 11th September 1803, lies on the left bank of the river, between five and six miles from Delhi.

Such, briefly, is the ground of interest to be covered at Delhi; full details will be found in the following chapters, and a brief itinerary is appended here.

The following general statistics of Delhi will no doubt be of interest :—

Population, according to census of 1901 :—

Total	208,000
Muhammedans . . .	88,000
Hindus	114,000
Christians	2,000
Others	4,000

Average municipal income of the last five years—Rs.435,000.

Average value of rail-borne trade for last five years :—

Exports . .	Rs. 100,51.00,000
Imports . .	68,000,000

Numbers under instruction in recognised educational establishments 3,500

St Stephen's College and Schools, the recently inaugurated Hindu College, and the Municipal High School are the principal educational institutions.

There are four places of Christian worship: St James' Church, at the Kashmir Gate; St Stephen's Church, at the Cambridge Mission; the Baptist Chapel, near the Delhi Bank, at the east end of the Chandni Chauk; the Roman Catholic Church, east of the Mor Sarai.

The Missions are the S.P.G. Mission, specially represented by the Cambridge Mission (ten European and twenty-three lady workers), and the Baptist Mission (four European and eight lady workers). The present Bishop of Lahore, the Rev. Dr Lefroy, was for many years head of the Cambridge Mission. The Hospitals are the Municipal Dufferin Hospital, on the north side of the Jama Masjid—one of the best found institutions of its class in North India; St Stephen's Hospital for Women, in the Chandni Chauk, which has won a great reputation for itself among the people of the city by the devoted labours of its staff; and the Baptist Hospital, on the south side of the open space in front of the Jama Masjid, to which will shortly be added the Empress Victoria Memorial Hospital,[1] on the south-west flank of the Jama Masjid.

Delhi is served by five different railways, viz. the East Indian, the Oudh and Rohilcand, the

[1] No less a sum than Rs. 125,000 has been subscribed for this Hospital by all classes of the Delhi community, under the auspices of a committee of citizens. This remarkable result is largely due to the devoted labours of the members of the committee, and especially of the Rev. Mr S. S. Thomas, of the Baptist Mission; Captain M. Douglas, Deputy Commissioner, and Mrs Douglas, the ladies of Delhi having contributed a very considerable sum. I have confident hopes that many of the great Chiefs of India will mark their presence at the Coronation Darbar by adding to the endowment of the proposed Hospital, and thus enabling it to become a real centre of female medical education in North India, as well as a local medical institution.—H. C. F.

Rajputana - Malwa and Bombay, Barodah, the Southern Panjab, and the North-Western, and is placed in an extremely favourable position for railway and sea-borne trade, being 940 miles distant from Karachi, 950 miles from Calcutta, and 960 miles from Bombay by the shortest route, which is likely to be made shorter than either of the first two by the construction of a chord line from Rewari to Jeypur. This route of the Rajputana-Malwa Railway involves, however, a break of gauge, and the shortest broad-gauge route to Bombay by the Midland Railway is 982 miles. There is direct communication now with the Oudh and Rohilcand Railway system by Moradabad, and with Lahore by the Southern Panjab Railway, which the East India Railway, as far as Amballah, and the North-West Railway, also connect with Delhi. The distance to Lahore by these routes is 310 miles and 348 miles, and to Peshawar 588 miles and 626 miles. Owing to these advantages, there is every reason to think that Delhi will become one of the greatest trade centres in India, and to hope that it will also become a large manufacturing centre. At present the place boasts three spinning-mills, and eleven other mills worked by steam. Several others, started unwisely or managed improperly, have unfortunately failed, and this has tended to discourage manufacturing enterprise for the present. The Municipal Committee has always been distinguished for its enlightenment, and has spent twelve lakhs of rupees on its Water Works, and is about to spend as much on a complete system of city drainage. It consists of seven Hindu, ten Muhammadan, and seven European members, five of the last being district officials. Twelve of the members are elected and twelve nominated; the number of registered electors is 10,000. The place is unusually healthy, and the once well-known Delhi boil or sore has almost entirely disappeared. The heat is very great in May and June, and until the rains fall. The cold weather is much milder than that in the northern portions of the Punjab. Of late years the district has suffered from a series of bad seasons, which further west have resulted in actual famine. As a great centre of vernacular education, Delhi has produced a number of eminent scholars. Among those recently distinguished may be named the Shams-ul-ulemas Maulavis Zakaullah[1] Khan, Khan Bahadur, Nisar Ahmad Khan, Ziauddin Khan, Khan Bahadur, the two last of whom have received the distinction of hon. D.C.L. from the University of Edinburgh. To these may be added the well-known mathematician, Ram Chandar. Among local institutions may be specially mentioned the Hindu College and the Yunani School of Medicine, maintained by the late Hazik-ul-Mulk, Hakim Abdul Majid Khan, and now continued by his brothers. During the last two years the city has had to lament the losses of this distinguished practitioner, of its leading, generous-minded citizen, Rai Bahadur Ram Kishan Das, and of its late Deputy-Commissioner and Commissioner, Mr Robert Clarke, B.C.S., who was closely connected with

[1] This gentleman, who is a well-known Indian historian, has kindly afforded me much information regarding Delhi.

Delhi and its development for a period of nearly ten years, and was greatly beloved by all classes of its citizens.

Delhi is famous for its art wares of gold and silver embroidery, and its jewellers, whose shops will be found on the north side of the Chandni Chauk. Many of the firms have a wide and well-established reputation. Minor art products are ivory miniatures and ivory carvings, but these are no longer of high quality, while the manufacture of the finer blue Delhi pottery has entirely ceased. The shops of photographers will be found for the most part inside the Kashmir Gate, near the Municipal Board School. The exhibition which will be held in connection with the Coronation Darbar will no doubt enable visitors to judge of the art products of all parts of India. The Delhi bazars offer little or nothing, either by way of curiosities or picturesque bits, and are not worth a special visit. The Chandni Chauk is sadly spoilt by the very modern frontages of many of the shops and houses, and it may be hoped that these will be gradually improved. As it stands, the city, apart from the old Imperial and other public buildings, will be found a sad disappointment as the seat of a whilom Eastern capital.

The principal hotel is Maiden's Hotel, well situated in the civil station, close to Ludlow Castle, and excellently managed. Laurie's Hotel is outside the Mori Gate, and another hotel is just inside; and there are usually two or three hotels inside the Kashmir Gate, near St James' Church. The management of most of these frequently changes, and it is not possible, therefore, to say much about them. There are two small rest-houses at the Kutab, and a good breakfast or lunch may be obtained at them; if it is proposed to sleep there, bedding, etc., for the night must be taken from Delhi. Permission to occupy the rest-house in Adham Khan's tomb at the Kutab must be specially obtained from the Deputy-Commissioner of Delhi.

There are a number of banks in Delhi, including a branch bank of the Bank of Bengal and the Bank of Delhi. Most of them are situated off the Chandni Chauk.

The Telegraph and Post-Offices are situated 600 yards inside the Kashmir Gate, the latter in the enclosure of the Old Magazine (p. 18).

A week, or at least five days, may well be devoted to Delhi, many of the sights of which deserve repeated visits. For those who can spend only three days to the place, the following plan of sight-seeing will perhaps be found the most convenient :—

First Day—*Morning.*—Drive through the Kashmir Gate to the Fort and Palace, the Jama Masjid, and the Chandni Chauk (Chapter II. Part I.).

Afternoon.—Drive to further end of Ridge, and from there along it to the south end. Then proceed along the route of the sites of the siege batteries and the breaches, finishing with the spot where General Nicholson was shot and grave where he lies buried (Chapter III. Part I.).

Second Day.—In the morning drive to the Kutab (12 miles), by the direct route of the Ajmir Gate and Safdar Jang's tomb (Chapter V.). Spend the day there—one cannot see well all that is worth seeing in less than some four hours—and return in the evening by the same road, pausing if there is time to see the group of tombs at Khairpur. (By starting at 7.30 A.M., and having a second relay of horses, it is possible to include Tughlakabad in the day's trip; this, however, involves a drive of 35 miles, and five to six hours' sight-seeing).

THIRD DAY—*Morning.*—Visit the Purana Kila, Humayun's tomb, and Nizam-ud-din; if possible also the tomb of Isa Khan, and of Khan Khanan (Chapter IV.).

Afternoon.—Visit the Delhi Palace again, the Kala Masjid, and the tomb and College of Ghazi-ud-din at the Ajmir Gate (Chapter II. Part II.), and anything else that seems of most interest in that Chapter, Part II.

It will be readily understood from this that two days more can be well filled up with a visit to Tughlakabad, and seeing the Begam, Roshanara and Kudsia Gardens, all beautiful in their way, and minor buildings of interest, such as the Fatehpuri Mosque, the Zinat-ul-Masajid Mosque, the pretty little golden mosque to the south of the Delhi Gate of the Fort, the Kudam Sharif, etc., detailed in Chapter II. Part II.

Those who can give only two days to Delhi will perhaps make the best disposition of their time by devoting the first day as above indicated, and the second to (1) the drive in the morning to the Kutab by the Kotila of Firoz Shah, Purana Kila, Humayun's Mausoleum, and Nizam-ud-din—it is hopeless to attempt to see more; and (2) the principal sights of the Kutab in the afternoon, visiting Safdar Jang's tomb on the way back in the evening.

Whenever drives are likely to be prolonged into the

evening, and especially till some time after sunset, between 1st November and 15th March, wraps should always be taken.

A pleasant morning or evening walk may be taken by following the Ridge towards the north to Wazirabad, three and a half miles distant from the Kashmir Gate, where the picturesque shrine of Shah Alam will be found (p. 59). The path along the Ridge gives the finer view, but a better route for walking is through the Old Cantonment north of the Grand Trunk Road. The walks through the Metcalfe Estate and through the old ruined Cantonment are also pretty ones.

CHAPTER II

THE CITY OF MODERN DELHI OR SHAHJAHANABAD

PART I.—THE CITY INSIDE THE WALLS, AND IN PARTICULAR THE MOGHAL FORT AND PALACE, AND THE JAMA MASJID.

APPROACHING the Kashmir Gate from the north, the vistas from the two portions of No. II Siege Battery are crossed, and a full view is obtained of the breach at the Kashmir Bastion, and of the battered face of the Bastion itself. The gate and its neighbourhood are described at pp. 91-93. Proceeding towards the city from the space inside, once occupied by the Main Guard, the road passes through open ground cleared after 1857, with St James' Church on the left hand, the Fakhr-ul-Masajid Mosque and the house of Colonel James Skinner, standing a little back, and St Stephen's College of the Cambridge Mission on the right hand. **St James' Church**, built by Colonel Skinner, C.B., at a cost of Rs.80,000, is in the form of a Greek cross, surmounted by a high dome, which indicates the position of the Kashmir Gate in all views of the city from the Ridge and from the north. The graves of Colonel Skinner and of various members of his family lie to the north side of the church; among these graves is that of Mr William Fraser, Commissioner of Delhi, murdered in 1835, of whom Colonel Skinner was the close friend, and of whom Victor Jacquemont wrote so enthusiastically. In the south-east corner of the churchyard is the grave of Sir T. T. Metcalfe, the builder of Metcalfe House; and near the south-west corner of the church is the old gilded ball and cross, bearing marks of bullets fired at it in 1857. In front of the church is a memorial cross, and inside it are a number of memorial tablets. Opposite St Stephen's College is the boarding-house of the students. On the same side of the road, 600 yards from the Kashmir Gate, is the municipal High School, in a building with high pseudo-classical columns in the front. This was originally the house of the famous Mardan Ali Khan, and was for many years after 1803 occupied by the Resident at the Court of Delhi, and afterwards by the Delhi Government College, given up in 1883. In front of the next large building on the left—well known as the Delhi Dak Bungalow between 1860 and 1885, and now the telegraph office—is the obelisk, inaugurated on 19th April 1902 by the officers of the telegraph department, in memory of the members of their service who fell in the Mutiny. The quarter of the old city on the right hand of the road here was entirely removed after 1860, to make room for the railway premises. Adjoining the telegraph office, and 800 yards from the Kashmir Gate, is the north-west gate of the **Old Magazine**, with a tablet to the memory of its gallant defenders on 11th May 1857, and beyond this again

Gate of the Old Magazine.

[*To face p.* 19.

are the second gate and the south-west tower of the magazine. On the opposite side of the road, in 1857, were the magazine workshops, which were looted before the magazine itself was attacked. The inscription on the tablet over the first gate is as follows:—

ON 11TH MAY 1857,

NINE RESOLUTE ENGLISHMEN,

LT. GEO. DOBREE WILLOUGHBY, BENGAL ARTILLERY,

In Command.

LIEUTENANT WILLIAM RAYNOR.	LIEUTENANT GEO. FORREST.
CONDUCTOR G. WILLIAM SHAW.	CONDUCTOR JOHN BUCKLEY.
CONDUCTOR JOHN SCULLY.	SUB-CONDUCTOR WILLIAM CROW.
SERGEANT BRYAN EDWARDS.	SERGEANT PETER STEWART.

Defended the Magazine of Delhi for more than four hours against large numbers of the rebels and mutineers, until the walls being scaled, and all hope of succour gone, these brave men fired the Magazine. Five of the gallant band perished in the explosion, which at the same time destroyed many of the enemy.

THIS TABLET

MARKING THE FORMER ENTRANCE GATE TO THE MAGAZINE IS PLACED HERE BY THE GOVERNMENT OF INDIA.

A few of the actual buildings of the magazine still exist, and the river wicket by which Willoughby and some of his companions escaped to the Main Guard after the magazine was blown up, will be found in the south-east corner of the enclosure.

Under the south wall of the magazine is the first Christian graveyard in Delhi. The earliest date on any grave is that of 1808 A.D. Among the collection of grave tablets near the memorial cross is one to the memory of a baby girl of Mr, afterwards Sir H. M. Elliott, K.C.B. The road descends from the old magazine under the railway bridge, and rises again to the level of the tail of the Western Jumna canal; in the hollow of depression a broad approach leads on the right past the Mor Sarai, and between the Begam Bagh and Railway Station to the Kabul Gate, and on the left to the site of the old Calcutta Gate and the Jumna bridge, beyond the Salimgarh outwork of the Fort. From the crest of the depression the road to the **Fort and Palace** turns to the left, and in 500 yards reaches the Lahore Gate, which faces the end of Chandni Chauk. On the west side of the canal, and below the level of the aqueduct, by which it is carried to its re-union with the river, are a number of water-mills and several picturesque temples and monasteries. The road by which the Hindus of the city go down to the Jumna waters every morning passes along the foot of the Fort glacis.

The **Lal Kila** of the Emperor Shah Jehan was commenced in 1638 A.D., and was completed some ten years later, when the Emperor himself held Court in the Diwan-i-Khas. The effect of the extremely beautiful walls of the Fort, built of deep red sandstone and rising 110 feet from the ditch below, is sadly spoilt by the glacis which was made in front of them after 1857, and is needlessly obstructed by the trees which have grown up at the foot of this. A number of these have, however, been cut down lately, and a full view can now be obtained of the south end of the west wall, opposite which the Ellenborough tank, known as the Lal Diggi,

Lahore Gate of Fort—View from the Exterior.

[To face p. 20.

existed till 1857. The beauty of the wall can be best judged by walking under it from outside the Lahore Gate to the north-west corner, and from outside the Delhi Gate to the south-east bastion on the river. The evening view of the wall under the level rays of the setting sun is particularly charming, especially as seen from the Jama Masjid.

As designed by the Emperor Shah Jehan, a garden existed in front of the Lahore Gate: it was doubtless ruined when the barbican was built by his successor. In front of this again was a great square, like that which up till 1857 lay between the Fort and Jama Masjid at Agra. Very different now is the scene of approach from what it was in the days when the palace was still a new structure, thus described by Bernier:

Nothing can be conceived much more brilliant than the great square in front of the Fortress at the hours when the Omrahs, Rajas, and Mansabdars repair to the citadel to mount guard, or attend the assembly of the Am-Khas. The Mansabdars flock thither from all parts, well mounted and equipped, and splendidly accompanied by four servants, two behind and two before, to clear the street for their masters. Omrahs and Rajas ride thither, some on horseback, some on majestic elephants; but the greater part are conveyed on the shoulders of six men in rich palankins, leaning upon a thick cushion of brocade, and chewing their betel for the double purpose of sweetening their breath and reddening their lips. On one side of every palankin is seen a servant bearing a spitoon of porcelain or silver; on the other side two more servants fan the luxurious lord, and flap away the flies, or brush off the dust with a peacock's-tail fan; three or four footmen march in front to clear the way, and a chosen number of the best groomed and best mounted horsemen follow in the rear.

Entering the outwork of the Lahore Gate, constructed by the Emperor Aurangzeb over a bridge rebuilt early last century, the Lahore Gate with its splendid side towers and great central arch is found to rise grandly in front. The proportions of the gate are exceedingly noble, and it is in every respect a great advance upon the Hathi Pul Gate of the Emperor Akbar in the Agra Fort. The description by Mr Fergusson of the palace, of the approach from the gate to the inner portions of it, and of those parts, is well known, but may be quoted all the same; some will possibly think that the architectural effect of the approach is rather over-estimated.

The Palace of Delhi, which is situated, like that at Agra, close to the edge of the Jumna, is a nearly regular parallelogram, with the angles slightly canted off, and measures 1600 feet east and west, by 3200 feet north and south, exclusive of the gateways. It is surrounded on all sides by a very noble wall of red sandstone, relieved at intervals by towers surmounted by kiosks. The principal entrance faces the Chandni Chauk, a noble wide street, nearly a mile long, planted with two rows of trees, and with a stream of water running down its centre.[1] Entering within its deeply-recessed portal, you find yourself beneath the vaulted hall, the sides of which are in two storeys, and with an octagonal break in the centre. This hall, which is 375 feet in length over all, has very much the effect of the nave of a gigantic Gothic cathedral, and forms the noblest entrance known to belong to any existing palace. At its inner end this hall opened into a courtyard, 540 feet by 360 feet, from the centre

[1] The stream was covered over many years ago.—H. C. F.

Lahore Gate of Fort—View from Interior.

[*To face p.* 22.

DELHI AND ENVIRONS

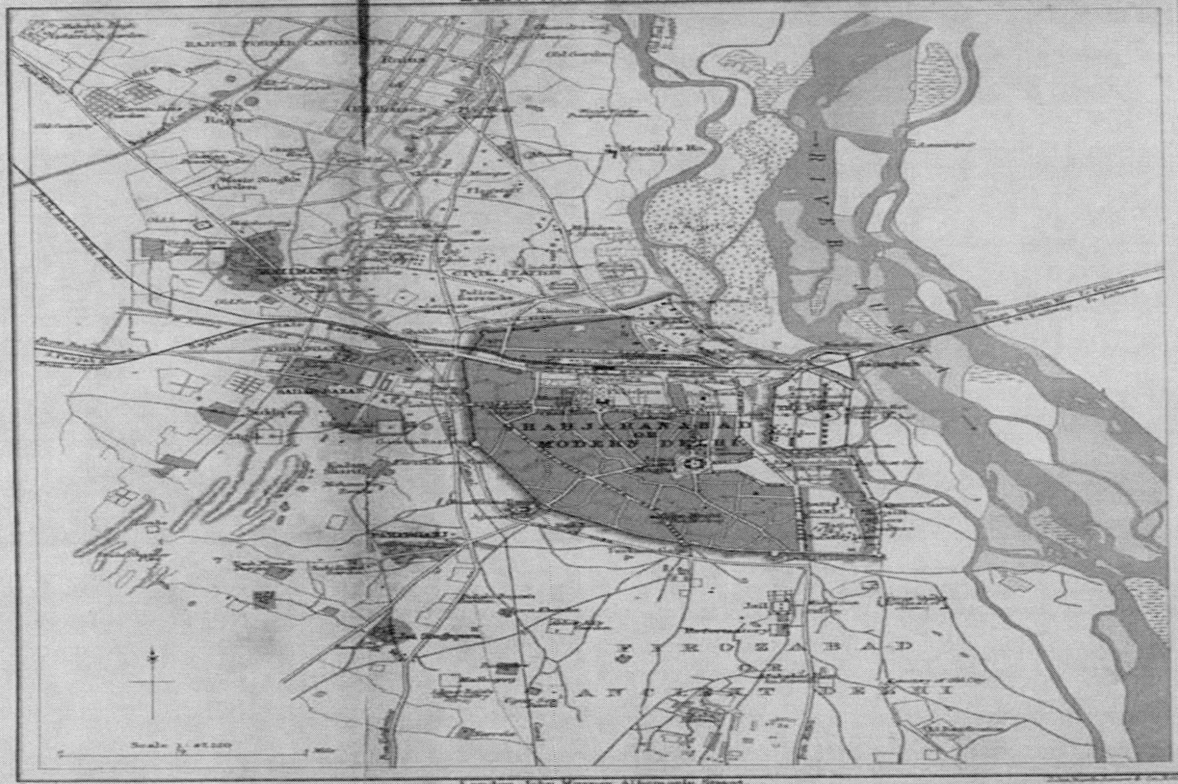

London, John Murray, Albemarle Street.

of which a noble bazar extended right and left, like the hall two storeys in height, but not vaulted. One of these led to the Delhi Gate, the other, which I believe was never quite finished, to the garden. In front, at the entrance, was the Naubat (or Nakkar) Khana [1] (8), or music hall, beneath which the visitors entered the second or great court of the palace, measuring 540 feet north and south, by 420 feet east and west. In the centre of this stood the Diwan-i-'Am (7), or great audience hall of the palace, very similar in design to that at Agra, but more magnificent. Its dimensions are, 180 feet by 160 feet over all. In its centre is a highly ornamental niche, in which, on a platform of marble richly inlaid with precious stones, and directly facing the entrance, once stood the celebrated peacock throne, the most

[1] I have substituted another plan, reduced from an original of double the scale, for that given by Mr Fergusson, which was not altogether correct, and have altered his references to this plan. For instance, the two courts of the Nakkar Khana and Diwan-i-'Am were of the same breadth, and the latter was not wider than the former, as shown on his plan, and I have corrected these and other measurements in the text of the quotation. On the substituted plan the buildings which still exist inside the Palace and Fort are shown in dark shading; all the rest have been removed, many quite unnecessarily, since 1857. Before that time the north side of the Palace, between the King's Garden and the outer wall, had become filled with mean buildings, and the garden of the Commandant at the sides of the vaulted hall, and the Artillery and Magazine quarters to the north of this, had ceased to exist; and all the south side of the Fort was full of debased buildings which were veritable rabbit warrens, occupied by the countless descendants of decayed royalty which clung around the King of Delhi.* It has been the fashion of late years to condemn the utilitarian tendencies of the Indian

* Captain Archer, writing in 1828, says that on issuing from the vaulted hall his party entered "a square, presenting all the miserable and squalid wretchedness of the most common village"—(probably the appearance presented was much inferior to that now presented by the interior of the Begampur Mosque, p. 255), and that after passing "through dirty lanes, and under low ruined arches," they dismounted at the Lal Pardah door.—H. C. F.

gorgeous example of its class that perhaps even the East could ever boast of. Behind this again was a garden court; on its eastern side was the Rang Mahal (5), or painted hall, containing a bath and other apartments.

This range of buildings, extending 1600 feet east and west, divided the palace into two nearly equal halves. In the northern division[1] of it were a series of small courts, surrounded by buildings apparently appropriated to the use of distinguished guests; and in one of them overhanging the river stood the celebrated Diwan-i-Khas (3), or private audience hall, if not the most beautiful, certainly the most highly ornamented of all Shah Jehan's buildings. It is larger, certainly, and far richer in ornament than that at Agra, though hardly so elegant in design; but nothing can exceed the beauty of the inlay of precious

Government for more detailed damage to antiquarian buildings than it is really responsible for, as may be seen by referring to the accounts of the Delhi Palace by Bishop Heber and Colonel Sleeman, and the following notices by Bayard Taylor, written shortly before the Mutiny:—"The vaulted gallery" (leading to inner palace) "must have once been an imposing prelude to the splendours of the palace; but it is now dirty and dilapidated, and the quadrangle into which it ushers the visitor resembles a great barn yard filled with tattered grooms, lean horses, and mangy elephants. The buildings surrounding it were heavy masses of brick and sandstone, rapidly falling into ruin." "Porticoes of marble, spoiled by dust and white-wash, exquisite mosaics, with all the precious stones gouged out, gilded domes glittering over courts filled with filth, and populated with a retinue of beggarly menials." Bishop Heber, who was twice beset by a crowd of beggars during his progress inside the palace, tells the same tale at a date earlier by twenty-five years:—"All was dirty, desolate, and forlorn. Half the flowers and leaves (of the pietra-dura work) had been picked and otherwise defaced, and the doors and windows were in a state of dilapidation." Even the Moti Masjid was neglected and dilapidated, and the throne recess in the Diwan-i-'Am was utterly befouled by birds which had built their nests in it.

[1] The north division was mainly occupied by the royal gardens, as stated below.—H. C. F.

stones with which it was adorned, or the general poetry of the design. It is round the roof[1] of this hall that the famous inscription runs: "If there is a heaven on earth, it is this, it is this," which may safely be rendered into the sober English assertion that no palace now existing in the world possesses an apartment of such singular elegance as this.

Beyond this to the northward were the gardens of the palace, laid out in the usual formal style of the East, but adorned with fountains and little pavilions, and kiosks of white marble, that render these so beautiful and so appropriate to such a climate.

The whole of the area between the central range of buildings to the south, and eastward from the bazar, measuring about 1000 feet each way, was occupied by the haram and private apartments of the palace, covering, consequently, more than twice the area of the Escurial, or, in fact, of any palace in Europe. According to the native plan I possess, which I see no reason for distrusting, it contained three garden courts, and some thirteen or fourteen other courts, arranged some for state, some for convenience; but what they were like we have no means of knowing.[2] Not one vestige of them now remains. Judging from the corresponding parts of the palace at Agra, built by the same monarch, they must have vied with the public apartments in richness and in beauty when originally erected, but having continued to be used as an abode down to the time of the Mutiny, they were probably very much disfigured and debased.[3]

[1] This is a commonly repeated error. The inscription is repeated twice in panels above the two smaller side arches of each end of the hall and below the cornice.—H. C. F.

[2] There were three garden courts on the river front, and three other courts of considerable size between these and the bazar road from the Delhi Gate. The rest were all very small.—H. C. F.

[3] It is probable that the interior of the Delhi Fort was never so fully finished as that of Agra, the Emperor Shah Jehan having been

From the octagonal space in the centre of the vaulted hall, openings lead to north and south, the former conducting to the northern flight of steps up to the rooms above the **Lahore Gate.** These, which are now tenanted by the officers of the Royal Artillery, and are private quarters, were occupied by the Commandant of the Fort Guard, and by the Chaplain, Mr Jennings, in 1857, and in them these persons and three others were murdered on 11th May (p. 99), while the Commissioner, Mr Simon Fraser, was murdered at the foot of the steps, the second of his family to lose his life in the service of his Government at Delhi (p. 18). Above the Lahore Gate flies the British flag, forming the crowning point in every distant view of Delhi.

At the east end of the vaulted hall the court of the **Nakkar** or **Naubat Khana**, or **Music Gallery**, was entered. This court measured 540 feet north and

deposed while his designs were still incomplete, and his successor, the Emperor Aurangzeb, not being interested in buildings of a secular nature, and never having resided at Delhi during the last twenty-five years of his reign, and that the buildings of the south side of the palace bore no relation in cost and magnificence to these in the centre and on the north end of the east face of the palace. We know from Bernier that there were many workshops in the palace ("kar-khanays," according to his spelling), and these would not have been in buildings of marble or red sandstone. The north side, beyond the king's private gardens, was called the Bunyad Mubarik, or Fortunate Foundation, for the reason that the work of the palace was first commenced here, and the Emperor Shah Jehan first entered it from this side. The inner palace, including the courts of the Nakkar Khana and Diwan-i-'Am, was usually called the Kila Mubarik, or Fortunate Fort or Palace, and the innermost portion, including the Diwan-i-Khas and the buildings round it, was entitled the Jalau Khana, or Abode of Splendour.

—H. C. F.

Nakkar Khana, or Music Gallery.

[To face p. 26.

south by 360 feet east and west, and was surrounded by a lofty arcade on all sides: part of the back wall of this exists to the south of the end of the entrance gallery. In the centre of the court was a tank marking the point where the two main roadways of the fort running east from the Lahore Gate and north from the Delhi Gate met. Along the edge of this tank, on the morning of 16th May 1857, were seated and were murdered the Christians who had been captured in the city, and chiefly in Daryaganj, during the five previous days—in number some fifty souls.

At the Nakkar Khana, which was separated from the rest of the court by a stone railing, all persons admitted to the palace, except princes of the royal blood, were required to dismount and proceed to the king's presence on foot. One of the bitterest complaints of the last *roi fainéant* of Delhi was that the mutinied soldiers used to ride through this gate, up to the Hall of Special Audience even, and walked about that hall with their shoes on, things which, he said plaintively, neither Nadir Shah nor Ahmad Shah, nor any British Governor-General (!) had ever done.

The music gallery is a handsome and well-proportioned building, with a fine archway through the centre,[1] and a large open gallery, 100 feet long by 80 feet broad, for the musicians above, but the effect of it is spoilt above by additions in the upper storey, and below by trees, and, on the further side, by menial offices, all of which should be removed. The carving

[1] Dresses of honour, conferred by the Emperor, were placed in the side-rooms, and were carried from there through the assembled crowd to the Darbar Hall.

of flowers on the panels round the bottom of the exterior of the building is unusually good for work of the kind in red sandstone. Bernier, who was in Delhi off and on between 1660 and 1665, writes of the music that it consisted of hautboys and cymbals, and was overpowering when heard near, but that heard far off in his bed—the recollection was perhaps a half-awakened one—the sound was solemn, grand, and melodious. The Nakkar Khana was also known as the Hathia Pul, but certainly not because the Chitor stone elephants stood in front of it, as some have gratuitously supposed, probably because the nobles alighted from their elephants here. In it the Emperors Jehandar Shah and Farukhsiyar were murdered, the latter after having been first blinded.

From the Nakkar Khana was entered the court in front of the **Diwan-i-'Am** or **Hall of Public Audience.** This was deeper than that of the Nakkar, being 420 feet from west to east. Like the latter it was surrounded by an arcade of arched rooms and recesses, but in two storeys. In front of the Diwan-i-'Am building was a space enclosed by a red sandstone rail, ornamented by gilded spikes: this enclosure was called the Gulál Bari, and was allotted to the minor officials and the court attendants, the higher officials and classes only being admitted to the actual Hall, and the ordinary crowd being kept outside the red railing. The Hall measures 100 feet by 60 feet, and is a splendid building: as noted by Bernier, it was once painted, *i.e.* plastered with chunam and laid over with gold: it was sometimes described as the Chihal Situn, or Forty-Pillared—a common Persian designa-

Diwam-i-Am—Exterior.

[To face p. 28.

tion of a Royal Hall. The majesty of the engrailed arches, the fine effect of strength in the four clustered columns at the corners, and the handsome proportions of their bases, are all very striking. In the centre of the back wall of the Hall was the recess for the royal throne, in front of which stood or were seated the principal grandees, separated from the rest of the Hall by a silver rail. Under the recess may still be seen the marble platform from which the Wazir or his secretaries could hand up petitions to the king. In the recess stood the Peacock Throne, of which Tavernier gives so elaborate an account—presumably, it was placed there on special occasions only, and was at other times kept in the Jewel House, situated on the north side of this court. On the back walls of the recess were panels of pietra-dura work, the most elaborate ever executed in India, with representations of birds [1] and foliage, restored since 1857 in lac. The panel with the scene of Orpheus, in the likeness of the designer, Austin of

[1] Col. Sleeman was told these indicated the various limits of the Empire! He says Austin was known as Oastan Isa, and had the title of Nádir-ul-Asár. A sketch of the recess in the South Kensington Museum shows that there were two square panels on either side of the gilded doors in the centre of the back wall, and a rounded head to the wall above these. All five spaces were enclosed by a narrow border of small reliefs of birds on a dark ground, and the interior of the panels was relieved by similar inlaid designs on larger cross-shaped frames, between which were painted representations of birds on the white marble wall. The relief of Orpheus was at the top of all, and touched the apex of the rounded head; it was smaller than the frames of the bird reliefs, and much too small to be a marked feature in the scheme of decoration. It is a very rough piece of work, the lapis lazuli and cornelian of the robes of the Italo-Thracian being extremely coarse in execution.

Bordeaux, charming the beasts, which was removed with the others in 1857, is now with some of them in the Indian Section of the South Kensington Exhibition, and might well be restored with them to its original place. Of the splendour of court displays in the great Hall of Audience, we may judge from the following account by Bernier, written in July 1663, five years after the deposition of the Emperor Shah Jehan.

The King appeared, seated upon his throne at the end of the great Hall, in the most magnificent attire. His vest was of white and delicately-flowered satin, with a silk and gold embroidery of the finest texture. His turban of gold cloth had an aigrette, whose base was composed of diamonds of an extraordinary size and value, besides an oriental topaz, which may be pronounced unparalleled, exhibiting a lustre like the sun. A necklace of immense pearls suspended from his neck reached to the stomach. (Bernier then describes the Peacock Throne).

At the foot of the throne were assembled all the omrahs in splendid apparel, upon a platform surrounded by a silver railing and covered by a spacious canopy of brocade, with deep fringes of gold. The pillars of the hall were hung with brocades of a gold ground, and flowered satin canopies were raised over the whole expanse of the extensive apartment, fastened with red silken cords, from which were suspended large tassels of silk and gold. The floor was covered entirely with carpets of the richest silk, of immense length and breadth. A tent was pitched outside, larger than the hall to which it joined by the top.[1] It could cover half the court, and was completely enclosed by a great balustrade covered with plates of silver. Its supporters were pillars

[1] The upper rings on the front of the hall were used to join these tent canopies to it.

Diwan-i-Am—Interior.

[*To face p.* 31.

overlaid with silver, three of which were as thick and as high as the masts of a barque, the others smaller. The outside of this magnificent tent was red, and the inside lined with elegant Masulipatam chintzes, figured expressly for that very purpose, with flowers so natural, and colours so vivid, that the tent seemed to be encompassed into fine parterres. As to the arcade galleries round the court, every omrah had received orders to decorate one of them at his own expense, and there appeared a spirit of emulation who should best acquit himself to the monarch's satisfaction. Consequently, all the arcades and galleries were covered from top to bottom with brocade, and the pavement with rich carpets.

Truly a scene of Oriental display and splendour, and worthy of the "Arabian Nights." With it may be compared the description of the court of the Palace of Artaxerxes in the Book of Esther—

Where were white and green and blue hangings, fastened with cords of fine linen and purple to silver rings and pillars of marble; the beds were of gold and silver upon a pavement of red and blue and black and white marble.

Of the **Peacock Throne**, Bernier writes only that it was supported by six feet of solid gold—(Tavernier says four, and is no doubt right)—sprinkled over with rubies, emeralds and diamonds; that it consisted of an aigrette of diamonds and other jewels, valued at four and a half millions of pounds, and that the construction and workmanship of it were not equal to the materials, though *two* peacocks, covered with jewels and pearls, were well conceived and executed. Tavernier, the professional jeweller and gentleman, who saw Delhi two years later (in 1665), describes the throne as of the shape of a bed, six feet by four feet, supported by four golden feet, twenty to twenty-five inches high, from the bars above which rose twelve columns to support the canopy: the bars were decorated with crosses of rubies and emeralds, and also with diamonds and pearls. Three steps led up to one of the longer sides of the throne, on which were three golden cushions; round it were suspended a mace, a shield, a bow and a quiver of arrows. In all, there were 108 large rubies on the throne, and 116 emeralds, but many of the latter had flaws. The twelve columns supporting the canopy were decorated with rows of splendid pearls, and Tavernier considered these to be the most valuable part of the throne. The inside of the canopy was covered with diamonds and pearls, and had a fringe of pearls all round it; and on the four-sided dome stood a peacock with large bouquets of gold inlaid with precious stones on either side of it. The peacock's tail was "made of sapphires and other coloured stones, the body being of gold inlaid with precious stones, having a large ruby in front of the breast, from whence hangs a pear-shaped pearl of fifty-six carats or thereabouts, and of a somewhat yellow water." On the front side of the canopy was a jewel, consisting of a diamond from eighty to ninety[1] carats weight, with rubies and emeralds round it. Placed in front of the throne at the sides were two umbrellas of red

[1] The Koh-i-nur now weighs 106 carats English: when received in 1849 it weighed 186 carats; when Tavernier saw it, it weighed 268 carats; and when found it is said to have weighed 756 carats.

Royal Buildings on east wall of Fort above the Zer Jharokha. [To face p. 33]

velvet, embroidered and fringed with pearls, with sticks seven to eight feet high, covered with diamonds, rubies and pearls. This throne was carried off by the Persian invader, Nadir Shah, in 1739. During the nineteenth century it was rumoured that it still existed in the Treasure House of the Shah of Persia; but Lord Curzon, who was allowed a unique opportunity of examining the thrones there, is satisfied that nothing now exists of the famous Delhi throne, except perhaps some portions worked up in a modern Persian throne ("Persia," vol. i. pp. 320-22), and no one is likely to differ from this conclusion. The present throne is, moreover, certainly that which Morier saw early in the century, more than half the distance back in time to the date of the removal of the Peacock Throne from Delhi.

In the arcade to the north side of the Diwan-i-'Am was a gateway leading to a small court, from which another gate, called the Lal Pardah, or Red Curtain, gave admission to the **Jalau Khana**, or **Abode of Splendour**, in front of the Diwan-i-Khas, or Hall of Private Audience. At this gate was stationed the king's body-guard from 1803 to 1857. In the centre of the innermost court, and on the edge of the wall rising from the river-bed, here known as the Zer Jharokha, or Beneath the Windows[1] stood the Diwan-i-Khas, with the Royal Bath and Moti Masjid,

[1] Regarding the Zer Jharokha (see note on p. 96) and the ceremony of "darshan," or the king's showing himself to the people, an annalist of the reign of the Emperor Aurangzeb writes as follows:—"In the reigns of former kings, and up to this year (1668 A.D.), the jharokha-i-darshan had been a regular institution. Although the king might be suffering from bodily indisposition, he went to the

or Pearl Mosque, added afterwards, on the north side, and the king's private apartments on the south side. From these approaches led to the Rang Mahal and the Zenana courts south of it on the wall, while the buildings on the north side were enclosed by the Hyat Bakhsh Garden. The dimensions of the court in front of the **Diwan-i-Khas** was 190 feet by 160 feet (east and west), the Hall of Private Audience itself measuring 90 feet by 67 feet. In front of it was a marble pavement, and at the sides low marble screens separated off the other buildings, as in the case of the Khas Mahal in the Agra Fort. Why these and the fountain in front of the Diwan-i-Khas, which fell over niches containing lighted lamps, and the arcades of the court should have been removed after 1857, is inconceivable, as they could not possibly have been objectionable on sanitary grounds, and the area which they covered was not needed for any military purpose. The two pavilions at either side of the Diwan-i-Khas, with roofs of curved Bengal

jharokha once or twice a day at stated times, and put his head out of the window to show he was safe. This window at Agra and Delhi was constructed on the side looking towards the Jumna. . . . Many Hindus were known by the name of darshanis, for until they had seen the person of the king at the window, they would not put a morsel of food in their mouths." The practice was abandoned by Aurangzeb, as savouring of idolatry. It was the failure of Shah Jahan to appear at the lattice during his illness in 1657, which led to the rumours of his death, and the determination of his younger sons to contest the empire. Coryat recorded of the custom which he saw practised in Agra : " The king presenteth himself thrice a day without fail to his nobles. He standeth aloft alone by himself and looketh upon them from a window that hath an embroidered sumptuous coverture, supported with two silver pilasters to yield shadow unto him."

Diwan-i-Khas, Exterior.

[To face p. 34.

Diwan-i-Khas—Interior.

[*To face p.* 35.

pattern similar to those flanking the Khas Mahal, were removed apparently before 1857, as they do not appear in the photographs of that year of the river-side of the palace. The Khas Mahal in the Anguri Bagh, or Vine Court, of the palace at Agra, was the model of the Diwan-i-Khas of Delhi, rather than the Diwan-i-Khas of the former place. Like the Diwan-i-'Am, the hall of the Diwan-i-Khas stands up finely on a raised plinth, a portion of which, however, is now buried in the ground. The flower bed in front of it, and all the bushes in that, should be removed, to allow of its being properly seen. The most beautiful views of it are perhaps obtained from the north-west corner and from the south side in front of the Khwabgah. In spite of the somewhat inferior quality of the white marble, of which it is built, it is a strikingly beautiful structure. The arrangement of the arches on the shorter sides of the Hall is particularly happy, and with the exception of the Moti Masjid, at Agra, in no Moghal building is an effect of elegance and beauty so simply produced. The interior, with its silver ceiling of flowered patterns removed by the Mahrattas, and its decorations of gold and inlay work, was, no doubt, once a dream of beauty, which, even now, it is possible to realise, in spite of the badly restored floor, disfigured piers, and tawdry roof. It is much to be desired that a single pier should be fully restored—and when restored, be fully protected from modern Vandals—with gold decoration and inlay of precious stones, to enable the visitor to gain a complete idea of the whole: it would probably be best to make a new ceiling of white marble, according to the analogy of the Diwan-i-Khas at Agra, any restoration of the original silver roof being out of the question. The stream passing from the Rang Mahal to the Baths ran under the centre of the Hall. The famous inscription which runs: "Agar Fardus ba rue zamin ast, Hamin ast wa hamin ast wa hamin ast" ("If a Paradise be on the face of the earth, it is this, it is this, it is this"), is given twice in the panels over the narrow arches at the ends of the middle Hall, beginning from the east on the north side, and from the west on the south side; many judges will perhaps be disposed to reckon the writing as but an indifferent specimen of Oriental caligraphy. At the back of the Hall is a marble platform seat, used as a throne by the later powerless Emperors of Delhi. The marble lattice frames in the east side of the Hall are heavy and ugly, and are probably of late date, and the effect of this side would be much improved by substituting grilles of better work for these: marks of the bombardment of the fort by the Rohillas may still be seen here. Whether the designer and builder of the Hall ever saw it in its complete glory may be doubted, but ever since the time of the Emperor Shah Jahan it formed the very arcana of the Moghal Empire, and in the later days of it contained the Peacock Throne. Here Nadir Shah and Ahmad Shah were received by their unhappy and unwilling hosts; here the Jats and Mahrattas and Rohillas set an example for the mutineers of 1857 of disregard of everything due to royalty; here Ghulam Kadir, the Rohilla, blinded the Emperor Shah Alam;

Interior of Royal Apartments of Palace. [To face p. 36.

and here, in 1803, the latter received his rescuer, Lord Lake, and conferred high-sounding titles upon him. Here, in May 1857, the mutinous soldiers declared Bahadur Shah king *de facto*; here, in September of that year, the Queen's health was proposed by Colonel Jones of the 60th Rifles, upon the capture of the palace, which, as a mark of special honour, was placed under a guard of the Rifles and the Sirmur Battalion of Goorkhas; here the Thanksgiving Service for the capture of Delhi was held on Sunday, 29th September; and here the trial of the ex-King, Bahadur Shah, took place between 27th January and 9th March 1858. And possibly few more brilliant displays were ever seen in it, even while the Moghal power was at its zenith, than the ball given by the Army at Delhi to his present Majesty, when, as Prince of Wales, he visited Delhi in January 1876, a year before the assumption of the Imperial title of India by the late Queen Empress.

Crossing a small open space to the south, the **King's Private Apartments**, known as the Khwabgah, or Sleeping-Room, the Tasbih Khanah, or Private Chapel, and the Baithak, or Sitting-Room, are reached. It was from the edge of this that Captain Douglas addressed the mutineers of the 3rd Light Cavalry in the river-bed, on the morning of 11th May 1857. The marble water-channel from the Rång Mahal passes under the centre of these rooms also, and in the arches above it are pierced marble grilles, with luminous marble or alabaster heads; that on the north side bearing a representation of the Mizan-i-Adal, or Scales of Justice, between the moon and stars under an Oriental sun on the inner side; the inscriptions on the walls of the centre room date from the time of Shah Jahan, and are considered to be extremely beautiful. The decoration of the walls of all three rooms is noticeable—that in the west room is particularly fine. In the recesses in the walls were placed no doubt china and vases of flowers, as Bernier notes was done in the houses of the nobles of the court. On the south side of these rooms, towards the Rang Mahal, is a verandah with beautiful tapering columns; and on the river-side of them is a projecting room, known as the Musamman Burj, or Octagonal Tower,[1] corresponding with that in the Agra Fort, but without the delicate and beautiful inlay work of it. In front of the tower is a balcony, with an inscription added in the beginning of last century. Under these rooms and the balcony a flight of steps leads to a postern gate, called the Khizri Gate, opening on the river-bed. It was this gate which Captain Douglas desired might be thrown open on the morning of 11th May 1857, in order that he might go down and speak with the mutineers.

On the north side of the Diwan-i-Khas, across an open space similar to that on the south side, are the **Royal Baths**, consisting of three chambers, once surmounted by three marble domes, with streams and fountains of water, and tanks and baths; from these the whole of the Diwan-i-Khas buildings were sometimes termed the Ghusal Khana, as by Bernier. The passage in the centre probably divided off the

[1] It was also known as the Tilla Burj, from its gilded cupola.

Interior of Royal Baths.

[To face p. 38.

baths for the women and men. The marble inlaid floor of the water-channels of the middle chamber, and the inlay work on the walls of several of the chambers, are specially worthy of notice; the coloured ceilings have been ruined by repeated coats of utilitarian white-wash. The general resemblance between the arrangements of these baths and of those at Pompeii is very striking. Separated from the baths by a narrow strip on the west side, is the **Moti Masjid**, or Private Mosque of the court, added to his father's buildings by the Emperor Aurangzeb in 1659. In simple beauty it is far inferior to the Nagina Mosque, built with the same object in the Agra Palace about 1640, and betrays weakness in the use of meaningless ornament: the rounded tapering shafts are a common feature in the latest buildings of the Moghal period. In the north wall is a covered way, by which the royal ladies could once reach the mosque. The bronze door of the gateway is a handsome piece of work, and looks as if it might be the handicraft of some Italian artificer. The court of the mosque measures 40 feet by 35 feet. The building is said to have cost Rs. 160,000.

On leaving the buildings of the enclosure of the Abode of Glory a brief visit may be paid to a small marble pavilion irregularly placed on the river wall to the north, to the large and fine marble pavilion by the Shah Burj, and the two others called the Bhadon (north side), and the Sawan (south side), which once decorated the Hyat Bakhsh (Life Giving) garden. This garden, which also contained a menagerie, and the Mihtab (moon) Bagh, lying west of it, were the private gardens of the king. The second pavilion stood at the north-east angle of the garden, under the Shah Burj, and the last two in the centre of the two long sides of the garden. They were once decorated with fountains in the centre, and cascades in the front walls, but these were removed after 1857. A pretty stone baoli outside the west end of the Mihtab garden, and just west of the main road from the Delhi Gate, is the only other structure on this side of the palace left intact.

Special permission (apply to the Station Staff Officer) is needed for a visit to the **Salimgarh Fort**, on the north side of the Lal Kila, formerly approached by a bridge said to have been built by the Emperor Jahangir—his only work in Delhi, if it is his, but more likely the work of Farid Khan, who held Salimgarh in Jagir (p. 227). This graceful bridge, noticed by Mr Fergusson, exists no longer now, but the railway bridge has been built upon the lines of it. The fort, which was built by Salim Shah, son of the Emperor Sher Shah, in 1546 A.D., as a bulwark against the return of the ex-Emperor Humayun, and which reminds one of the walls of the Purana Kila, has no object of interest in it (indeed, the only old structure remaining in it is a heavy mosque near the gate in the north wall above the road leading to the railway bridge across the Jumna), but affords a fine view of the river and of the west side of the Moghal palace. In later Moghal times the fort was used chiefly for the purposes of a prison, and in it the Emperor Aurangzeb confined his too-confiding brother, Murad Bakhsh, entrapped at Muttra, before sending him to Gwalior and his death. Ghulam Kadir fled through the fort when he made his escape from Delhi in 1788, and went to his well-merited fate; and the mutineers are said, but incorrectly said, to have first entered the palace by it on 11th May 1857.

On the south of the Jalau Khana enclosure is the **Rang Mahal**, formerly one of the principal buildings of the Royal Zananah, and now used as the mess-house of the officers stationed in the fort. Once it was an extremely beautiful palace, famous for the coloured decorations from which it was named. It is quite possible that some of these might still be recovered, and it is highly desirable that this building should be added to the protected group round the Diwan-i-Khas. In front of it formerly stood the large marble bath now placed in the Queen's Gardens in the city. A little further south, also on the wall of the fort, and the sole remaining structure on this side, is the Mumtaz Mahal, a hall with five arches on each face. In the south-east corner of the fort is a Water Gate, with a picturesque descent to it; the effect from the bottom of a blue dome of sky over bright red sandstone walls, forming as it were a well, is extremely beautiful.

From this point the road running under the south wall of the fort may be followed to the **Delhi Gate**, so called from its facing Old Delhi. This gate is a less striking structure than the principal, or Lahore Gate, but, like the latter, has a barbican. On the west side of the main road leading northwards through the palace from the Delhi Gate were the rooms in which the ex-King Bahadur Shah was confined after his capture by Major Hodson at Humayun's tomb. Colonel Ommaney, C.S.I., late Commissioner of the Peshawar Division, who, as Lieutenant Ommaney, in 1857, was in charge of the king, and ultimately escorted him to his place of exile at Rangoon, describes the final surroundings of the last Emperor of Delhi in the glorious palace of his ancestors, as follows:—

The house was on the west side of the street leading from the Delhi Gate. The ground floor on the street side had been used for shops, so that the house was well above the street. It consisted of three rooms, with a courtyard on the north and south sides. There was a European sentry posted in each courtyard, and one native sentry on the garden side to the west below, and one in the street. The plan of the house thus admitted of its being effectually protected by four sentries, and being so near the Delhi Gate the guard there could assist the guard over the king if necessary. The ex-king was about eighty-five years old, and must have been a striking man in his prime; his face was of an aristocratic type, with marked features, especially the nose. He must have been a powerful man too, as the muscles of his arms hung long and flabby in his old age. He had a pleasant expression, and a sense of humour. . . . . I should say he was too old to have initiated or taken any active part in he horrors of these days, and was the tool of the bolder and more truculent spirits, male and female, about him.

The rebel chiefs, who were tried for their lives and hung after September 1857, were confined in quarters under the Fort Wall to the west of the

Delhi Gate. Outside the gate originally stood the Chitor stone elephants[1] brought from Agra, and from it two principal streets, the Feiz Bazar and the Khas Bazar, led to the Delhi Gate of the city and the Jama Masjid.

Not far from the front of the Fort Gate is the elegant **Sonahri Mosque** of Javed Khan, built in 1751. It is constructed of fawn-coloured sandstone, like the tomb of Safdar Jang, which is of the same date. The builder was the confidential adviser of the Kudsia Begam, the mother of Ahmad Shah, and was murdered when the king, together with his mother, was deposed and blinded. The inscription on the mosque calls it the mosque of Bethlehem. Between it and the Fort Gate stood the large Akbarabadi mosque, constructed with the Feiz Bazar by the Akbarabadi Begam, wife of the Emperor Shah Jahan. This mosque, with all the buildings on the south and west sides of the palace, was removed after 1857: in style it seems to have resembled the Fatehpur mosque.

[1] There cannot be any doubt about this. Bernier, who must have passed them hundreds of times, says the elephants stood in front of the Palace Gate which led to the street through which the canal flowed, and this road, with the canal running down to our day, was that from the Delhi Gate. He also says the *other* gate led to a street or bazar with a divan with shops on both sides, and with an *arched* roof, in which round apertures admitted air and light, and this, we know, was the Lahore Gate. The suggestions that the elephants stood outside before the Lahore Gate or in front of the Hathia Pul are altogether baseless. They could never, however, have stood on the platforms in front of the upper gate of the Agra Fort, as the bulk of the body of the elephant, as restored at least, is much too great to have allowed this. The remains of the elephants were found inside the palace on the east side of the road leading to the Delhi Gate.

From near the Sonahri mosque a road affording beautiful views of the building leads west to the Jama Masjid, named, but practically never known as, the Masjid Jahannuma, built in 1648-50. The Khas Bazar, which was the original approach to it from the fort, had a ten-sided "chauk" in the middle, corresponding to the octagonal space in front of the Begam Serai of the Chandni Chauk. The Jama Masjid should be visited with the morning sun shining on it, and, if possible, under the full moon, which gives a lovely softness to the facade and domes: it is specially beautiful when it can be seen of a morning with a bank of dark clouds behind it. Mr Fergusson writes of it as follows:—

The Jama Masjid at Delhi is not unlike the Moti Masjid of Agra in plan, though built on a very much larger scale and adorned with two noble minarets, which are wanting in the Agra example; while from the somewhat capricious admixture of red sandstone with white marble, it is far from possessing the same elegance and purity of effect. It is, however, one of the few mosques, either in India or elsewhere, hat is designed to produce a pleasing effect externally. . . .[1] It is raised on a lofty basement, and its three gateways, combined with the four angle towers and the frontispiece and domes of the mosque itself, make up a design where all the parts are pleasingly subordinated to one another, but at the same time produce a whole of great variety and elegance. Its principal gateway cannot be compared with that at Fatehpur Sikri; but it is a noble portal, and from

[1] The external effect has been unconsciously enhanced by the clearances of 1857. The lofty basement is built round an outcrop of Aravalli rock, as the Mosque of Omar is built over the so-called rock of Abraham in Jerusalem.—H. C. F.

Jama Masjid—Distant View.

[To face p. 44.

its smaller dimensions more in harmony with the objects by which it is surrounded.

It is not a little singular, looking at the magnificent mosque which Akbar built in his palace at Fatehpur Sikri, and the Moti Masjid, with which Shah Jahan adorned the palace at Agra, that he should have provided no place of worship in his palace at Delhi. The little Moti Masjid that is now found there was added by Aurangzeb, and though pretty enough in itself, is very small, only sixty feet square over all, and utterly unworthy of such a palace. There is no place of prayer within the palace walls, of the time of Shah Jahan, nor, apparently, any intention of providing one. The Jama Masjid was so near, and so apparently part of the same design, that it seems to have been considered sufficient to supply this apparently anomalous deficiency.[1]

It is interesting to read in continuation of this the opinion of one who had no trained architectural eye, but had all the instincts of an artist, Dr François Bernier.

I grant that this building is not constructed according to those rules of architecture which we seem to think ought to be implicitly followed; yet I can perceive no fault that offends the taste; every part appears well contrived, properly executed, and correctly proportioned. . . . With the exception of the three great domes and the numerous turrets which are all of white marble, the mosque is of red colour, as if built with large slabs of red marble.

Tavernier has left us a description of how the

[1] The Moti Masjid of the Agra Fort was constructed last of all the buildings there, and was finished *after* the Jama Masjid of Delhi, its date being 1647-54. The Jama Masjid of Delhi was built two years after the palace was completed. It is said to have cost ten lakhs of rupees.—H. C. F.

Emperor Aurangzeb used to proceed to the mosque on Fridays, in a palanquin, with one son mounted on horseback at his side, and all the nobles of the court on foot. Four elephants with standards and four with howdahs headed the procession, and a bodyguard of 500–600 pikemen and 300–400 matchlock men accompanied it. If the king rode on horseback the nobles again walked on foot, but if he went on an elephant they accompanied him on horses. The following prayer (Khutba) for the king and his people offered at public worship will probably be read with interest :—

O Lord! Do thou grant honour to the faith of Islam and to the professors of that faith through the perpetual power and majesty of thy Slave the Sultan, the son of the Sultan, the Emperor (Khâkán), the son of the Emperor, the Ruler of the two Continents, and the Master of the two Seas, the Ghâzi (the conqueror), the Mujáhid (the warrior in the cause of God), the Emperor Abul Muzaffar Shahabuddin Muhammad Sháh Jahán Ghâzi. (May God perpetuate his dominions and empire.) O Lord! defend him and his armies: Be thou his Guardian, his Helper and his Defender. Give his sword the power to slay the rebellious and the wicked. O Lord who directest the affairs of this world and of the world to come, destroy the infidels and the innovators and the idolaters. O Lord give peace and rest to all cities of the Musalmans, and appoint protection, safety and health for us and for thy servants, the pilgrims, the ghâzis, and all Musalmans travelling by sea or land.

Three flights of steps and three doorways lead to the interior, the steps and the gate on the eastern side being extremely fine; the great doors of this

Jama Masjid—Near View.

[*To face p. 46.*

gate were never opened in old times except for the king, and are opened now only for Royalty, for the Viceroy, and for the Lieutenant-Governor of the Punjab. The exterior of the building is built wholly of red sandstone, and the open arcades present a very beautiful appearance above the high red walls of the basement. The interior courtyard measures nearly 400 feet each way, and the roofed western portion, 260 feet by 90 feet.[1] The effect of the arcades and the views seen through them from inside the court are both unique and charming. The view of the Fort and the Delhi Gate of it from the arcade on either side of the great centre door should be specially observed, and no one should fail to look from outside at the splendid wall of red sandstone, unhappily rather spoilt by the shops, at the back of the mosque. The front of the western covered hall of the mosque containing the pulpit and kiblagah, or prayer niche, pointing towards Mecca, is decorated with white marble panels, set in black frames of the same material; above it rise the three fine white marble domes, relieved by black vertical bands, and from the corners soar the two red sandstone minarets softened by white marble inlay. The marble panels on the front of the mosque simply recite the history of its construction — guides assert unblushingly that they contain the *whole* Koran!—the centre one bearing

[1] The regulations of the mosque, approved by authority, provide that the shoes of European visitors should be covered when entering the roofed western portion, where covers are provided. Visitors to the mosque during the hours of prayer will naturally remain in the background on the east side.

only the words, "Ya Hádi" ("Ah the Guide"). In the centre of the court is a tank for the necessary ablutions of worshippers before prayers: in the north-west corner was once a railed-off space, where in the dream of a devotee the Prophet appeared to him, and in a room in the north-east corridor are some relics of the Prophet. The minarets are reached by a staircase in the south gate, and thence over the roof of the arcade of the courtyard to their base: the view of the city obtained from the top of them is very extensive and curious. The pulpit in front of the principal bay of the facade was given to the mosque in 1829, in order that all persons in the court might be able to hear the preachers.

The mosque being the Royal Cathedral Mosque of India, is under the management of a committee appointed by Government, subject to the control of the Deputy-Commissioner of the District. It was repaired by Government at considerable cost some seventy or eighty years back, and has recently been again well and successfully restored, under the supervision of Government, by means of a gift of Rs.100,000, made by the Nawab of Rampur, and a smaller donation by the Nawab of Bhawalpur. Previous to 1857 a school and a hospital — the Dar-ul-Baka and the Dar-ush-Shafa—stood in the two spaces at the back corner of the mosque; these are now about to be again occupied by a Primary School for the boys of Delhi, and the Empress Victoria Memorial Hospital for Women.

Adjoining the mosque on the east is the Delhi

Jama Masjid—Congregational Prayers.

[*To face p.* 48.

Municipal Hospital, called after Lord Dufferin, by whom the foundation-stone was laid, one of the largest and best organised institutions in the Province. From this the **Dariba** leads to the Chandni Chauk, upon which it formerly opened through the Khuni Darwazah. This gate was so-called from the special massacre which took place near it, under the orders of Nadir Shah, and it was through it—opened by the plucky daring of a chaprassi and four British soldiers—and down the Dariba that the 3rd assaulting Column advanced on 14th September 1857 up to the angle which then existed in the street near the Jama Masjid, but had ultimately to fall back. The portion of the **Chandni Chauk** from the fort, as far as the Dariba, was originally called the Urdu, or military bazar. On the north side of it stands the fine building now occupied by the Delhi Bank, which was once the residence of the Begam Samru.[1] It was on the roof of an outhouse of this building that the Manager of the Bank, Mr Beresford, desperately defended himself and his family on 11th May 1857, until overborne by numbers. West of the Dariba came the Phul-ki-Mandi, or Flower Market, up to the Kotwali, followed by the Jauhri, or Jewellers' Bazar, and Chandni Chauk proper, the name of which was gradually extended to the whole street. It was originally built with arcades of shops one storey high to the front, the warehouses and residences of the traders being behind these. Unhappily, this once

[1] Another house of the Begam Samru, known as the Barud Khana, or Powder Magazine, is situated in the Churiwalan quarter. It was in this that a terrific explosion took place on the 7th August 1857, and killed a number of the enemy.

famous eastern street has now hardly anything eastern in appearance about it. At the end of the last century houses had been built both across it and down the centre of it, but these were all removed after 1803.

Further west a fountain and the south-west gates of the Queen's (Begam) Gardens are reached on the right hand, and the Kotwali, or Police Station, and the **Golden Mosque of Roshan-ud-daulah** (who was Bakhshi under the Emperor Muhammad Shah, and is remembered as a notorious and successful bribe-taker), on the left. The front part of the **Kotwali** has always served the purposes of a police station, but the portion behind was once the residence of a well-known man, Maulana Fakhruddin (p. 283). In the middle of the bazar in front of the Kotwali were erected gallows, on which many leading mutineers and encouragers of disloyalty and disturbance met their fate after September 1857, including Nawab Abdurrahman Khan of Jhajjar and Raja Nahar Singh of Ballabgarh, and on this spot were exposed the bodies of the three royal princes, one a son and one a grandson of the king, shot by Captain Hodson on 18th September. The Golden Mosque has an earlier and darker memory, as the place where the Persian invader, Nadir Shah, sat during the massacre of the people of the city in March 1739. The incident is thus described by an historian of the time:—

On the morning of the 11th, an order went forth from the Persian Emperor for the slaughter of the inhabitants. The result may be imagined; one moment seemed to have sufficed for universal de-

Kotwali and Roshan-ud-daulah Mosque, 1857.

Bourne & Shepherd, Photographers.]

[*To face p.* 50.

struction. The Chandni Chauk, the fruit market, the Daribah Bazar, and the buildings around the Masjid-i-Jama were set fire to and reduced to ashes. The inhabitants, one and all, were slaughtered. Here and there some opposition was offered, but in most places people were butchered unresistingly. The Persians laid violent hands on everything and everybody; cloth, jewels, dishes of gold and silver, were acceptable spoil. The author beheld these horrors from his mansion, situated in the Wakilpura Muhalla outside the city, resolved to fight to the last if necessary, and with the help of God to fall at least with honour. But, the Lord be praised, the work of destruction did not extend beyond the above-named parts of the capital. Since the days of Hazrat Sahib-Kiran Amir Timur, who captured Old Delhi and ordered the inhabitants to be massacred, up to the present time, A.H. 1151, a period of 348 years, the capital had been free from such visitations. The ruin in which its beautiful streets and buildings were now involved was such that the labour of years could alone restore the town to its former state of grandeur.

But to return to the miserable inhabitants. The massacre lasted half the day, when the Persian Emperor ordered Haji Fulad Khan, the Kotwal, to proceed through the streets accompanied by a body of Persian Nasakchis, and proclaim an order for the soldiers to desist from carnage. By degrees the violence of the flames subsided, but the bloodshed, the devastation, and the ruin of families were irreparable. For a long time the streets remained strewn with corpses, as the walks of a garden with dead flowers and leaves. The town was reduced to ashes, and had the appearance of a plain consumed with fire. All the regal jewels and property, and the contents of the treasury were seized by the Persian conqueror in the citadel. He thus became possessed of treasure to the amount of sixty lacs of rupees and several thousand ashrafis; plate of gold to the value of one kror of rupees, and the jewels, many of which were unrivalled in beauty by any in the world, were valued at about fifty krors. The Peacock Throne alone, constructed at great pains in the reign of Shah Jahan, had cost one kror of rupees. Elephants, horses, and precious stuffs, whatever pleased the conqueror's eye, more indeed than can be enumerated, became his spoil. In short, the accumulated wealth of 348 years changed masters in a moment.

Proceeding up the Chandni Chauk and passing many shops of the principal dealers in jewels, embroideries, and other products of Delhi handicrafts, the Northbrook Clock Tower and the principal entrance to the Queen's Gardens are reached. The former is situated at the site of the **Karavan Sarai of the Princess Jahanara Begam** (p. 239), known by the title of Shah Begam. The Sarai, the square in front of which projected across the street, was considered by Bernier one of the finest buildings in Delhi, and was compared by him with the Palais Royal, because of its arcades below and rooms with a gallery in front above. Bernier was of opinion that the population of Delhi in 1665 was much the same as that of Paris, a striking instance of how population follows the court in the East. The gardens must at one time have been extremely beautiful specimens of eastern pleasure retreats, and even now are very pretty. Inside the railings of the street will be placed the **Statue of the late Queen Empress of India**, presented to his fellow-citizens by Mr James Skinner, a grandson of Colonel Skinner, C.B. Further back are the Municipal Buildings, and a museum with a number of objects of much interest. In the gardens is also one of the restored stone elephants which stood before the Delhi Gate of the Fort. Through the middle of them runs the channel of the tail of the Western Jumna Canal, the water of which was held up at places along its course in reservoirs. Continuing down the Chandni Chauk to the end we reach the Fatahpur Masjid, nearly a mile from the Lahore Gate of the fort. This was built by one of the wives of the Emperor Shah Jahan in 1650 A.D.; from 1857 till the visit of His Majesty to Delhi in 1876, it was devoted to secular purposes, but was then restored to the Muhammadan community as a place of worship. The eastern portion of the enclosure is occupied by a garden and a tank and some graves; on the western side rises a well-proportioned mosque building, surmounted by a single dome of black and white stripes. From the front of the mosque one broad street leads along the south side to the Lal Kua Bazar, while the Lahore Bazar, which is the principal grain market of Delhi, leads past the north side to the Lahore Gate of the city. The road to the right leading along the west end of the Queen's Gardens takes us to the main road from the Railway Station to the Kabul Gate, and turning to the right short of this crosses the Dufferin Bridge to the Mori Gate and the Civil Station, outside the northern wall of the city. The fine native house on the left of the main road across the canal, now occupied by the Cambridge Mission, was once the mansion of Nawab Safdar Jang (p. 246) and the Nawab Wazirs of Oudh.

CHAPTER II—*continued*

THE CITY OF MODERN DELHI OR SHAHJAHANABAD

PART II.—THE SURROUNDINGS OF THE CITY, CHIEFLY ON THE NORTH AND WEST SIDES, THE MINOR BUILDINGS WITHIN THE WALLS, AND THE FIELD OF THE BATTLE OF DELHI, 11TH SEPTEMBER 1803.

ON the north of the city, outside the Kashmir Gate, are the pretty **Kudsia Gardens**, on the Jumna bank. These were constructed by the Kudsi Begam, mother of the Emperor Ahmad Shah, whose reign was the culminating period of the decay of the Moghal Empire. The walls which formerly enclosed it have been removed for the most part, and the river which once flowed under the terrace, on the east side, is now far away from it; but the fine though ruined gateway remains, and a handsome mosque, still bearing marks of the siege of 1857, stands near the south-east corner of the public recreation grounds. In the Kudsia Garden are the sites of the Mortar Battery, and of Siege Battery No. III, described at pages 88 and 167. Opposite the south end are the breaches of the Water Bastion and Kashmir Bastion, and outside the south-west corner are the Nicholson Garden and the cemetery where General Nicholson lies (p. 92). At the north-west corner stands Ludlow Castle, the residence of the Commissioner, Mr Simon Fraser, in 1857, and now the Delhi Club. The site of the left section of No. II Siege Battery is in the grounds of the Club, near the east wall (pp. 87 and 167).

As the longest portion of the **City Walls** generally seen by visitors to Delhi is that on the north side, it may be noted here that these defences as they now stand were constructed between 1804 and 1811 by the British Government, after the attack on the city by the Mahrattas,[1] at which time the Kashmir Gate was also reconstructed. The Moghal walls were apparently never properly completed, and after they

[1] The attack on Delhi by the troops of Jaswant Rao Holkar lasted from 7th October to 15th October, 1804: the defence was conducted under Colonel Ochterlony by Colonel Burn, after whom the Burn Bastion is named. The first attack was made at the south-east angle. After the batteries here had been destroyed by a sally, the curtain between the Turkman and Ajmir Gates was breached, but fresh defences were constructed inside the wall, and no assault of the breach was pressed home. Finally an attack, also repulsed, was made on the Lahore Gate, a demonstration being made on the Kashmir Gate. Like the actual siege of 1857, which began on 6th September and ended on the 14th, the siege of 1804 lasted for nine days only. The Mahratta forces consisted of 70,000 men and 130 guns; the British force of two battalions and four companies of sepoys, two corps of irregular cavalry, and some 800 Tilangas, who had recently deserted from the enemy; and of these eight companies were lost to the defence, as they were needed to protect the palace and secure the person of the king, whom Holkar desired to get into his own hands. General Lake had ordered that if the city could not be successfully defended, the troops were to retire into the palace and hold that; Colonel Ochterlony wished to do this, but Colonel Burn, who was in military command, refused. The extraordinary achievement of the defence was allowed to pass practically unnoticed, and Colonel Burn never received any recognition of his gallant feat of arms.

had been seriously damaged by a severe earthquake in 1720, offered no serious obstacle to any enemy; and it was by a special irony of fate that in the summer of 1857 the British forces found themselves unable to batter down the ramparts which the British Government had itself raised. The walls were never any real defence against the fire of heavy artillery, as was proved in less than a week in September 1857, and under the conditions of modern warfare are an entirely negligable item. They are fully described, from a military point of view, by Colonel Baird Smith, in his report upon the Siege and Assault (p. 200), and as they were in 1857, so they are now. They are well built for the most part, though some curiously rough bits exist between the Kashmir Bastion and the river.

The **Ridge** is described in detail in the first part of the following chapter, and only the objects ot antiquarian interest, situated on it, will be noticed here. The Lat of Asoka, and the so-called Observatory were situated in the **Kushk-i-Shikar**, or country palace of Firoz Shah, known also as **Jahannuma**, or World-displayed, and the Chauburji Mosque probably stood outside that. The origin of this palace is thus described by the annalist of the king:—

In the year 774 H.=1373 A.D., the Wizir Malik Mukbil, entitled Khan Jahan, died, and his eldest son, Juna Shah, succeeded to his office and titles. During the year 776 H., on the 12th of Safar, the king was plunged into affliction by the death of his favourite son, Fatah Khan, a prince of great promise, and the back of his strength was bent by the burden of grief.

Finding no remedy, except in patience and resignation, he buried him in his own garden (now the Kadam Sharif, p. 63), and performed the customary ceremonies upon the occasion. On account of the excess of his grief, the shadow of his regard was withdrawn from the cares of state, and he abandoned himself entirely to his sorrows. His nobles and counsellors placed their heads on the ground, and represented that there was no course left but to submit to the divine will, and that he should not show further repugnance to administer the affairs of his kingdom. The wise king acceded to the supplications of his friends and well-wishers, and, in order to dispel his sorrows, devoted himself to sport, and in the vicinity of new Delhi he built a wall of two or three parasangs in circumference, planted within the enclosure shady trees, and converted it into a hunting park. The ruins of it remain to this day.

Mr Finch, in the memoirs of his travels as far as Lahore, specially mentions this site in the following terms :—

A little beyond Delhy are the relicks of a stately hunting house, built by an ancient Indian king, which has great curiosities of stone work about it. Amongst the rest there is a pillar all of one entire stone, some 24 feet high, and as many under ground (as the Indians say), having a globe and half moon at top, and divers inscriptions upon it. This, according to the tradition of the country, a certain Indian king would have taken up and removed, but was prevented in his design by the multitude of scorpions that infested the workmen.

An account of the removal of the Buddhist columns to Delhi will be found on p. 223. The **Lat on the Ridge** was broken by an explosion early in the eighteenth century, and lay on the ground for 150 years; and, in consequence, the surface of the stone is rougher, and the letters of the original inscription are less distinct than in the case of the Lat in the Kotila of Firoz Shah, which has stood erect there for 550 years, and no doubt stood erect at Topra for 1600 years.

The Observatory, which stands on the highest point of the Ridge, was in all probability the tower upon which a chiming clock was erected by the king. It is popularly known as the Pir Ghaib, or the Hidden Saint, perhaps from the underground galleries which connected it with the plain to the west, and of which vestiges may be seen throughout the slope on that side. On this side too, near the south corner of the area round Hindu Rao's house, and at the level of the plain, is a fine baoli, with a very long flight ot steps, belonging to the same period as the Kushk-i-Shikar.

Opposite Jahannuma, and probably by the ford under Metcalfe House, Timur and his horde crossed the Jumna in 1398, after taking and destroying Luni, the site of which still rises prominently on the left bank of the river, and after slaying all the captives with the army to a number, it is alleged, of 100,000. At Jahannuma the Moghal camp was attacked by the Sultan, Mahmud Khan, and his minister, Mallu Khan, but the attack was repulsed, and the camp was carefully secured by abattis of trees, and by chaining lines of buffaloes, and placing iron caltrops in front of these, to break the charge of the war elephants.

The **Chauburji Mosque**, so called from the

Shrine of Shah Alam near Wazirabad.

[To face p. 59.

four domed corner rooms which once stood upon the raised platform, is a structure of the time of Firoz Shah, which was used as a mausoleum, and altered in certain respects in the last century. The restoration, made since 1857, has almost entirely destroyed all resemblance to the building of the Mutiny time.

Near the extreme north end of the Ridge, where it ceases abruptly on the bank of the river, is the picturesque shrine of a local Muhammadan saint, by name Shah Alam, in the limits of the village of **Wazirabad**. This is built on the banks of a channel which drains the Bawari plain, and is spanned by a fine bridge above the north-west corner of the building. Shrine, gateway and courtyard, and mosque, bridge, and paved causeway alike, belong to the period of Firoz Shah Tughlak (1365-1390 A.D.), and in spite of vile whitewash, they form one of the prettiest architectura groups at Delhi, when viewed from the north side of the bed of the stream, from which two flights of steps ascend to the enclosure. It was at Wazirabad that Timur and his Moghal horde encamped and crossed the Jumna on 1st January 1399 A.D., after having deluged Old Delhi with blood and utterly destroyed the central Muhammadan power of the day in North India. Six years later the great Sultan died on the borders of China, having meanwhile sacked Baghdad and captured the Turkish Emperor, Bajazet.

West of Wazirabad and north of the Grand Trunk Road is the Bawari plain, the site of the **Imperial Darbar** of 1st January 1877, and the **Coronation Darbar** of 1st January 1903. Two miles further west along the main road at the site of **Badli-ki Sarai** and the village of Pipal Thalla is the battle-field of 8th June 1857 (p. 117).

Less than a mile to the north-west of the Sarai and across the railway line are the scanty remains of the **Shalimar Gardens**, which must be visited on foot. It may be doubted if these were ever fully finished, as they were begun by the Emperor Shah Jahan only in 1653. though Bernier speaks of them as fine gardens, with handsome and noble buildings (inferior, however, in his opinion, to Versailles or St Germain), and the Emperor Aurangzeb was formally crowned there. At any rate, they were no doubt ruined at an early date by some one of the many invaders of Delhi in the eighteenth century—Nadir Shah encamped here on quitting Delhi—and but little now exists to mark their former grandeur. The depressions of the three principal tanks, and the long water-channel connecting these, lie outside a fine grove of mango trees, which still shades the highest pool, overgrown by lotus, and forming a very picturesque bit; and a half-ruined summer-house, called the Shish Mahal, stands at the south-west corner of the garden. The designation given to it by the Emperor was Khanah-i-Aish-wa-Ashrat, the Home of Joy and Companionship; the name by which it and the more famous gardens of the Emperor Jahangir, or, more properly of his consort. Nur Jahan, at Lahore and Kashmir are known, is derived from two Hindi, or Sanscrit words, also meaning the Abode (shála) of Joy (már). For a time after 1803 the gardens were used by the Resident at Delhi as a summer retreat, and General Ochterlony contracted in them the fever of which he died thirty-two years after his defence of Delhi.

Returning from the Badli-ki Sarai and Shalimar, the road to the right at Azadpur may be followed to the Roshanara Gardens. The point of separation is that where our force divided after the battle on 8th June 1857, and advanced in two bodies on the Ridge (p. 118). This road runs through gardens on both sides, passing on the left hand the Ochterlony Garden, or **Mubarik Bagh**, which was one of the finest round Delhi. Near the Sabzi Mandi and the Roshanara Gardens are two handsome gateways, each of three arches, and known as **Tirpulia**, built in 1728 by one Mahaldar Khan Nazir, or Superintendent of the household of the King Muhammad Shah, and bearing his name. They formed the entrances of a bazar, on the right side of which is a garden made by the same official, approached by a handsome portal. There are very few notable buildings in or near Delhi of subsequent date to this, the principal being two of the Golden Mosques (pp. 43 and 50), and the tombs of Safdar Jang and Ghazi-ud-din Khan.

Half a mile nearer to Delhi, and two miles from the Kashmir Gate, are the gardens of **Roshanara Begam**, standing a little back on the right. The present grounds, which are extremely pretty, have been formed by the combination of several gardens into one, that from which the whole is named lying on the east side. It was made in 1650 by the Princess Roshanara Begam, a daughter of the Emperor Shah-jahan, and the devoted adherent of Aurangzeb against Dara Sheko and his partisan sister, Jahanara Begam (p. 239), and she lies buried in it, after having survived her brother's accession for thirteen years. The grave enclosure, which is open to the sky, is placed in the middle of a pavilion which no doubt once stood in the centre of the garden; the tomb itself carries earth in the recess hollowed in it, like that of her sister at Nizam-ud-din. The gate of the garden on the east side was once decorated with beautiful encaustic work.

Across the canal, and reached by the road which

runs south from the front of this gate is an interesting Armenian graveyard, containing a number of tombs which are much the oldest Christian graves in Delhi. It is known by the name of the family of D'Eremao, which was once connected with the imperial court.

About three miles from here, and four miles from Delhi, down the Rohtak road is a fine old masonry aqueduct, called the Pul Chaddar, by which the Western Jumna Canal was carried towards the city across the cut from the Najafgarh Jhil. This, and various bridges across the canal were blown up in 1857 to prevent the enemy crossing to the rear of our position.

Returning through the Sabzi Mandi from the Roshanara Gardens to the city, the quarters of Kishanganj and Paharipur, from which the enemy so persistently annoyed and attacked our position in 1857, are passed on the south side of the Western Jumna Canal. The bridge across this on the road running south from the end of the Ridge leads in 300 yards to a solitary grave and monument in an open space on the right hand. The former marks the resting-place of Captain G. C. M'Barnett, killed in the attack of the 4th Column on 14th September 1857, and the latter records the bravery and losses (four sergeants, three corporals, and twelve privates) of the 1st Bengal Fusiliers near this spot on that day. "Familiar with the aspect of Death which they had confronted in so many battles from which they had always emerged victorious, they met his last inevitable call here with intrepidity, falling on the 14th September 1857 in the faithful discharge of their duty. This monument, erected by the officers and fellow soldiers of the 1st Regiment

The Kadam Sharif.

[To face p. 63.

European Bengal Fusiliers, is their remembrance, which is part of its glory. The rest remains with the Lord."

Outside the Kabul Gate of the city once stood the fine garden and tomb, known as Tis Hazari, of Malika Zamani Begam, the high-spirited mother of the Emperor Muhammad Shah, who freed her son from the Syad tyranny; and outside the Lahore Gate stands a third mosque built by a wife of Shahjahan, known as the Sarhandi Begam. It is not perhaps generally recollected that the Lady of the Taj died in 1630, two years after this Emperor ascended the throne, and that the bereaved husband proved by no means inconsolable during the thirty years of his reign. Both in size and in architectural merit, this is the poorest of all the buildings inaugurated under the auspices of the founder of modern Delhi, the domes being low and ungainly in shape; they are constructed of red sandstone, which is very unusual in domes of such a size.

Nearly a mile south of this gate and mosque, and across the channel which connects the Western Jumna and Agra Canals, is a fine old Sarai, known as the Idgah Sarai, and behind it to the south is the Dargah, or Sacred Enclosure, of the **Kadam Sharif**—the Holy Footprint, which must be approached on foot. This is a very interesting and picturesque building of the time of Firoz Shah, having been raised by that king as the last resting-place of his eldest son, Fatah Khan, in the year 1375 (p. 57). The tomb enclosure is surrounded by a citadel wall, like the tomb of Tughlak Shah, constructed, no doubt, to protect it against the attacks of the Moghals, as it lay, of course, outside the city of Firozabad. The shrine is approached by two fine outer gateways, and consists of a quaint arcaded enclosure round the grave of the prince, over which the sacred imprint, sent by the Khalifa of Baghdad to Firoz Shah, is placed in a trough of water. It is worth while descending the steps on the north side of the mosque, in order to view the west end of the enclosure from the outside. South of the outermost gate of the outer walls is a fine stone tank; and on this side is situated the principal Muhammadan cemetery of Delhi, unhappily much neglected. On the Ridge west of the Kadam Sharif is the **Idgah**, a fine enclosure which merits a visit, which also must be made on foot. The view of the city from this point is very pleasing.

Following the road to the left from the main road past the west of the city to Paharganj and the Kutab, we pass round the hornwork enclosing the **Mausoleum and College of Ghazi-ud-din Khan,** and reach the Ajmir Gate. The former specially deserves to be seen, as one of the few remaining specimens of a religious endowment, similar to those of the middle ages in Europe, comprising a place of worship, the tomb of the founder, and a residence and place of instruction for those who were to have charge of both, all built in his lifetime. Ghazi-ud-din was son of the first Nizam-ul-Mulk of Hydrabad. He became the leading noble of the Delhi Court when his father returned to the Deccan after the events of 1739, and died in 1752 A.D., on

Kalan or Kala Masjid of Firoz Shah.

[To face p. 63.

his way to assert his succession to the Hyderabad Territories. The courtyard, approached through a gateway of which the wings are thrown forward, is surrounded on three sides by a double tier of chambers for students, like the colleges of Samarkand and Bokhara: on the west side the mosque, built of very deep coloured red sandstone, and with very rounded domes, fills the centre, and the south of it is the grave of the founder, enclosed by a beautiful pierced screen of fawn-coloured stone, with doors elaborately carved with flowers. This corner is, perhaps, quite one of the most picturesque bits in Delhi. For a long time the building, which had been closed eighty years after the founder's death for want of funds, was occupied by the police: it is now again devoted to educational purposes in connection with the Anglo-Arabic school. From the Ajmir Gate—the wooden doors, which are no doubt much what those in the Kashmir Gate were in September 1857, should be noticed — the straight road runs to the Sita Ram Bazar (p. 6), which turns to the right to the **Kala** or **Kalan Masjid**, standing a little back on the west side from the main street. This was probably the principal mosque of the city of Firozabad, which extended further west than this, as distinguished from the Citadel or Kotila of Firoz Shah and its mosque, and is a curious building, well meriting a visit. It is reached by a high flight of steps, and like other mosques built about 1380 by the latter of the two great Wazirs who bore the name of Khan Jahan in the reign of Firoz Shah, consists of a courtyard, surrounded on three sides by a simple arcade, borne by plain squared columns of quartzose stone, with a dripstone over the arches, and on the west side by a mosque chamber of three rows of similar columns, each carrying five arches. The corner towers and outer walls of the mosque are all sloped inwards; there are no minarets, and the call to prayer was made from the roof of the terrace. It would appear from Bishop Heber's journals that for a long time prayers were not held in this mosque. The graves of the founder of it and of his father were destroyed in the troubles of 1857. Three other mosques, built by them in the same style (see p. 319), but of more interesting arrangement, exist at Nizam-ud-din, Khirki, and Begampur (pages 235, 251, and 286). Near the Kalan Masjid are two historically interesting graves of a date of 150 years earlier. On the left side of the road opposite the mosque is the tomb and cemetery of Turkman Shah, after whom the Turkman Gate of the city is called, a militant saint of the first period of Muhammadan conquest and settlement, who died in 1240 A.D. A little to the north, reached by the Bulbuli Khana lane at the point where the Sita Ram Bazar ends, is a small isolated enclosure containing two graves, of which the larger is, according to old tradition, that of the **Sultan Raziyah**, El Malika Raziyah, Ibn Batuta calls her (p. 295), who was killed and buried in the same year as the above. There is no reason, I think, for distrusting the popular tradition in this case, as it is on contemporaneous record that the Sultan was buried on the banks of the Jumna, and that the city of Firozabad included the area of her grave; and we may reasonably believe that we see in this humble tomb the last resting-place of the first Empress of India, known like her predecessors and successors as Sultan.

About 200 yards to the north-west from the Jumna Mosque, and conveniently reached from there, is the **Jain** or **Saraogi Temple** of Delhi, the elegant decoration of the porch of which is specially commended by Mr Fergusson, and well deserves a visit, which must be made on foot. The times and conditions for visiting the interior can be ascertained at the Temple, and are known to the local guides.

To the east of the Sonahri Mosque of Javed Khan (p. 43), may be seen a cross at the bottom of the slope of the southern glacis of the fort, marking the site of the old Daryaganj cemetery. East of this again is the Raj Ghat Gate, with a ramp ascending from the river below, and south of both is the garden of the little cantonment of **Daryaganj**, in which the native regiment of the Delhi garrison is quartered, and the officers of the regiment reside. This was the original cantonment of Delhi after 1803; but the garrison was subsequently located beyond the Ridge, and in the Mutiny the quarter was mainly occupied by subordinates of the Arsenal, and of various departments of Government. The tale of the strenuous defence made by a number of these against the mutineers will be found on page 106. The house held by them was that now numbered five, the first on the left beyond the road leading up from the Khairati Gate, by which, as by the Raj Ghat Gate, the mutineers of the 3rd Light Cavalry entered the city on finding the Calcutta Gate closed, and being directed by Captain Douglas to leave the ground below the king's apartments in the palace. On the north side of the road above the Khairati Gate is the mosque of the Zinat-ul-Masajid, or Beauty of Mosques, built in 1700 by one[1] of the daughters of the Emperor Aurangzeb. The building is a fine one, and well deserves a visit: the steps leading up to it from the roadway are particularly picturesque. The mosque was used for military purposes for many years after 1857, and during that time the tomb of the foundress, which stood on the north side of the enclosure, was removed.

The only other buildings in Delhi which call for any notice are the Mosque of Roshan-ud-daulah (1745 A.D.), on the right hand of the Feiz Bazar, leading to the Delhi Gate of the city, and the Fakhr-ul-Masajid, or Pride of the Mosques, built in 1728 A.D. inside the Kashmir Gate. The latter is a very graceful mosque—the former is a clumsy one, far inferior to the Sonahri Masjid of Javed Khan, built three years subsequently to it (p. 43).

The site of the field of the **Battle of Delhi**, fought by General Lake on 11th September 1803, lies some five miles south-west of the city, on the left bank of the river, and almost exactly opposite the tomb of the Emperor Humayun. It is nearly as far from the railway station of

[1] Another of these, it will be recollected, is represented by Thomas Moore as Lalla Rookh (Lala Rukh).

Shahdara[1] as from the east end of the iron Jumna Bridge, and it is therefore better to drive there direct from Delhi—a light trap can go down the road along the embankment from the bridge to Patparganj.

On the way to the Jumna Bridge the road passes the traditional sites of the Das-Aswa-Medh (or Ten-Horse-Sacrifice), and Nigambodh (or Veda-Knowledge) Ghats, connected with the earliest dawn of Hindu history. The former commemorates the great sacrifice of Yudisthara, the Pandu Prince of Indrapastha, now Indrapat, which was famous before Delhi was known, and the latter the recovery of the knowledge of the Hindu scriptures by the god Shiva. The road also passes the Nili Chattri, an old temple restored by the Mahrattas, at or near which once stood inscriptions by the Emperors Humayun and Jehangir. An extremely picturesque view of the north end of the Moghal Fort is obtained from the masonry bridge across the right arm of the Jumna here, and further on a full survey can be made of the walls of Salimgarh (p. 40), rising at the side of the road. From the end of the bridge an unmetalled road leads along the left bank of the river to Patparganj, once a flourishing rural town, but now nearly deserted. This place, from which the battle-field is named locally, is slightly in advance of the right of the position occupied by the Mahrattas,

[1] Ahmad Shah, the Durani, was encamped at Shahdara before he moved to Panipat, and placed himself between the capital and the Mahratta army, which had gone north to attack the Kunjpura chief, and Suraj Mal, the first great Jat leader, was killed here in a cavalry skirmish in 1764.

which extended along a stretch of elevated ground from the village of Kotla to that of Ghazipur, thus described, and accurately described, with reference to the configuration of the ground at the present day by Major Thorn; the best general view of it is obtained from the summit of a brick-kiln lying north-east of Patparganj. "The enemy," he writes, "were discovered by Lord Lake, drawn up on rising ground, in full force and complete order of battle, posted very strongly, having each flank covered by a swamp beyond which were stationed the cavalry, while numerous artillery defended the front, the whole being concealed by a high grass jungle. This front was the only point which could be attacked." The rising ground is situated between two depressions connected at the west end—the right of the enemy's line—where the water is the deepest, the northern depression being, however, much more shallow than the southern one. Water stands in the latter from three to four and a half feet deep from August till October or November.

The following account of the engagement is abstracted mainly from Major Thorn's "Memoir of the Late Great War in India," after careful study of the battle-field, and the necessary additions for its elucidation with reference to the ground and its surroundings have been made to the map published in the Memoirs.

Lord Lake's force had left Allygurh on 7th September, and arrived at an encampment two miles south of the battle-field and six miles from Delhi, about 11 A.M., on 11th of that month, having been under arms since 3 A.M. Learning that

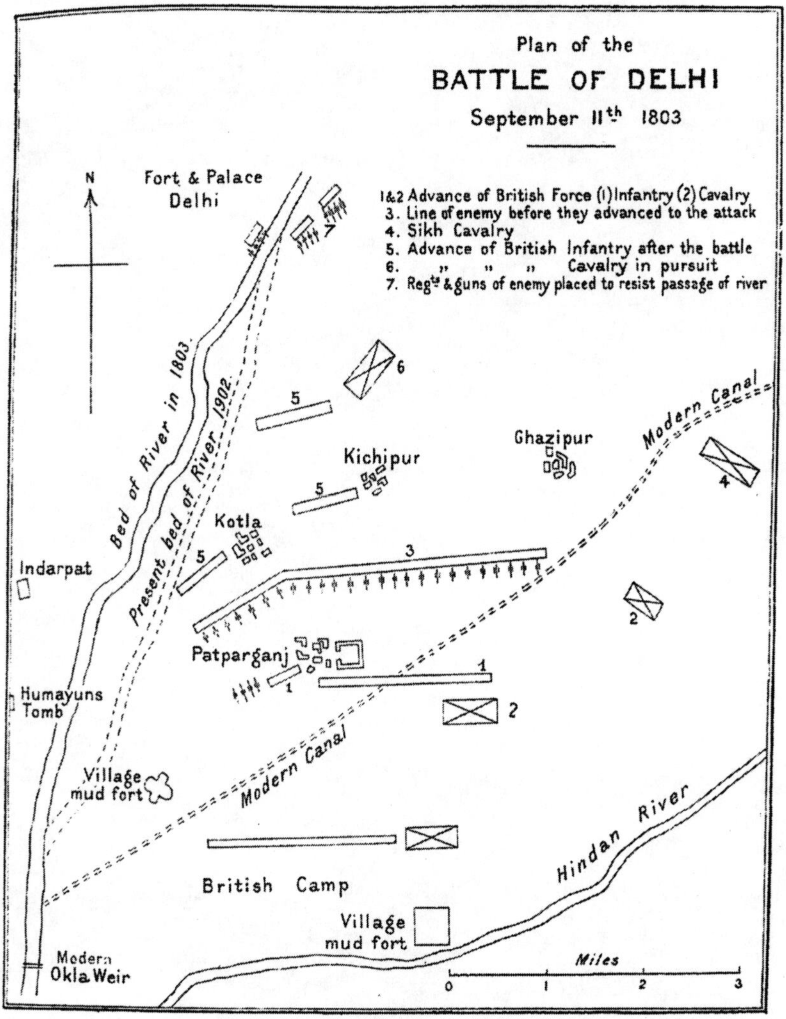
Plan of the
BATTLE OF DELHI
September 11th 1803
1&2 Advance of British Force (1) Infantry (2) Cavalry
3. Line of enemy before they advanced to the attack
4. Sikh Cavalry
5. Advance of British Infantry after the battle
6. " " " Cavalry in pursuit
7. Regts & guns of enemy placed to resist passage of river
N
Fort & Palace Delhi
Bed of River in 1803
Present bed of River 1902
Kichipur
Ghazipur
Modern Canal
Kotla
Indarpat
Patparganj
Humayuns Tomb
Village mud fort
British Camp
Hindan River
Modern Okla Weir
Miles
0
1
2
3

[To face p. 70.

the enemy had marched out of Delhi, under Mons. Bourquin, and was strongly posted on the left bank of the Jumna, Lord Lake went forward with the cavalry to find them. Their strength was about 19,000 men, including 6000 cavalry, and seventy guns of every sort and calibre. The British force comprised 4500 fighting men in all, with but a small body of cavalry, and some galloper guns. The troops engaged were the following:—H.M. 76th Regiment, posted on the right of the advance; 1st Battalion 4th Native Infantry; 2nd Battalion 12th Native Infantry; 1st and 2nd Battalion 15th Native Infantry; 1st and 2nd Battalion 2nd Native Infantry; 1st Battalion 14th Native Infantry; 27th Dragoons; 2nd and 3rd Native Cavalry Artillery. They were under the command of Major-General St John and Major-General Ware. To turn either flank of the enemy with so small a force was impossible, and to attack either would have been almost impossible; while a front attack on the position, defended as it was with artillery, would have entailed tremendous losses. Lord Lake, therefore, decided to make a feigned retreat, while the infantry were being hurried up to the front, and this move was crowned with complete success, though the cavalry were sharply pressed for a time, both the Commander-in-Chief and his son (who fell at the head of his regiment in one of the earliest Peninsular battles) having a horse killed under them; for while the enemy immediately deserted their post of advantage and moved forward in pursuit, our infantry was concealed from them by the high river grass, and on our cavalry passing between the regiments to the rear of the line, the Mahrattas suddenly found themselves face to face with it, and subjected to an immediate attack. The troops, with the General himself leading the 76th Regiment, advanced to within one hundred yards of the enemy with their muskets to their shoulders, then fired a single volley and charged, and the Mahratta force at once gave way and broke everywhere in wild flight towards Delhi. The cavalry and galloper guns immediately advanced again in pursuit in their turn, and did great execution among the fugitives, and drove in the troops which had been left to guard the passage of the river; while the infantry also swept up to the north along the river bank, then much further to the west than now, and the whole force ultimately encamped opposite Delhi, after a most exhausting day, which lasted nearly up to 7 P.M. Our casualties were 117 killed and 292 wounded; the enemy is believed to have lost 3000 men, and the whole of their guns and tumbrils were captured. The fight was watched from Delhi and the buildings opposite the battlefield on the right bank of the river. A full view of the mausoleum of the Emperor Humayun and of the Purana Kila is still obtained from the site of the monument of the battle; but the trees planted along the River Protective Works shut off the general view of the Delhi Palace; through the tops of the gates the Jama Masjid and the minarets of the Zinat-ul-Masajid Mosque (p. 68) can be seen from it, as also may the needle-like Kutab Minar far down to the south-west.

On 14th Sept. the British army crossed the Jumna and entered Delhi; and that date is therefore doubly marked in British military annals in connection with the once Imperial Moghal City. On the 16th Lord Lake was escorted to the palace by the heir-apparent Mirza Akbar, and met the blind king, Shah Alam, in the Diwan-i-Khas. Major Thorn describes him "as an object of pity, blind and aged, stripped of authority, and reduced to poverty, seated under a tattered canopy." Lord Lake received from this lowly representative of the great Moghal the titles of "Samsam-i-Daulah, Ashjah-ul-Mulk, Khan Dauran"[1]; and in the following August he was invested with the insignia of the Mahi (Fish) and Muratib (a ball of copper gilt, surrounded by a deep fringe) at Cawnpur. Our force left Delhi on 24th September to meet the other Mahratta armies near Agra. The site of the battle on the south side of the depression, in front of the original position of the enemy, is marked by a small obelisk, recently restored. The plain is peaceful enough now, and will probably be found frequented by deer and large wading birds. On the cross are engraved the words of the Governor-General of India, the Marquess of Wellesley, in memory of the officers killed in the engagement:—

The Governor-General in Council sincerely laments the loss of Major Middleton, 3rd Regi-

[1] Their meaning is Sword of the State, the Hero of the Realm, the Chief of the Age. Twenty-five years later Lord Combermere received the same insignia and the titles of Rustam-i-jang, Seif-ud-dowlah, the Hero of Battle and the Sword of State.

ment Native Cavalry; Captain MacGregor, Persian Interpreter; Lieutenant Hill, 2nd Battalion 12th Native Infantry; Lieutenant Preston, 2nd Battalion 13th Native Infantry; Cornet Sanquire, 27th Dragoons; Quarter-Master Richardson, 27th Dragoons, and of the brave soldiers who fell in the exemplary execution of deliberate valour and disciplined spirit at the battle of Delhi. The names of these brave men will be commemorated with the glorious events of the day on which they fell, and will be honoured and revered while the fame of that signal victory shall endure.

And now, a hundred years later, how many have ever heard of the names of these brave men, or recall the 11th September, even though its glory, as the Governor-General further wrote, and as may be fairly said, "is not surpassed by any recorded triumph of the British arms in India, and is attended by every circumstance calculated to elevate the fame of British valour, to illustrate the character of British humanity, and to secure the stability of the British Empire in the East"?

CHAPTER III

DELHI IN 1857

PART I.—THE SCENE OF THE SIEGE AND ASSAULT DESCRIBED WITH SPECIAL REFERENCE TO PRESENT CONDITIONS.

STARTING from the south-east corner of Ludlow Castle (p. 54) as the centre of the final siege operations in September 1857, the Grand Trunk Road leading to Karnal and Amballah passes on the right the office of the Great Western Jumna Canal and Maiden's Hotel, and leads in 600 yards to the present residence of the Commissioner of the Delhi Division, Flagstaff House, on the left. Immediately behind this house is a platform upon which another building once stood. This building was the **Telegraph Office** in 1857 (p. 107), and the "bhisti," who used to supply water to the tatties, or grass screens, is still alive, and can tell the tale of what happened at the office up to mid-day. He then left to get his morning meal, and when he plucked up courage to return two days afterwards, he found only a heap of smouldering ruins on the spot. A little further on the road crosses the bed of a deep nulla, or ravine, which carries the drainage of the north end of the river-face of the Ridge through the Metcalfe estate to the Jumna. Just beyond this on the left, stood the Station Assembly Rooms previous to May 1857, and near this spot after the return of the troops, Showers' piquet was constructed on the road, and the **Mound and Metcalfe House Piquets** were established further east to protect the extreme left of our position, resting on the river. Later on, the last was broken up into the Stable, Farm and Cow-House Piquets, of which the two latter were placed on the south side of the ravine. In the middle of August a battery was established by the enemy on the left bank of the Jumna at Shamgarh, specially to annoy these piquets, and was subsequently used against the Siege Batteries. From the top of the mound, still crowned by the entrenchments of 1857, a fine view is obtained of Metcalfe House, 600 yards to the east, and of the Mosque or Chauburji Piquet on the Ridge, and of the whole of our position on that down to the extreme right now marked by the Mutiny Monument. **Metcalfe House** must once have been a very fine mansion, and it still rises effectively on the high right bank of the Jumna. Beneath it were a number of apartments, and below the terrace on the river side of it was a series of underground rooms, arranged for occupation in the summer. It was in the latter that the refugees with whom Lieut. Vibart escaped from Delhi were concealed for a brief period by the servants of the house. North of the ravine the Grand Trunk Road divides, the branch to the left going straight to the

The Flagstaff Tower, 1857.

Bourne & Shepherd, Photographers.] [To face p. 77.

Flagstaff Tower by a steep ascent, and that to the right reaching the crest of the Ridge by an easier incline from a cutting through the rocky barrier. Near the point of separation inside the Metcalfe estate, the General Field Hospital was established on 14th September 1857. The road along the Ridge from the above cutting passes southwards through the site of the Old Sadr Bazar of the cantonment, and beyond a Guard House to the Flagstaff Tower. Fifty yards before this is reached is a walled enclosure, containing the grave of four officers murdered at the Main Guard of the Kashmir Gate, on 11th May 1857, whose remains were found here when the Ridge was re-occupied on 8th June, still lying on the cart on which they had been sent to the cantonment. The inscription on the gravestone runs thus: "Sacred to the memory of Captain R. M. Smith, Captain C. Burrowes, Lt. C. A. Edwards, Lt. W. Waterfield, all of the 34th Regiment, B.N.I. They were killed by the mutineers of the 3rd Bengal Light Cavalry, on 11th May 1857, opposite the church in the city of Delhi. This tribute to their memory is erected by their surviving brother officers." There is also a separate gravestone erected to the memory of Lieut. Edwards by his widow.

The Flagstaff Tower was the sad spot where the ladies of the cantonment gathered with their children on the afternoon of 11th May, and waited vainly for help from Meerut, or for something to be done, and from which they finally started in sad disorganised flight towards Karnal; and it is only too easy to imagine what their sufferings of that afternoon must have been. It was at the Flagstaff Tower too, that the enemy made their last stand, on 8th June, before falling back behind the shelter of the city walls; and four days later, on 12th June, delivered one of their most determined attacks on our position, which compelled us to occupy Metcalfe House. From the top of the tower a very peaceful scene is now beheld, with general features doubtless much the same as might have been seen on the Sunday preceding 11th May, but with gaps and ruins which still vividly recall the memory of that time. On the top of the Ridge are scattered indications of the old Sadr Bazar. At the foot of the west slope are trees and walls and pillars of garden gates, which mark the site of the officers' bungalows, and part of the native lines. Beyond these, seen at intervals through the further trees, is a line of Bells-of-Arms on the edge of an open space, once the general parade ground, in the summer of 1857 the encampment of our troops, and at the Christmasses of 1876 and 1903 the site of the Viceregal and other camps on the occasions of the Imperial Assemblage and the Coronation Darbar. This space is again lined by trees on its further side along the drainage cut from the Najafgarh Jhil, or swamp, while a darker cluster of foliage in the centre marks the site of the graveyard where so many brave men sleep their last sleep, and of the bridge crossed by our troops on 8th June in their advance upon the right of the Ridge. Beyond this, again, in the distance, are the trees of the Mubarik Bagh (p. 61), which hide from view the village of Azadpur, and the more distant Badli-ki Sarai (p. 115). On the north side of the Great Trunk Road and of the garden is the village of Dahirpur, and to the north-west of the latter is seen the large low-lying plain of Bawari, the scene of the Imperial Assemblage of 1st January 1877, and of the Coronation Darbar of 1st January 1903.

Looking round further north up the line of the Ridge, are seen the ruins of the Artillery Hospital and the village of Wazirabad beyond it, and on the river bank the old and still intact Powder Magazine. Across the blue Jumna is a plain of dull green tamarisk, and in spring of bright green crops, extending up to the higher permanent left bank in the river. Down stream from the Magazine rises the minaret of a ruined mosque, the dark chimney of the pumping station of the Delhi Water-Works, and the pale yellow walls of Metcalfe House, with the high piquet mound lying to the west of it. The road running nearly straight to the Kashmir Gate carries the eye past the grey battlements of Ludlow Castle to the white dome of St James' Church, with the barracks in the fort beyond, and the iron railway bridge to the left of them. Looking towards the right of these are seen first the Lahore and Delhi Gates of the fort, mixed up with the minarets of the Zinat-ul-Masajid mosque, next the spire of the Mor Sarai, then the gateway and domes of the Jama Masjid, and the Northbrook Clock Tower, while further on the right is the square-headed building—an effect due to a tank on the top of a mill—which marks the site of the Mori Bastion. Looking south along the crest of the Ridge—just here unusually broad and flat—

are seen a Guard House and the Chauburji Mosque, and beyond them the dark walls of the Observatory on the left, the flat roof of Hindu Rao's House on the right, and the summit of the Mutiny Memorial over all. In the cantonment below to the south-west are seen the ruined walls of the old Station Hospital, and further west the General's Mound, the background being filled, as in 1857, with the trees of Sabzi Mandi, and of the village of Rajpur.

The road running down into the old cantonment from the Flagstaff Tower leads to the **Military Cemetery**,[1] alongside of which a new cemetery has now been opened, that near the Kashmir Gate no longer affording resting-room, so quickly do graveyards fill in India. In this graveyard lie buried Sir Henry Barnard, K.C.B., Colonel Chester, Colonel Yule, Captain Fagan, and many other brave officers and men, some named, but most nameless, who fell before Delhi, upholding the cause of their country.[2]

Sir Henry Barnard's grave lies to the left of the path down the centre, and Colonel Chester's on the right; the former bears the following inscription:—

"Beneath this cross are buried the mortal remains of Major-General Sir Henry Barnard, K.C.B., who

[1] The oldest grave here dates from 1833; one tombstone is to the memory of a husband and a wife, who died the same day in 1855.

[2] On my recommendation, Government has recently approved of the erection of a memorial cross in this cemetery. It is extraordinary, and would, I should hope, be impossible anywhere, except in India, that this should have been neglected for over forty years. The English cemetery at Sebastopol, and the cemetery in the Residency, Lucknow, are now at least well and lovingly cared for, and the same may be hoped for Delhi.—H. C. F.

The Chauburji Mosque, 1857.

Bourne & Shepherd, Photographers.

[*To face p.* 81.

died on the vii July MDCCCLVII, when in chief command of the troops besieging Delhi.

"This monument is erected to his memory by brother officers who served with him before Sebastopol."

To the right of the entrance is the general grave of those killed in the assault of Delhi, and near Sir Henry Barnard's tomb is a monument, with three broken columns, to the memory of Captain Law, Lieutenant Travers, and Lieutenant W. A. Lumsden, all of 1st Punjab Infantry:—

"Among the brave soldiers who gave their lives for their country at the siege of Delhi in 1857, none more gallant and true-hearted here rest from their labour."

Across the drainage-cut towards the Grand Trunk Road was the heavy rear battery of two 18-pounders, erected to protect our position from attacks on this side.

Proceeding south from the Flagstaff Tower, and passing a second old Guard House, where the road makes a considerable angle, the **Mosque Piquet at the Chauburji Mosque** (p. 59), which formed the extreme left of our position on the Ridge, is reached at 800 yards, and 750 yards further south the so-called **Observatory** (p. 58) and Hindu Rao's House. The remains of the battery in front of the Observatory are the best preserved of any of the defences made for the protection of our position before Delhi, and the breastworks on the edge of the slope of the Ridge here can be traced for a considerable way north of it. The **House of Hindu Rao**, a refugee from the Gwalior State, was formerly the residence of Mr William Fraser (p. 18). This formed the headquarters of the centre of our position, and was held by the late General Sir Charles Reid, G.C.B., then Major Reid, and his gallant Sirmoor Goorkhas, and the no less gallant 60th Rifles and Guides. The building was the special mark of the enemy's artillery, and it is on record[1] that it was a cause of wonder to all at the end of the siege how the walls still stood—a conclusion of which the correctness is fully borne out by the photograph of it taken shortly after September 1857. In a brief publication of the year 1861, Colonel Charles Reid, C.B., wrote thus of the disposition of his force:—

"My own regiment and one company of the Rifles occupied the house, and one company of the Rifles the Observatory, where a battery of three heavy guns was constructed on the night of the 9th June. The Guides were located in and about the outhouses."

When His Majesty visited Delhi in 1876, and proceeded to his camp along a route lined by troops, the portion adjoining this point was again held by the 2nd Goorkhas and the 60th Rifles.

From the back of the Observatory ran the nearest road to the camp from the centre and right of the Ridge: this, owing to the command which the fire of the enemy had over it, was named the Valley of

[1] "How men could have held a building so battered and riddled with shot and shell, the very target of the enemy, is a marvel; yet as the siege progressed, when it was proposed to remove even the sick and wounded in hospital, they violently protested against being carried away from their comrades even to a place of safety."—(Raikes' "Notes on the Late Mutiny.")

Hindu Rao's House and Sirmoor Battalion, 1857.

Bourne & Shepherd, Photographers.]

[*To face p.* 82.

The Mutiny Memorial on the Ridge.

[To face p. 83.

Death. At the head of it is the grave of Lieutenant Murray, killed on 14th September, in the assault on Kishanganj, bearing the following legend:—

"Sacred to the memory of Alexander William Murray, Lieutenant in the 42nd Regiment Bengal Native Infantry, attached during the siege of Delhi to the corps of Guides, who fell, whilst encouraging his men to follow his own brave example, on the 14th September 1857."

The two monuments on the Ridge are therefore memorials of the first day of Mutiny inside Delhi, and the last day of our enforced stay outside.

To the east of Hindu Rao's House, which is used still from time to time as a convalescent military hospital, is the reservoir of the Water-Works of the city, which, unfortunately, partly spoils the prospect towards the city from this historic spot. From the south edge of the tank, however, an uninterrupted view can be obtained of the slope from here and from the Mutiny Monument, up which so many attacks of the enemy were made. It must be remembered that in 1857 this site was very much more bare of trees than it is now. Half-way towards the Memorial Monument, rises the second Lat of Asoka (p. 57).

The **Memorial** stands on the spot of the extreme right of our position, which was constantly the object of severe attacks. Two hundred yards to the south-east of it is seen the white stunted cone of the "**Sammy House**," in which there was always a strong piquet, and in front of which much desperate fighting took place. The breastworks on either side of the temple enclosure can still be traced, that to the north as far as the Sammy House Battery, which was constructed on 6th September to control the fire of the Mori Bastion, 800 yards distant, and was officially named Reid's Battery.

The temple, quaintly named by our soldiers from the word Swámi, is a shrine of Bhairon Ji, built in the middle of a small monastery of Kanphattá Sadhs, recluses whose ears are pierced with very large holes for wooden rings which they wear. To the south-west of the right of our position a breastwork ran to the Crow's Nest perched above a pool in an old quarry at this corner of the Ridge, which here sinks practically to the level of the plain, but rises again half a mile to the south to the great Idgah just a mile distant (p. 64). Beyond the pool and across the road leading through Sabzi Mandi to Karnal, is the Sarai, and at the parting of two roads, a little further to the west, is a temple which was held by us to prevent the enemy turning our right flank and penetrating through the walled gardens to our encampment below the Ridge. All these sites—the Mori Bastion, the situation of the Kashmir Bastion, marked by the white church dome, and the principal buildings of the city, are finely seen from the platform of the monument,[1]

[1] The memorial monument, which was erected by the Army before Delhi, is but a sorry specimen of architectural art, and the material used in parts does little credit to the Government Agency charged with the erection. It is much to be desired that a worthier monument should take its place, and I would venture to express the hope that this will be found feasible on the occasion of the Coronation Darbar. It is due to the Army which fought before Delhi that the design of the monument approved by it should be maintained, but the present memorial can readily be recast, while retaining its essential shape, so

from which also the Kutab Minar, over ten miles away as the crow flies, and the tomb of Safdar Jang are usually visible, lying far south of the city, while the marble dome of Humayun's mausoleum may also be seen on very clear days, but it is apt to be lost at once in any haze from the river or ground.

A walk of 300 yards to the east of the memorial leads by a recently constructed path to the **Sammy House Battery**. The legend on it is—

[BATTERY. SAMMY HOUSE [Commanding. Major REMINGTON, R.A.,	Armament, eight 9-pounders. [Mori Bastion. To command ground near

A further walk of about the same distance conducts to the right section of **No. I Siege Battery**: carriages should be sent down the Ridge

as to make it look less like a telescope badly drawn out, and the details of ornamentation can be supplied in good Gothic style in place of the carpenter's work, which alone, perhaps, was possible in 1857, while the marble-backed recesses, which bear the record of the deeds of our brave men, and the names of their dead brave leaders, need not present the shabby appearance caused by the use of three separate pieces of bad stone in one panel. That record will be read by all Englishmen with a glow of admiration for what our army did then, and perhaps a feeling of generous shame that we should have so far forgotten this in the din of subsequent exploits in almost every corner of the world—perhaps, also, with a tinge of contempt for the Government which does so little to hallow the memories of its dead servants. Would any other Government than the British have left such a memorial to stand up gaunt and solitary on the end of a mountain ridge, without an attempt to show that honouring and loving hands had charge of it, or have permitted the stones, once marked by the life-blood of our men, to be quarried for railway ballast and the profit of cantonment funds?—H. C. F.

to the south and round to this point. The right section is situated inside the Police lines to the south of the road to the Kashmir Gate; the left section will be found on the north of the road in the corner of the compound of a house next to the Court of the Sessions Judge, Delhi, upon the edge of the deep ravine, which presented a most valuable natural parallel for our attack. The inscriptions on the two sections of the Battery are as follows:—

[R. MANSELL, R.E.
Right Attack—Lieutenant F.
No. I BATTERY—*Right*,
[Commanding.
Major JAMES BRIND, R.A.,

Directing Engineer.
Arma-ment { Five 18-pounders. One 18-inch howitzer.
To silence Mori Bastion.

No. I BATTERY—*Left*,
Commanding.
Major FRANK TURNER, R.A.,

Armament, four 24-pounders.
To silence Kashmir Bastion.

Proceeding down the road towards the Kashmir Gate, and turning left to the south-west entrance to Ludlow Castle, the site of **No. II Siege Battery** is reached, the right section being close to the cemetery wall and the left[1] section near the wall,

[1] The left section is the private grounds of the Delhi Club, but it is needless to say the members are always glad that any person should walk or drive through the grounds to see the site. The right section can be well seen from over the north wall of the cemetery, or

along the Grand Trunk Road. The legend on them is as follows:—

No. II BATTERY—*Right*, [Commanding. Major EDWARD KAYE, R.A.,	Arma- ment { Two 18-pounders. Seven 8-in. howitzers, To breach Kashmir Bastion.

No. II BATTERY—*Left*, Major CAMPBELL, and subsequently Capt. E. B. JOHNSON } Com- manding	Armament nine 24-pounders. To breach curtain of Kashmir Bastion.

It will interest all visitors to be reminded that the two right guns of the left section of this battery were commanded by Field-Marshal Lord Roberts.

The vistas cut through the trees at these sites, as from that in the Police lines, allow one to see freely the battered wall faces upon which the artillery fire was directed: the vista from the left section of No. I Battery is unfortunately crossed and closed by private property. From the roof of Ludlow Castle General Wilson and his staff watched the attack on the breaches.

From the Ludlow Castle grounds and the Grand Trunk Road, a thoroughfare leads east into the Kudsia Gardens, and at a distance of about 100 yards inside these, a path to the left runs to the

can be reached by a gate into the garden in which it is now enclosed, opposite the aqueduct, near the south-west entrance to the Club grounds.

site[1] of No. IV Siege Mortar Battery on the edge of high ground.

The inscription in this case is as follows:

[Directing Engineer.
Left Attack—Lieut. W. A. GREATHEAD, Bengal Engineers,

No. IV BATTERY. Armament, 10 mortars.

Captain and Brevet-Major TOMBS, Royal Artillery, Commanding.

To shell Kashmir Gate and Kashmir and Water Bastions.

Proceeding east towards the river bank and past the ruined gate of the Kudsia Garden proper, and then turning to the right, the road leads under the mosque to **No. III Siege Battery**, which was constructed behind the Old Customs House, only 200 yards distant from the **Water Bastion and from the Breach** in the corner of the curtain just west of that.

The legend on the miniature battery reads thus:—

[GREATHEAD, R.E.
Left Attack—Lieut. W. A.
No. III BATTERY,
Major WILLIAM SCOTT, R.A.,
Commanding.

Directing Engineer.
Armament, six 18-pounders.
To breach the curtain of the Water Bastion.

[1] The site of this battery which had been left unindicated, was determined at my instance in 1900 by bearings and offsets from the other batteries and sites marked on the plans of 1857, and is now marked by a miniature battery like the others.—H. C. F.

Walking down the vista to this breach, and taking the path to the right along the edge of the city ditch, the **Kashmir Breach and Bastion** (the carriage should be sent round from the site of No. III Siege Battery to this point) are reached in 350 yards. The view of the breaches, the bastions, and the wall of the ditch, with its scarp and counterscarp, and of the glacis outside the ditch, permit a vivid picture of the conditions of the assault on the morning of the 14th September 1857, and one can well imagine the first and second Columns issuing from out of the trees of the Kudsia Gardens under cover of the fire of the Rifles, and pressing on dauntlessly to the breaches. All traces of the shelter ditch thrown up by the enemy in front of this part of their line of defence, and from which they kept up a smart fire on our batteries, have long since disappeared; it formed no actual obstacle to the advance of our troops. Passing the battered and shattered front of the Kashmir bastion, and turning to the left to the Kashmir Gate, it is not hard, with the walls still stripped of their parapets, and their faces scarred with the marks of artillery, to conceive the exploding party advancing to that desperate deed, recorded on the slab erected between the two gateways by Lord Napier of Magdala, when Commander-in-Chief of India. The inscription on the slab is given on p. 90. Curiously enough, the names of two of the men mentioned by Colonel Baird Smith and Lieutenant Home, for "the most determined bravery and coolness," viz., Havildar Ram Taroy and Sepoy Sahib Singh, do not appear on it. Colonel Baird Smith states in his Report (p. 207) that fourteen Bengal Sappers and Miners, and ten Punjab Sappers and Miners, made up the native portion of the party.

On the 14th September 1857, the British Force stormed Delhi. It was after sunrise on that day that the undermentioned party, advancing from Ludlow Castle in the face of heavy fire, and crossing this bridge which had been almost totally destroyed, lodged powder-bags against and blew in the right leaf of this gate, thus opening the way for the assaulting Columns.

Bengal Engineers.[1]

Lieutenant Duncan Home.
Lieutenant Philip Salkeld—mortally wounded.

Bengal Sappers and Miners.

Sergeant John Smith.
Sergeant A. B. Carmichael—killed.
Corporal F. Burgess—killed.

Bugler Hawthorne, 52nd Foot.

Bengal Sappers and Miners.

Soobadar Toola Ram.
Jamadar Bis Ram.
Havildar Madho—wounded.
Havildar Tilok Singh—mortally wounded.
Sepoy Ram Heth—killed.

This memorial is placed here as a tribute of respect to those gallant soldiers by General Lord Napier of Magdala, Colonel, Royal Engineers, and Commander-in-Chief in India, 1876.

Passing through the gate which was blown in—the present wooden doors are subsequent to 1857

[1] Lieutenant Salkeld had escaped from the Kashmir Gate on 11th May with Colonel Vibart's party. Colonel Vibart has not explained how Lieutenant Salkeld happened to be at the Kashmir Gate; Lieut. Home, who was recommended for the V.C., subsequently blew in the gate of the Delhi Fort, and unhappily lost his life in blowing up the fortress of Malagarh not long afterwards, while accompanying the Delhi Field Force.

The Kashmir Gate, 1857.

Bourne & Shepherd, Photographers.]

[*To face p.* 90.

—those which then existed probably resembled the ones still in the Ajmir Gate—entry is made into the **Main Guard** in or near which so many officers were murdered on the fatal 11th May. It was a twelve-sided enclosure, with the outer gate of the city on its west side, the inner city gate on its south side, a gate to the District Courts and Offices, which, as in 1857, lie in the north-east angle of the city, on its east side, and a ramp to the Kashmir Bastion on its north side. All round the enclosure were rooms for the guard, and over the gate were quarters for the officer in command. Ascending the ramp, we find ourselves on the wall at the head of the Kashmir breach, and can look down the vista from it to the left portion of No. II Battery in the grounds of Ludlow Castle. Those to the right portion of this battery and towards the left half of No. II Siege Battery, can be viewed from the Bastion itself; and from the top of the gate is seen the whole length of the northern wall up to the smashed defences of the Mori Bastion. About half way between them is a bit of wall broken by artillery fire, where the enemy contrived to mount a gun, so as to enfilade No. II Siege Battery; one martello tower also breaks the long front of the curtain here.

From the Main Guard the Columns which assaulted the breaches moved inside the city wall to the Mori Gate and the Mori Bastion beyond it, and this route should now be followed. From the **Mori Bastion**, the front of which is more battered and broken than that of the Kashmir Bastion, a full view is obtained of the right of our position on the

Ridge, and of the red Mutiny Memorial with the white Sammy House in the trees below it. General Sir J. Hope Grant has recorded in his Memoirs how he saw General Nicholson on the top of the Mori Bastion, and how the latter shouted to him that the fight was going well for us. Turning south from the bastion, and skirting the railway to the Dufferin Bridge, the route onwards crosses this, and then turns right again to the gap in the city walls where the **Kabul Gate** once stood. From this point it is necessary to walk over the Western Jumna Canal, and to turn southwards for sixty yards under the wall, when the spot will be reached where a tablet over a recess under the raised way behind the battlements bears the following inscription:—

THIS TABLET
MARKS THE SPOT WHERE
BRIGADIER-GENERAL JOHN NICHOLSON
WAS MORTALLY WOUNDED
DURING THE ASSAULT
ON THE 14TH SEPTEMBER 1857.

The narrow lane beyond, with two guns at the end, and the houses on the east side filled with armed mutineers, must have formed a veritable "Gate of Hell" into which to advance.

Returning over the Dufferin Bridge, and passing through the Mori Gate, the usual road to the Civil Station leads to the entrance of the **Kashmir Gate Cemetery**, thirty yards from which, to the right, following a path indicated by small piles of cannon

The Grave of Brigadier-General Nicholson.

[*To face p.* 93.

balls, is the grave of Brigadier-General John Nicholson. The large stone slab over it, which was taken from the king's palace, says simply :—

THE GRAVE

OF

BRIGADIER-GENERAL JOHN NICHOLSON

WHO

LED THE ASSAULT OF DELHI

BUT FELL

IN THE HOUR OF VICTORY

MORTALLY WOUNDED

AND DIED

23RD SEPTEMBER 1857

AGED 35.

The funeral, which took place early on the 24th September, was entirely without military honours, so fully were the troops still available engaged; only Colonel Chamberlain (the late Field-Marshal Sir Neville Chamberlain), Mr Saunders, who had succeeded Mr Greathead as Commissioner of Delhi, and a few other officers, were present at it. The day was marked, however, in a way which General Nicholson would have preferred above all others—the departure from Delhi of the avenging Field Force which he was to have commanded. His mother, to whom his last thoughts turned, survived him for seventeen years, dying in 1874 at the age of eighty-eight.

One hundred yards from the entrance to the cemetery on the left of the main path, is the grave of

Harvey Greathead, who was Commissioner and Political Agent with the Delhi Field Force, and died of cholera four days after the fall of Delhi. This was the first grave made here, but a number of memorial tablets from some earlier burial-ground are placed in the wall to the left of the entrance. Among the memorials of 1857 is one of Mr Clifford, killed in the Gurgaon district, in October of that year, and of his sister, killed in the Delhi Fort on 11th May.

With the grave of General Nicholson ends the record of the spots of special interest connected with the Siege and Assault of Delhi.

CHAPTER III—*continued*

DELHI IN 1857

PART II.—THE OUTBREAK OF THE MUTINY ON 11TH MAY

THE mutiny of the 38th, 54th, and 74th[1] Regiments of Bengal Native Infantry, and of a battery of Native Artillery, at Delhi, on 11th May, was the direct outcome of the mutiny on the preceding Sunday evening of the 3rd Bengal Light Cavalry,

[1] The 38th was known as the Ballamteer or Volunteer Regiment, the 54th as the Mapert Regiment, and the 74th as the Sikander Regiment. The battery was No. 5 Light Field Battery. The soldiers of the Native Army in 1857 were usually known and referred to as Talangas.

and the 11th and 20th Regiments of Native Infantry at Meerut, which lies thirty-six miles to the north-east. A number of the native officers of the Delhi regiments had been members of the courts of enquiry at Meerut into the conduct of the troopers in refusing to take and use the new greased cartridges; and it is clear from the evidence given at the trial of the King of Delhi, that the Delhi regiments were well aware of the reasons of the mutiny of the Meerut regiments, and had prepared to join them. That they did not do so at once upon the arrival of the latter, must have been due to the knowledge that the plan of murdering all the Europeans at Meerut had failed, and that there was, therefore, a possibility of these turning up in fierce pursuit at any moment. Of the conduct of the authorities at Meerut in first insisting at that moment upon the use of the cartridges, and subsequently subjecting the men who had refused them to a peculiarly degrading form of punishment in public, and of their utter failure either to foresee the general outbreak, or to take instant steps to crush it after it occurred, it is useless to write at this distance of time. One has only to read the appalling account of what occurred on and after the Meerut outbreak, recorded by General Sir Hugh Gough, V.C., and by Colonel A. R. D. Mackenzie in his Mutiny Memoirs, to realise only too vividly why nothing was done there; as was said of another similar occasion, "firmness, decision, and self-reliance were absolutely necessary for the crisis, and were unfortunately not sufficiently displayed." An attempt was made by offering a large money reward to forward news of the Mutiny to Delhi by native agency that night—no one apparently thought of using the services of a Gough or a Mackenzie—and a native news-letter writer of the time recorded that information did reach the Commissioner, Mr Simon Fraser. Be this as it may, it is certain that the Commissioner and the Collector, Mr Hutchinson, received intimation of something untoward early on the morning of the 11th May, which caused them to send a message to cantonments, and to proceed to the Calcutta Gate and Bridge of Boats before 8 A.M., and perhaps before 7 A.M.—it is extraordinary how variously the times of events throughout that sad and terribly long day are stated. Previous to this, at least one of the mutineers of the 3rd Light Cavalry had ridden into the city and up to the Lahore Gate of the fort, where he was spoken to by Captain Douglas, Commandant of the Palace Guard; and others arrived immediately afterwards at the ground in the river bed, under the walls of the king's apartments, known as the Zer Jharokha[1] (p. 33), and called upon the

[1] Nearly all the writers upon the events of 1857 in Delhi have gone wrong regarding this incident, and have imagined that these mutineers were gathered in a courtyard *inside* the palace, under some window of the king which never existed. The term Zer Jharokha was a well-known one, used to designate the space in the river bed below a window in the royal apartments, from which the king used formerly to show himself to the crowd below (p. 33), and it was on this space that the troopers were assembled. Captain Douglas wished to go down to them by the staircase and wicket under the Musamman Burj (p. 38), but this the king refused to permit; and he accordingly addressed them from the platform between the Diwan-i-Khas and the private apartments of the king.

king to do them justice, and to place himself at their head.

The king immediately sent for Captain Douglas, who at once went to the royal apartments on the south side of the Diwan-i-Khas, and spoke to the troopers, telling them not to annoy the king, but to pass on to the Kotila of Firoz Shah, when their complaints would be heard. The men who had found the Calcutta Gate closed on them, and now found themselves repulsed at the palace, proceeded presently to the Raj Ghat,[1] and probably the Khairati Gate, and were there admitted to the city, their arrival being clearly expected by the dangerous classes of the place. From that point they galloped up past the Ellenborough Tank to the Lahore Gate of the Fort. This also they found closed by the orders of Captain Douglas, who, on returning from the king, had directed it to be secured, and had proceeded to the Calcutta Gate in compliance with a message left for him by the Commissioner. The mutineers no doubt learnt this from the guard, which was furnished by the 38th Regiment, and immediately passed on to that point. There they found Captain Douglas with the Commissioner and the Collector—these officers, with the aid of Sir Theophilus Metcalfe, who had meanwhile gone on to the Kotwali, or

[1] I can find no authority for the common statement that the mutineers who first arrived entered the fort from the Salimgarh, and feel sure this is a mistake, based upon that connected with the real position of the Zer Jharokha. Quite possibly, however, after the British officers had been murdered and the palace guard had mutinied, the later arrivals among the mutineers were admitted to the fort and palace by this route; but at that time every gate on the south side of the city was open to them.

principal police station, to make arrangements there, had succeeded in closing the gate,—and this group they immediately attacked, wounding Mr Hutchinson. The Commissioner's escort of Jhajjar Sawars refused to fire or draw sword in defence of the officers, but the Commissioner seized a musket and shot one cavalryman dead, and his companions at once made off. Meanwhile a crowd, intent on evil designs, had gathered on the spot; but the Commissioner forced his way through them in his buggy, with Mr Hutchinson, while Captain Douglas got away into the Fort Ditch, badly injuring his ankle, however, in so doing; and ultimately all three arrived at the Lahore Gate, and entered the fort. During a pause in the gateway, for both Captain Douglas and Mr Hutchinson were severely hurt, the Chaplain, the Rev. Mr Jennings, joined them, and shortly afterward they all proceeded to the rooms over the gate occupied by the Commandant and the chaplain. Meanwhile the Commissioner had summoned two of the principal advisers of the king, and on their arriving at these rooms, he requested them to move the king to send two guns down to the gate, and two palanquins to remove to his own protection Miss Jennings and Miss Clifford, who were also in the fort. When these men left to carry out their instructions, Mr Fraser accompanied them down to the bottom of the northern flight of steps leading to the upper portion of the gate, and saw them on their way. A crowd of ruffians from the palace precincts had now gathered at the foot of the steps, and this Mr Fraser faced and addressed. On turning to go up the steps again he was instantly attacked from behind, and cut down by an Abyssinian, who was happily brought to justice some years afterwards. The mob, which had now tasted blood, at once invaded the staircase, and sought to enter the rooms above. The native servants with the Europeans played the man so far as was possible, and managed to close the doors on this staircase; but some of the mob ascended the southern staircase, and passing over the rooms, descended by the upper portion of the northern staircase, and opened the doors to the murderers. No resistance could be offered by the inmates of the rooms, and the deed of blood was accomplished in a few seconds. All this occurred before 10 A.M. The mutinous troopers and the guard of the 38th at once presented themselves before the king, and as other mutineers arrived from Meerut (accounts as to when they arrived, and in what array they did so, differ widely), plans were no doubt laid for more serious mischief, upon which the mob was already actively engaged. Many Englishmen were murdered at this time in the city by the mob, among them Mr Beresford, Manager of the Delhi Bank, and his family, after a desperate resistance on the roof of an out-house. The prisoners of the jail had been set free, and the houses of Daryaganj were generally in flames; and now the king's personal troops[1] and the mutineers issued forth to attack the Magazine.

[1] The king had a body-guard of some 1,200 soldiers and a few artillerymen. Mr Minturn, who visited Delhi about eight months before the outbreak of the Mutiny, describes the guards as shabby-looking soldiers, dressed in a clumsily-made uniform after the English pattern.

The officer in charge, Lieut. G. D. Willoughby, had been warned by the Commissioner and Sir Theophilus Metcalfe as they went down to the city, and he and his assistants (Lieutenants Raynor and Forrest, Conductors Buckley, Shaw, and Scully, Sub-Conductor Crow, Sergeants Edwards and Stewart) had prepared as best they could to resist attack, which they probably considered would not be persistent, until the Meerut troops should arrive. Little, however, it is needless to say, could be done to effectively repel assaults on a position of considerable extent, with no British guard,[1] and a garrison of only eight British subordinates, surrounded by native houses, and occupied by a treacherous guard of the 38th, and a native establishment, probably as treacherous, and which could not be expected to fight. No notice was taken of various summons to surrender, but the little garrison was quite powerless to prevent or check the plunder of the Magazine workshops on the other side of the road, and reserved its strength for the real attack when it should be made.

Long before this, probably about 9 A.M., the 38th and 54th regiments had been paraded in the cantonment, and an hour later had marched to check the mutineers, the eight leading companies of the latter to the Main Guard at the Kashmir Gate, already held by two companies of the 38th, and two companies of

[1] Arsenals at least are efficiently protected now in India, and there is no longer any arsenal at Delhi. But many, perhaps most people, will hear with surprise, I think, that the European garrison of Delhi consists of only a garrison battery, and two companies of a British regiment sent over from Meerut.—H. C. F.

the former to the Powder Magazine[1] on the bank of the Jumna, near the north end of the Ridge (p. 79). Both regiments seem to have started off with alacrity; but on the leading companies of the 54th[2] reaching the main guard with unloaded muskets, and proceeding beyond it into the open space towards the city, a number of rebel troopers rode up and proceeded to shoot and cut down the officers, no less than five of whom were killed outright, their own men looking on all the while, and the men of the 38th even assisting in the attack. This portion of the 54th regiment then entirely disappeared for a time, but was subsequently brought back by its native officers from the Sabzi Mandi direction. Two other companies of the regiment, which arrived later, escorting two guns, and with which Lieutenant (afterwards Colonel) Vibart was, remained at the Quarter Guard with the two companies of the 38th Native Infantry. Upon the news of what had happened to the officers of the 54th reaching cantonments, the 74th regiment was also paraded, and sent down to the Kashmir Main Guard by the General commanding the Station; but beyond recovering the bodies of the officers killed at this enclosure, no move was made by any one, and a force of men from three separate regiments,

[1] This Magazine had been established outside the city only seven years previously. Had it still been at the Arsenal in 1857, its explosion would probably have destroyed most of the munitions of war which fell into the hands of the mutineers, after the explosion of the small Powder Magazine left in it.

[2] One of the last of the enemy killed facing our troops in September 1857 was a private of the 54th Regiment, who stood as a solitary sentinel at the approach from the Salimgarh to the palace.

all over ripe for mutiny, was kept inactive for hours with the sound of desperate fighting at the Magazine, only 700 yards away, in their ears, until the certainty that no avenging troops from Meerut were to be feared, encouraged them to openly complete their mutiny. The attack on the Arsenal began apparently soon after one o'clock, though the actual assault was not made till considerably later, and seems to have lasted only for some forty minutes, during which the gallant defenders did all that such a handful of men could do. At last, hopeless of succour either from the troops at Delhi or those at Meerut, and having been deserted by all the native establishment, Lieutenant Willoughby gave the preconcerted signal, and the Magazine of the Arsenal was blown up, Conductor Scully firing the train and perishing in the act. The survivors escaped by the sally-port on the river face, and some of them reached the Kashmir Main Guard.[1] The destruction of the Arsenal naturally destroyed the last shreds of loyalty of the already half-mutinous regiments, at this spot, and after a further interval (some of the officers say they did not leave the Main Guard till 5 P.M.), they broke into open revolt upon the 74th regiment, being recalled with two guns to the cantonment. In this, the men of the 38th, who had already brought back two guns previously recalled, were as usual the leaders, and a few volleys laid many of the officers low. Some, however, had already

[1] The inscription on the tablet over the Main Gate of the Magazine which commemorates this heroic feat will be found on p. 19. The report of the senior surviving officer among the defenders, and the orders of the Governor-General thereon, are given at the end of this section of the chapter.

moved out of the Main Guard with the 74th, and others, including some unhappy ladies who had gathered there, escaped over the Kashmir Bastion walls, the mass of the mutinous soldiers being luckily attracted for the moment to the pillaging of the Government Treasury. Of the adventures which attended the escape of one party, a thrilling narrative will be found in the pages of Colonel Vibart's book, "The Sepoy Mutiny, as Seen by a Subaltern."

Upon the explosion of the Arsenal Magazine the two companies of the 38th posted on the powder stores made off to the city, considerately sparing their officers, with loud shouts of "Prithvi Raj ki Jai," a war-cry which had first been heard at Delhi 700 years previously, when the Chauhan Prince fell before the Muhammadan conquerors. The news of the final defection of the regiments at the Kashmir Gate, and of the further murder of officers there, was the signal to all Europeans left in the cantonment that they must betake themselves to immediate flight. All the afternoon the non-combatants and unhappy women and children had been gathered at the Flagstaff Tower, where also the officer commanding the Station, Brigadier-General Graves[1] looked in vain for the succour from Meerut which never came; and now they started off in disorganised flight, so disorganised that wounded men and ladies with infants were left to manage for themselves as best they could. The

[1] I am informed that no report by this officer upon the events at Delhi on 11th May 1857 is in existence. If it were, it would prove extremely interesting reading. I need not indicate upon what points. —H. C. F.

cantonments were burnt and destroyed by the mob and the neighbouring Gujars the same night, and when our forces reappeared on the 8th June, they found nothing but a heap of ruins. The Meerut and Delhi regiments at once imposed themselves upon the king as unwelcome guests, and took up their quarters in the Diwan-i-'Am and the Diwan-i-Khas, and in the royal palace gardens. The only persons who maintained their struggle against the mutinous mercenaries and murderous mob were a handful of humble individuals, six men and two lads, with a number of women and children, who, without food and without water, the latter all spilt by treacherous servants on leaving them, maintained themselves in a house[1] in Daryaganj till the 13th May, when Mr Aldwell and his son alone escaped, the rest having been killed or captured. Mrs Aldwell, who had been previously taken away by some native servants, escaped again, when fifty-two[2] captive Christians were murdered in the fort on 16th May. These unfortunates, who had been confined in a room of the king's kitchen, forty feet long, twelve feet broad, and ten feet high—simply imagine what that meant in the middle of May—were seated round the edge of the tank in front of the Nakkar Khana (p. 27), and were there killed by the king's servants, the mutineers

[1] The house is No. 5 in the cantonment, just south of the road from the Khairati Gate, and the military hospital above this. Mr Aldwell's son, who, as a lad of sixteen, shared the defence throughout, is still alive, and in the service of the Delhi municipality.

[2] This is the number given by the news-writer of the day. In the fourth charge framed against the king at his trial, the number is said to have been forty-nine.

refusing to their credit[1] to be the butchers; and with them all persons of British descent and Christian belief disappeared for the time being from Delhi.

The suddenness with which all English authority perished in Delhi is probably without a parallel in history. Lucknow and Cawnpur present no such phase in their sad chronicles. That there was a complete understanding between the Meerut and Delhi troops is beyond all doubt; but the latter did not immediately join the former, probably for the reason stated above, while the city mob seems to have risen to murder and burn upon the arrival of the very first mutinous troopers. Various survivors of the summer of 1857 in Delhi say, as was said at the king's trial, that the mutiny of the army and revolt of the people was mainly due to a deep-rooted fear that it was intended to impose the Christian religion on the country, and they refer, in support of this belief, to certain officials of the time as ardent advocates of the Christian religion in their relations

[1] A representation to the king by one Nabbi Bakhsh, found after the capture of the palace in September 1857, showed that he had had the courage to declare that the slaughter of women and children and other prisoners of war was contrary to the tenets of the Muhammadan religion. This paper was considered then to be of doubtful authenticity; but the news-writer in Delhi recorded on the 20th May that one Mahbub Ali had given a similar opinion, and that a certain Mirza Majhli tried to save some of the prisoners, and was nearly murdered himself in consequence. The royal physician, Ahsanullah Khan, deposed at the king's trial that if the king had chosen to say to the troops that they should kill him first, the lives of the prisoners might have been saved, but this would seem to be very doubtful.

with the natives. Such persons also say that the turbulent factions of the people talked openly of the mutiny of the troops and the fall of the British rule for some time before the 10th and 11th May, and this may account for the sudden appearance of the mob on the scene; but it seems extraordinary that all these indications should have escaped the notice of the authorities of the day. That the officers of the Delhi regiments had no suspicions of the disloyalty of their men is abundantly apparent. It seems certain, as stated by Major Abbott, commanding the 74th regiment, in his report of 13th May, that the 38th was at the bottom of the whole Mutiny, and coerced the other two regiments. That the 38th should have furnished the guards not only at the Kashmir Gate, but also at the Arsenal and Palace on the morning of 11th May, and should have done so only for that morning, is one of the many instances of extraordinary fatality of which the Mutiny of 1857 was so fruitful. At the same time, it should be noted that, according to Major Paterson of the 38th, 300 men of that regiment stood by Brigadier-General Graves till the last, and the Colonel and Adjutant of the regiment were allowed to leave the cantonment unharmed long after all other Europeans. That the King of Delhi had no direct connection with the mutiny of the troops is practically certain, though he perhaps was prepared to take advantage of it, as his sons assuredly were. From the first, he was wholly at the mercy of the mutinous soldiery who were controlled by a council named the Bàrah Topi, or Twelve Heads (Hats), and his papers seized after September are full of senile complaints of the disrespect and discourtesy which he suffered from them. Many things done by the British Government before 1857, out of regard for the past of the fallen Moghal Emperors, were used to our disadvantage then. For instance, in proclamations the wording used to run "Mulk-i-Badshah aur hukm Sirkar company ka" ("The King's Realm and the Company's Rule"), and it was industriously asseverated at the time that the Company had rebelled against the king, and that the native soldiers were bound to rally round him and against it.

One incident of that terrible day has still to be noticed—the incident of the Telegraph Office. A full and authentic account of this will be found in a chapter of Colonel Vibart's book, specially written by Mr P. V. Luke, C.I.E., of the Indian Telegraph Department, and a brief record must suffice here. The telegraph master, Mr Todd, had left Delhi very early in the morning to see what was wrong with the line which had been cut by the mutineers, and he was met and murdered by them. His two assistants, by name Brendish and Pilkington, remained at the office till two o'clock in the afternoon, and during all that time no message was despatched by the military authorities, who leant solely on that broken reed of expected aid from Meerut. The signallers, however, from time to time, informed the Amballah office of what was going on in Delhi. About three in the afternoon Pilkington returned to the office from the Flagstaff Tower, to which the telegraph party had been advised to retreat, with a military officer, and despatched a very meagre official telegram to Amballah; but it was really the irresponsible chatter of one clerk with another that gave the effective warning to the Punjab of what had happened at Delhi, and enabled the authorities there to take steps which at least scotched further mutiny and saved the position for the time being. The signaller, Pilkington, died a long time ago. Mr Brendish retired from Government service only four years back, on a special pension equivalent to his full pay, granted in recognition of his services on 11th May 1857, and is still alive. And yet Mr Cooper recorded in his "Guide of Delhi," written in 1862, that the signaller at Delhi was cut down with his hand still upon the telegraph instrument. Other recorded incidents in the history of the time are perhaps hardly much more authentic than this.

General Order by the Right Hon'ble the Governor-General of India in Council, dated Fort William, ——— 1857.

No. 940 of 1857.—The Right Hon'ble the Governor-General in Council is pleased to direct the publication of the following authentic report of the occurrences at the Delhi Magazine on the 11th of May last, when attacked by mutineers, and of the noble and cool soldiership of its gallant defenders, commanded by Lieutenant G. D. Willoughby, Commissary of Ordnance.

The Governor-General in Council desires to offer his cordial thanks to Lieutenants Raynor and Forrest and the other survivors amongst the brave men mentioned in this report, and to express the admiration with which he regards the daring and heroic conduct of Lieutenant G. D. Willoughby and the warrant and non-commissioned officers by whom he was supported on that occasion. Their names are Lieutenants Raynor and Forrest, Conductors Shaw, Buckley, and Scully, Sub-Conductor Crow, and Sergeants Edwards and Stewart.

The family of the late Conductor Scully, who so devotedly sacrificed himself in the explosion of the magazine, will be liberally provided for, should it be ascertained that they have survived him.[1]

From Lieutenant G. FORREST, *Assistant Commissary of Ordnance, to Colonel* A. ABBOTT, C.B., *Inspector-General of Ordnance and Magazines, Fort William, dated Meerut, 27th May* 1857.

I HAVE the honour to report, for the information of Government, and in the absence of my commanding officer, Lieutenant Willoughby, Artillery, supposed to be killed on his retreat from Delhi to this station, the following facts as regards the capture of the Delhi Magazine by the mutineers and insurgents on the 11th instant. On the morning of that date, between 7 and 8 A.M., Sir Theophilus Metcalfe came to my house, and requested that I would accompany him to the magazine, for the purpose of having two guns placed on the bridge, so as to prevent the mutineers from passing over. On our arrival at the magazine,

[1] Mrs Scully and three children were among those massacred in the palace on 16th May. One son of this gallant man was serving in the Indian Inland Customs some years ago.—H. C. F.

we found present Lieutenants Willoughby and Raynor, with Conductors Buckley, Shaw, and Scully, and Acting Sub-Conductor Crow, and Sergeants Edwards and Stewart, with the Native establishment. On Sir Theophilus Metcalfe alighting from his buggy, Lieutenant Willoughby and I accompanied him to the small bastion on the river face, which commanded a full view of the bridge, from which we could distinctly see the mutineers marching in open column, headed by the cavalry; and the Delhi side of the bridge was already in the possession of a body of cavalry. On Sir Theophilus Metcalfe observing this, he proceeded with Lieutenant Willoughby to see if the city gate was closed against the mutineers. However, this step was needless, as the mutineers were admitted directly to the palace, through which they passed cheering. On Lieutenant Willoughby's return to the magazine, the gates of the magazine were closed and barricaded, and every possible arrangement that could be made was at once commenced on. Inside the gate leading to the park were placed two 6-pounders, double charged with grape, one under Acting Sub-Conductor Crow and Sergeant Stewart, with the lighted matches in their hands, and with orders that if any attempt was made to force that gate, both guns were to be fired at once, and they were to fall back on that part of the magazine in which Lieutenant Willoughby and I were posted. The principal gate of the magazine was similarly defended by two guns, with the *chevaux de frieze* laid down on the inside. For the further defence of this gate and the magazine in its vicinity, there were two 6-pounders so placed as either to command the gate or a small bastion in its vicinity. Within sixty yards of the gate and in front of the office, and commanding two cross roads, were three 6-pounders and one 24-pounder howitzer, which could be so managed as to act upon any part of the magazine in that neighbourhood. After all these guns and howitzers had been placed in the several positions above-named, they were loaded with double charges of grape. The next step taken was to place arms in the hands of the Native establishment, which they most reluctantly received, and appeared to be in a state not only of excitement but also of insubordination, as they refused to obey any orders issued by the Europeans, particularly the Mussulman portion of the establishment. After the above arrangements had been made, a train was laid by Conductors Buckley and Scully and Sergeant Stewart, ready to be fired by a preconcerted signal, which was that of Conductor Buckley raising his hat from his head, on the order being given by Lieutenant Willoughby. The train was to be fired by Conductor Scully, but not until such time as the last round from the howitzers had been fired. So soon as the above arrangements had been made, guards from the palace came and demanded the possession of the magazine in the name of the King of Delhi, to which no reply was given. Immediately after this, the subadar of the guard on duty at the magazine informed Lieutenant Willoughby and me that the King of Delhi had sent down word to the mutineers that he would without delay send scaling ladders from the palace for the purpose of scaling the walls; and which shortly after arrived. On the ladders being erected against the wall, the whole of our Native establishment deserted us by climbing up the sloped sheds on the inside of the magazine and descending the ladders on the outside, after which the enemy appeared in great number on the top of the walls, and on whom we kept up an incessant fire of grape, every round of which told well, as long as a single round remained. Previous to the Natives deserting us, they hid the priming pouches; and one man in particular, Karim Bakhsh, a *durwan*, appeared to keep up a constant communication with the enemy on the outside, and keep them informed of our situation. Lieutenant Willoughby was so annoyed at this man's conduct, that he gave me an order to shoot him should he again approach the gate.

Lieutenant Raynor, with the other Europeans, did everything that possibly could be done for the defence of the magazine, and where all have behaved so bravely, it is almost impossible for me to point out any particular individual. However, I am in duty bound to bring to the notice of Government the gallantry of Conductors Buckley and Scully on this trying occasion. The former, assisted only by myself, loaded and fired in rapid succession the several guns above detailed, firing at least four rounds from each gun, and with the same steadiness as if standing on parade, although the enemy were then some hundreds in number, and kept up a continual fire of musketry on us within forty or fifty yards. After firing the last round, Conductor Buckley received a musket-ball in his arm, above the elbow, which has since been extracted here; I, at the same time, was struck in the left hand by two musket balls, which disabled me for the time. It was at this critical moment that Lieutenant Willoughby gave the order for firing the magazine, which was at once responded to by Conductor Scully firing the several trains. Indeed from the very commencement he evinced his gallantry by volunteering his services for blowing up the magazine, and remained true to his trust to the last moment. As soon as the explosion took place, such as escaped from beneath the ruins—and none escaped unhurt—retreated through the sally-port on the river face. Lieutenant Willoughby and I succeeded in reaching the Kashmir Gate. What became of the other parties it is impossible for me to say. Lieutenant Raynor and Conductor Buckley have escaped to this station. Severe indisposition prevented my sending in this report sooner.

CHAPTER III—*continued*

DELHI IN 1857

PART III.—NARRATIVE OF THE SIEGE AND ASSAULT OF DELHI, BY LIEUT. H. W. NORMAN, NOW FIELD-MARSHAL SIR HENRY NORMAN, G.C.B., G.C.M.G., WITH NOTES AND ADDITIONAL PAPERS.

WHEN the news of the outbreak at Delhi and Meerut reached the Commander-in-Chief, General Anson, in Simla on 12th and 13th May, he at once took steps to concentrate at Amballah such troops [1] as were available, and by the 17th a small force was pushed forward to Karnal. Apparently all that could be done by human energy at this moment was done; but, as usual, the crisis found us unprepared, and there were no tents and no supplies, and no spare ammunition either for muskets or field-guns on the spot, and carriage had to be collected. General Anson himself proceeded to Karnal on 25th May, and died there of cholera on the morning of the 27th, General Sir H. Barnard succeeding him in the command. Rai, two marches distant from Delhi, was reached by the advanced troops on 2nd June, and by the Headquarters on 4th June. On the 7th, Brigadier-General Wilson, marching *via* Baghpat, with the Meerut force, joined the camp at Alipur, 10 miles from Delhi. General Wilson's small force had

[1] At the time of the Mutiny there were 15,000 European troops, with 84 guns in the Punjab and at Meerut, and 65,000 native troops with 62 guns.—H. C. F.

fought two successful actions with the mutineers from Delhi, on 30th and 31st May, at the Hindan River, near Ghazi-ud-din-nagar, now Ghaziabad, and had captured five guns from them. The army under General Barnard's command then consisted of 600 cavalry, 2400 infantry, 22 field guns, and a small siege train; and with this force he advanced at 2 A.M. on the morning of the 8th June against the enemy's position, six miles in front of him, at Badli-ki Sarai. The account of the action which followed is thus told in

LIEUTENANT NORMAN'S NARRATIVE.[1]

The baggage was all left at Alipur with directions not to move on until the success of our attack at Badli-ki Sarai had declared itself and orders been sent back for its advance. The guard for its protection was composed of two guns of Major Scott's battery, a squadron of the Carabineers, a company of the 2nd Bengal European Fusiliers, and the contingent of the Rajah of Jhind, with the exception of about fifty sawars.

[1] I have no doubt that every one will prefer this simple, vigorous, original narrative of the Siege of Delhi, written at the time and on the spot, to any account which can be compiled now; and I therefore reproduce it here from the selection of Delhi Mutiny papers, edited by Mr Forrest, merely adding a few notes. To the extraordinary accuracy of the narrative I may perhaps venture to offer my testimony, after studying every portion of it on the ground. I have added to it the reports by Brigadier-General Nicholson on the Battle of Najafgarh, and of Colonel Baird Smith upon the operations of the actual siege, and the record of the Governor-General of India, and of various distinguished soldiers of the services rendered by the army before Delhi. The map of siege operations, contained in the end pocket, is adapted from that prepared authoritatively, in 1876, under the orders of the Quarter-Master-General in India, Major-General Fred. Roberts.
—H. C. F.

The mutineers' position was as follows:—They held the *sarai* of Badli[1] on the right of the Trunk Road as we advanced, and their camp was grouped about it. About a hundred and fifty yards in front of the *sarai*, on a small natural elevation, was a sand-bag battery for four heavy guns and an 8-inch howitzer. The ground on either side of the Trunk Road leading to this position is intersected with water-cuts and generally swampy; while nearly parallel to the road on the right, at the distance of about a mile, runs the canal, crossed by bridges at various places not far from each other.

The main attack was to be made in front, supported by a diversion on the enemy's left flank with cavalry and guns. Brigadier Grant, commanding the cavalry, accordingly quitted camp before the main column, passed the canal at a neighbouring bridge, and proceeded down its right bank with intent to cross in the enemy's left rear, and to attack simultaneously with the main body under Sir Henry Barnard. Brigadier Grant had with him ten horse artillery guns under Major Turner, consisting of four guns of Major Tombs' troop, and Major Turner's own troop under Lieutenant Bishop, three squadrons of the 9th Lancers under Brevet Lieutenant-Colonel

[1] It is an extraordinary fact that the battle-field of Badli-ki Sarai has been placed at an entirely wrong site in the map published by military authority in the volume of Mutiny papers referred to above. The battle took place in front of the old Moghal brick sarai in which the village of Pipal Thalla has been built, nearly a mile and a half south of the village of Badli, at which it has been located in the map. The Revenue Survey map of 1872-73 happened to show the site of an old deserted encamping-ground and mud sarai east of the village of Badli, while it indicated the Moghal Sarai in a very indefinite way, and hence the mistake of the actual site of the engagement arose, and corrections were made in Lieutenant Norman's narrative, and a line of march, which was never followed, was designed for General Graves. There is no doubt that it was fought at the position of the brick Moghal Sarai. Many villagers who viewed the fight from afar off can still recall vivid details of it; and

Yule, and about fifty Jhind horsemen under Lieutenant Hodson.

The main column proceeded down the Trunk Road, and consisted of Captain Money's troop of horse artillery, four guns of Major Scott's horse battery, four heavy guns hastily formed into a battery for field purposes, and principally manned by recruits, a squadron each of the Carabineers and 9th Lancers, and the five weak infantry regiments.

The total force to be engaged in the main attack was in round numbers 170 cavalry and 1900 infantry, with fourteen guns. That employed in the flank attack about 350 cavalry and ten guns.

It was intended that in the main attack our four heavy guns should open on the enemy from the road itself, with a light battery on either flank; that Brigadier Showers, with the 75th Foot and 1st Bengal European Fusiliers, should operate to the right; and Brigadier Graves, with the 60th Rifles, 2nd Bengal European Fusiliers and Sirmoor Battalion to the left of the road.

As the day broke the lights in the enemy's camp were visible, and our guns advanced to open fire. Their artillery, however, commenced the ball with a sharp cannonade, to which our guns were not slow

all the features of this site—the sarai itself, the mound in front on which the heavier guns of the enemy were placed, and which since then bears a European grave, that of Lieutenant Harrison of the 75th Regiment, and the buildings on both sides of the road—make its correctness unmistakably clear to any one who has visited the spot. A map of the actual battle-field is inserted in the text. The Grand Trunk Road, which had formerly led through the middle of the sarai, had been diverted to the east of it shortly before 1857, and was then without trees, and, in consequence, our troops advancing down it were exposed to the full fire of the enemy's guns. On the right of our troops as they advanced, and between Badli and the village of Haidarpur, lying north-west of Badli-ki Sarai, were the Shalimar Gardens, and to the west again of these was the West Jumna Canal, along which Brigadier-General Hope Grant advanced in order to take the enemy in the rear.—H. C. F.

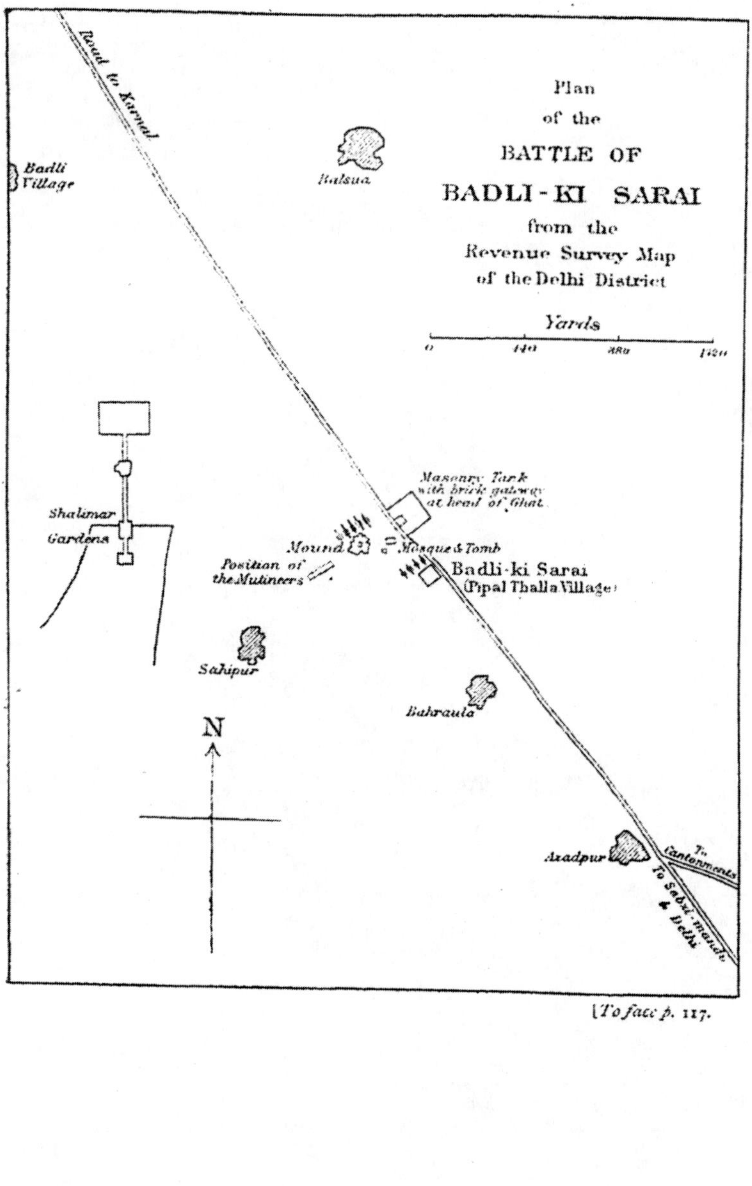
Plan
of the
BATTLE OF
BADLI-KI SARAI
from the
Revenue Survey Map
of the Delhi District
Yards
0
440
880
1320
Road to Karnal
Badli Village
Balsua
Masonry Tank with brick gateway at head of Ghat
Shalimar Gardens
Mound
Masque & Tomb
Position of the Mutineers
Badli-ki Sarai
(Pipal Thalla Village)
Sahipur
Bahraula
N
Azadpur
To Cantonments
To Sabzi-mandi & Delhi

[To face p. 117.

in replying. The leading infantry brigade moved off the road to the right and deployed, the 75th Regiment on the left, the 1st Bengal European Fusiliers partly in support and partly on the right of the 75th Regiment, and this brigade advanced in line under the cannonade towards the enemy. At this time the 2nd Brigade, which by some accident had fallen in rear, was not in sight, but orders were sent to hurry it up. The fire of the enemy's heavy battery, aided by several light guns, began to tell seriously, the bullock-drivers of our heavy guns ran away with the cattle, and one of the wagons blew up; our men fell fast, and the staff offering a tempting mark, two officers (Colonel Chester and Captain Russell) were killed, and several horses of the staff lost in the course of one or two minutes. Time was precious, there was no sign of any flank attack by our cavalry on the insurgents, and it was evident that our guns could not silence their artillery sheltered behind a parapet, so Sir Henry Barnard ordered the 75th Regiment to charge and take the heavy battery. This corps, led by Brigadier Showers and Colonel Herbert, carried out this duty in the most spirited manner. They were supported by the 1st Bengal European Fusiliers, who in their advance suffered somewhat from a musketry fire opened from an enclosure on their right.

The battery was hardly taken ere Brigadier Graves came up on our left; and Brigadier Grant [1] (who had been much delayed by the great difficulty experienced in getting his guns over some water-courses) appeared on the enemy's left rear, and at once attacked them. This completed the defeat, and the insurgents fell back, leaving several guns in our possession, besides their camp.

The troops pushed on in pursuit, clearing many gardens, until (*at Azadpur*) we reached the cross roads, one of which leads to the city through the

[1] His force crossed the canal by the Pembari Bridge, between Sahipur and Azadpur.—H. C. F.

Sabzi Mandi suburb, and the other (the left road) to the cantonment. From this point we could see the ridge beyond the cantonments held by the insurgents; and after a short halt Sir Henry Barnard, with Brigadier Graves' brigade of infantry, Captain Money's troop of horse artillery, and a squadron of the 9th Lancers, took the left or cantonment road, while Brigadier Wilson with the rest of the artillery and cavalry and Brigadier Showers' brigade of infantry took the road through the Sabzi Mandi. The Sirmoor Battalion was ordered to extend between the columns, but the distance was too great for the communication to be complete. It was intended thus simultaneously to attack both flanks of Hindu Rao's Ridge, the Sirmoor Battalion skirmishers threatening it at the same time in front.

In front of our left column on the ridge was the Flag Staff Tower, at which the insurgents had posted three guns, and from these a cannonade was opened on Sir Henry Barnard's column. The column moved across open ground to pass a wide and deep canal cut,[1] which ran nearly parallel to the ridge and at a distance of perhaps 1200 yards, by a masonry bridge. This was partially destroyed, but fortunately was left of a sufficient width for the guns to pass and no more. The insurgents had the range of the bridge, and kept up an accurate fire on it as the column and guns passed over. Proceeding onwards through the huts of the sepoy lines and then through the streets of ruined bungalows of officers, the column came out on the flank of the Flag Staff guns at a distance of a few hundred yards; and Captain Money's troop having moved to the front, wheeled up to its right and commenced a fire which almost immediately silenced the cannon of the insurgents. The

[1] This is the drainage cut from the Najafgarh Jhil, which subsequently proved so valuable a protection of the rear of our position behind the Ridge. The bridge in question is just 1400 yards from the Flag Staff Tower.—H. C. F.

60th Rifles and 2nd Bengal European Fusiliers having brought up their left shoulders then advanced and took the guns; and the Sirmoor Battalion coming up to the ridge, the whole column moved along its crest towards Hindu Rao's house, on reaching which it was joined by Brigadier Wilson's column, which had come by the road through the Sabzi Mandi suburb, and had been opposed *en route*, capturing an 18-pounder gun.

While Sir Henry Barnard's column was moving on the ridge, as well as after it had been joined by that of Brigadier Wilson, a cannonade was kept up from the city, and the shot ranged well up to and over the ridge, killing some men and blowing up a gun limber.

The camp was ordered to be pitched on the cantonment parade ground facing the lines, and with its rear protected by the canal cut, which could only be crossed by bridges at certain points. A mound[1] on the right of the camp offered an advantageous post for a piquet on that flank, which was much exposed to attacks from the Sabzi Mandi suburb. Cavalry piquets on the left flank patrolled to the river, while the ridge on our front was held by the Sirmoor Battalion and two companies of the 60th Rifles at Hindu Rao's house on the right, a piquet of infantry at the Flag Staff Tower in front of the left of the camp, and an infantry piquet at a mosque midway between Hindu Rao's house and the Flag Staff.

The heavy guns were ordered to be brought up to Hindu Rao's preparatory to being put into battery, and it was found necessary to have two light guns on piquet at the Flag Staff, Hindu Rao's, and the mosque.

The troops were withdrawn to the camp ground, but the tents were not up, and the heat was excessive, when about 2 P.M. the insurgents commenced a heavy

[1] This was known subsequently as the General's Mound, and lies near the south-east corner of the village of Rajpur.—H. C. F.

cannonade from the walls, their balls constantly flying far on our side of the ridge. A body of troops also came out of the city and threatened Hindu Rao's or the main piquet. The whole of the troops had again to move up to the ridge, and after a short time the attack was repulsed; but the cannonade did not altogether cease, and it became evident that as long as we occupied the ridge all our piquets on it would be exposed to the fire of the heavy guns, howitzers, and mortars within the city.

Before sunset the troops not on piquet had returned to camp, and no further attack was made that night.

In the action fought this day our losses were tolerably severe.

They are as follows:

Casualties in the Action of 8th June, 1857, before Delhi.

Corps.	Killed.				Wounded.					Missing.	
	Officers.	Non-Com. Officers.	Rank and File.	Horses.	Officers.	Native Officers.	Non-Com. Officers.	Rank and File.	Horses.	Rank and File.	Horses.
Staff	3	...	...	3	...	...	...	...	...	...	...
Artillery	...	1	3	5	4	...	5	12	14	...	11
Detacht., 6th Dragoon Guards	...	...	2	5	...	...	1	4	1	...	...
Her Majesty's 9th Lancers	...	3	12	20	...	...	3	7	4	...	...
Her Majesty's 60th Rifles	...	...	1	...	...	...	...	3	...	...	...
Her Majesty's 75th Regiment	1	2	20	...	7	...	2	41	...	2	...
1st Bengal European Fusiliers	...	...	3	...	2	...	1	25	...	...	...
2nd Bengal European Fusiliers	...	...	...	...	...	...	1	5	...	...	...
Sirmoor Battalion	...	...	...	...	...	1	1	6	...	...	...
Total	4	6	41	33	13	1	14	103	19	2	11
Grand Total	51			33	131				19	2	11

Of the troops opposed to us it was said that a thousand of those who came out never returned to Delhi. This may be an exaggeration, but their losses were undoubtedly heavy, probably three or four hundred killed and wounded, besides a good many who were said to have gone off to their homes after or during the action.

Thirteen guns were captured, viz., an 8-inch howitzer, two 24-pounder guns, two 18-pounders, and the remainder 9-pounder guns.

It is impossible to give anything like an estimate of the insurgent force; but we know that at this period the following corps or detachments were at Delhi, and though one or two portions of corps possibly arrived without arms, there was no difficulty in supplying their wants in this respect from the armoury in the Delhi Magazine :—

3rd Company, 7th Native Battalion Artillery, with No. 5 Horse Field Battery, 38th Regiment, Light Infantry, 54th and 74th Regiments, Native Infantry, from Delhi.

3rd Regiment, Light Cavalry, 11th and 20th Regiments, Native Infantry, from Meerut.

Head-Quarters of the 9th Regiment, Native Infantry, from Aligarh, and detachment from Bulandshahar.

Hurrianah Light Infantry Battalion and a large portion of the 4th Regiment, Irregular Cavalry, from Hansi, Hissar, and Sirsa.

Head-Quarters of the Corps of Sappers and Miners, from Meerut and Roorkee.

Detachments of the 44th and 67th Regiments, Native Infantry, from Muttra.

A large portion of the 45th Regiment, Native Infantry, from Ferozepore, and many deserters of the 5th Regiment, Native Infantry, from Umballa.

In addition to the above, there were known to be many Native soldiers on furlough, particularly of the irregular cavalry, a very large portion of which branch of the service reside within a circuit of a hundred miles from Delhi; also a miscellaneous collection of customs *chaprasis*, who had deserted their posts, police and jail guards, besides many loose characters of all kinds, and these, though far from formidable in the field, could do much mischief when firing from behind walls during our numerous subsequent actions in the suburbs, they being well aware that a secure and certain retreat into the city was always open behind them.

From the above it would seem that in the early part of the siege the mutineers had but one artillery company, but whether this company had been strongly reinforced by Native artillerymen on furlough, or whether the numerous magazine lascars (an intelligent body of men) assisted in working the guns, or both combined, certain it is that from the first day of our arrival before Delhi the mutineers seemed to have no want of trained artillerymen, and were always able to work as many guns as could conveniently be brought to bear upon us.

On the morning of the 9th June, the Guide Corps, consisting of three troops of cavalry and six companies of infantry (rifles), marched into camp under the command of Captain Daly. This distinguished body of men had marched at the hottest season of the year from Mardan, on the Peshawar Frontier, to Delhi, a distance of 580 miles, in twenty-two days, and though the infantry portion were occasionally assisted with camels or ponies on the line of road, the march was a surprising feat even for cavalry.

The same afternoon the mutineers, who had cannonaded at intervals during the day, moved out of the city, and threatened our position on the ridge, making a sharp attack on its right at Hindu Rao's House. The Guides moved up in support, and the insurgents were driven back into the city with considerable loss. On our side Lieutenant Quintin Battye, Commandant of the Guide Cavalry, an enthusiastic, gallant soldier, was mortally wounded, and several men killed and wounded.

During these two days our heavy guns were being

put in position on the ridge near Hindu Rao's house, to reply to the enemy's fire. They were too distant (from 1200 to 1500 yards) to do more than check that fire, and sometimes to silence the guns at the Mori Bastion. It was at once evident that our artillery and engineer means were insufficient to take Delhi, the guns of the rebels being infinitely superior in numbers and calibre to our own, and well served; while to make regular approaches was quite impossible, the Sappers being few in number, and so large a proportion of the infantry being at all times required for the defence of our position that no men could be spared for working parties.

On the 10th and 11th June, attacks similar to that of the 9th were made, and were similarly repulsed.

About this time the insurgents were reinforced by the 60th Regiment, Native Infantry, which mutinied at Rohtak, and at once proceeded to Delhi, their officers escaping to our camp without injury, but with the loss of all their property.

On the morning of the 12th, a very serious attack was made. A large body of the mutineer infantry having concealed themselves in the ravines in Sir Theophilus Metcalfe's compound, between the Flag Staff Tower and the river, soon after daylight made a sudden and vigorous onset on the piquet at the Tower consisting of two horse artillery guns and a detachment of the 75th Foot. They gained the summit of the ridge on the left of the Tower, and the piquet was hard pressed, losing Captain Knox, killed, and several men. The musketry fire was sharp and heavy, and the bullets fell into the camp; some of the enemy even descended to the camp side of the ridge, and three were killed in the sepoy lines within a short distance of the tents. Reinforcements moved rapidly up in support of the piquet, and the insurgents were driven off and pursued some way. To avoid a recurrence of anything of the kind, a large piquet was sent to occupy Sir Theophilus Metcalfe's ruined house close to the river, thus throwing up as it were the left flank of our defences, and rendering it almost impossible for the enemy to pass round on that side. This piquet eventually was thrown in advance of the house and divided into three portions—one of 150 men on a mound on the right of the compound, close to the road leading from the Kashmir Gate to the Cantonment Sadr Bazar, and from which a few men were detached to a house on and commanding the road; fifty men in a cow-house midway between this mound and the river bank; and 150 men in the stables close upon the river. All these posts were gradually strengthened by the engineers, and were of much use. Sir Theophilus Metcalfe's house would have been previously occupied had it not been for the difficulty of providing due relief for the piquets, and after this it sometimes was impossible to carry out the daily reliefs. The Flag Staff continued to be held by a hundred men with two guns, and at night the sentries from this piquet and the mound piquet in the Metcalfe compound communicated.

The attack at the Flag Staff had hardly been repulsed, when other bodies of insurgents advanced upon the Hindu Rao's piquet and through the Sabzi Mandi into the gardens on the right flank of camp. The first of these attacks was not serious, but the latter threatened the mound piquet, and supports of all arms had to be moved up. The 1st Bengal European Fusiliers, under Major Jacob, then advanced and drove the mutineers out of the gardens, killing a considerable number of them.

As it seemed certain that our means were insufficient regularly to besiege the place, a proposal was made to take it by a *coup de main*, and to this Sir Henry Barnard assented. There was considerable risk in the attempt, for not more than 1700 or 1800 infantry were available for the assault, and there was every reason to anticipate a prolonged struggle in the city and in capturing the palace, during which time the camp, with all its sick and wounded, stores, followers, etc., would be necessarily very weakly guarded.

Failure, moreover, would have been disastrous, not simply to the troops employed, but in all probability to the whole British population in Upper India and the Punjab. The General, however, was urged from all quarters "to take Delhi" by those who little comprehended his weakness or its strength.

Two gates were to be blown in by powder bags, by which two columns were to effect an entrance, and early on the morning of 13th June, corps were actually formed to move down to the assault, when the mistake of a superior officer[1] in delaying the withdrawal of the piquets without which the infantry regiments were mere skeletons, forced the plan to be abandoned as daylight was coming on, and it was felt that success was impossible if the blowing in process was not effected by surprise.

There are few who do not now feel that the accident which hindered this attempt[2] was one of those happy interpositions on our behalf of which we had such numbers to be thankful for. Defeat or even a partial success would have been ruin, and complete success would not have achieved for us the results subsequently obtained, or, as far as can be seen, would it have prevented a single massacre, most of which indeed had already taken place.

[1] This officer was Brigadier-General Graves, already mentioned on pp. 103. Brigadier-General Graves left the position before Delhi, when Brigadier-General Wilson was appointed to the command of the Delhi Field Force.—H. C. F.

[2] This is also the opinion of Field-Marshal Lord Roberts; but the natives of Delhi all held otherwise, and it may be permitted to think, that in similar circumstances again, an assault would be made. The one rule on such occasions in the East is *Toujours l'audace.* It must be remembered that up to 12th June the mutineers consisted of mên from eight infantry and two cavalry regiments only, who had been defeated and driven back in three engagements, and were not likely, therefore, to be in very good heart to meet another onslaught. As usual, when they found we were not going to attack them, they plucked up courage anew, and within a week they received considerable reinforcements.—H. C. F.

From this period almost daily attacks took place for some time, and though our losses were not heavy, the troops were much harassed.

Though our investment was only on one side of the city (happily securing, however, our left flank and the communication with the Punjab in our rear), very nearly half the effective force at this period was on piquet; and when the "alarm" sounded and all the piquets had been reinforced, there merely remained a few companies of infantry, besides some cavalry and guns, in reserve to succour any point seriously attacked, or to make a forward move against the insurgents.

The artillery fire from the city—principally directed against Hindu Rao's house and the neighbouring batteries, but sometimes with violence against the Metcalfe piquet as well as the mosque and ridge generally—was constantly kept up, and seldom an hour passed without some shots.

Mortar shells, too, were often thrown, and generally in the evening, over the ridge, the fragments sometimes coming into camp, sometimes falling near our right piquet at the mound. Our batteries replied at intervals, and always when the enemy's fire became very troublesome, and a mortar fire on the city was regularly maintained at night. The trunnions of our 8-inch howitzers giving way one after the other, these pieces were sunk in the ground and used as mortars, their shells having a very long range. In our batteries we used the enemy's ordnance captured at Badli-ki Serai; and as we had no ammunition for the captured 24-pounders, the shots of this calibre fired by the enemy were picked up and sent back again.

The position at Hindu Rao's was confided to the charge of Major Reid of the Sirmoor Battalion, who established his corps in the large house which gave its name to the whole ridge.

At first he had only his own battalion and two companies of the 60th Rifles, but after a time the Guide Infantry were added, and on an "alarm" he was reinforced by two more companies of the 60th

Rifles. He had the protection of all our heavy batteries, and throughout the siege held this honourable post. The house in which he resided with his corps was within perfect range of nearly all the enemy's heavy guns, and was riddled through and through with shot and shell. He never quitted the ridge save to attack the enemy below it, and never once visited the camp until carried to it wounded on the day of the final assault.

On the 15th June, a very sharp attack was made on the Metcalfe piquet, and the enemy taking advantage of the lowness of the river tried to turn our left flank by the sands below the high river bank. The party of the 75th Foot on piquet, however, repulsed the onset, and being reinforced, the assailants were driven back and lost a good number of men.

On the 17th the cannonade was more than usually severe, apparently to divert our attention from a battery which it was evident the enemy were constructing on a rising ground in the direction of the *Idgah* (a large walled enclosure on a hill), and the fire of which if completed would enfilade our position on the ridge. During this cannonade a shot came into a portico of Hindu Rao's house, killing or wounding ten men of different corps, including Ensign Wheatley, 54th Regiment, Native Infantry, attached to the Sirmoor Battalion, who was killed.

Sir Henry Barnard determined to drive the insurgents from the position they were taking up before their battery could be established, and to destroy the works that had been commenced, so at 4 P.M. two columns were detached on this duty.

The right column under Major H. Tombs, Horse Artillery, moved from camp towards the enemy's left. It consisted of four guns of his own troop, thirty Guide Cavalry, twenty Sappers and Miners, two companies of Her Majesty's 60th Rifles, and four companies of the 1st Bengal European Fusiliers, while Major Reid moved from Hindu Rao's towards Kishanganj and the enemy's right with four companies of the 60th Rifles and the Sirmoor Battalion. Both columns were completely successful, and each defeated and drove off considerable bodies of mutineers. Major Tombs captured and brought in a nine-pounder gun; and Major Reid, besides destroying a battery, burnt the village in which it was situated, a magazine (evidently made by Sappers) and the gates of three *serais*.

The column under Major Tombs had two killed; Captain Brown, 1st Bengal European Fusiliers (dangerously), and nine men wounded, with seven horses. Major Tombs himself was slightly wounded and had two horses shot, making five horses that, from the commencement of the campaign up to that date, had been shot under him.

The column under Major Reid had one man killed and five wounded.

On this and the previous day the mutineers were reinforced by the Nasirabad Brigade, consisting of the 2nd Company, 7th Battalion, Artillery, and No. 6 Horse Battery, the 15th and 30th Regiments, Native Infantry, with a few men of the 1st Bombay Light Cavalry (Lancers).

Early in the afternoon of the 19th the enemy began to issue from the city, and threatened nearly every part of our position. A very large body with guns, however, proceeded through the suburbs and gardens on our right, and re-appeared a mile and a half in our rear about an hour before sunset. Twelve guns and the available cavalry (between four and five hundred men), all under Brigadier Grant, immediately moved rapidly to meet them, and a sharp action ensued. The portion of the 60th Rifles in camp was also sent in support of the cavalry, followed by the few other infantry that were available; but altogether as attacks were threatened at other points not much over 300 infantry could be spared. Before these latter came up the enemy's infantry from gardens shot down our artillerymen and horses, while the insurgent guns kept up a remarkably quick and well-directed fire; and it was found absolutely necessary for a portion of the 9th Lancers and for the Guide Cavalry to charge the enemy, which was gallantly done, the two corps being led, respectively, by Brevet Lieutenant-Colonel Yule and Captain Daly.

By the time that the 60th Rifles had reached the ground it was nearly dusk, and quite so when the other infantry came up. After dark the action still raged for some time, and a waggon of Major Scott's battery was exploded by the enemy's fire.

The firing on both sides gradually ceased, and our infantry being much too weak in numbers to attack the enemy's extended line, our troops returned to camp about 8.30 P.M., the insurgents' fire totally ceasing.

At daylight next morning Brigadier Grant was again on the ground, and found it abandoned. A good many dead men and horses were lying about, and a nine-pounder gun which was brought in.

He had hardly returned to camp when the enemy again resumed their attack on the rear, and opened fire at so short a distance that their round shot came right through the camp. Some of our guns again moved to the rear and soon silenced their fire, and Brigadier Wilson with a body of troops proceeded towards the enemy only in time to find them hurrying away to their side of the canal.

The insurgent force was principally composed of the Nasirabad Brigade. Their loss must have been very severe, for numerous bodies were lying about, although they had the whole night for their removal. Thirty-five horses were found lying on the spot where their field battery (the famous Jellalabad Battery) was drawn up.

Our own loss in this affair amounted to three officers, 17 men, and 25 horses killed; seven officers, 70 men, and 35 horses wounded; and two men missing. The portions of the artillery, the 9th Lancers and the 60th Rifles engaged, as well as the Guide Cavalry, all suffered heavily. The officers who were killed or died of wounds were Brevet Lieutenant-Colonel Yule, 9th Lancers, Lieutenant Humphrys,

20th Regiment, Native Infantry, attached to the 60th Rifles, and Lieutenant Alexander, 3rd Regiment, Native Infantry, who had come to Delhi with magazine stores, and accompanied the troops into action.

The officers wounded were Colonel Becher, Quartermaster-General, severely; Captain Daly, Commandant of the Guide Corps, severely; Captain Williams, 60th Rifles, severely; Lieutenant Bishop, Horse Artillery, slightly; and Lieutenants McGill and Dundas, 60th Rifles, and Ensign Lisle-Phillipps, 11th Regiment, Native Infantry, attached to the 60th Rifles, slightly.

Brigadier J. Hope Grant, commanding the troops engaged in the action of the 19th, had his horse shot under him in a charge, and was only saved by the devotion of two men of his own regiment and his two orderly sawars of the 4th Regiment, Irregular Cavalry.

The artillery employed on our side (twelve guns) consisted of portions of the four troops and batteries in camp, under their respective commanders, Majors Scott, Turner and Tombs, and Captain Money. This employment of portions of troops and batteries, as well as of regiments, instead of whole troops, batteries, or corps, was an evil which, owing to our numerical weakness and the necessarily large force always on piquet duty, was often obliged to be tolerated. In fact, from our proximity to the enemy when an attack took place, the first and most important object was always to bring up such troops as were most ready to hand, and could, without danger, be spared.

To render it less easy to make attacks in rear, which might have led to a stoppage of our communications with the Punjab, a battery for two 18-pounders was constructed behind the camp and armed, and the rear piquets of cavalry and infantry were posted at it. Prior to this, three 18-pounders had been placed in battery on the mound to the right of camp,[1] to check

[1] This was the General's Mound.—H. C. F.

any attack from the side of the Sabzi Mandi suburbs. An infantry piquet had been here all along, and a cavalry piquet on the ground below, together with two horse artillery guns.

A day or two after the action in rear of camp, the mutineers from Jullundur and Phillour reached Delhi, consisting of the 6th Light Cavalry, and the 3rd, 36th and 61st Regiments of Native Infantry, and very confident information was given that an attack was again to be made in rear on the morning of the 23rd. On the 22nd, a detachment was at Rai, twenty-two miles from Delhi, under command of Major Olpherts, Horse Artillery, consisting of four guns of the 1st (European) Troop, 1st Brigade and two guns of the 5th (Native) Troop, 1st Brigade, Horse Artillery, a weak wing of the 2nd Punjab Cavalry, a company of the 75th Foot, and the detachment of the 2nd Fusiliers, that had been left at Umballa, with the head-quarters of the 4th Sikh Infantry,—a total force of about 850 men and six guns. On the evening of the 22nd, a staff officer was sent to Rai to order Major Olpherts to march early in the night, to leave the treasure, etc., to which he was giving escort under a strong guard at Alipur until he found that the road was clear, and should the enemy really be engaged in rear of camp to come upon their rear and attack with vigour. No attempt was made, however, on the rear of camp, but as Major Olpherts' baggage was coming up some cavalry came across the canal and threatened it. They, however, at once retreated on Lieutenant Nicholson moving towards them with his sawars.

It was not destined, however, that the centenary of Plassey should pass over in a bloodless manner. The rear of these troops had not reached camp when a furious cannonade was opened from the city walls, while guns that had been brought into the suburbs opened on our right and kept up a heavy enfilading fire on Hindu Rao's ridge, which the few guns we had in position were unable to silence. The mutineer infantry occupied Kishanganj and Sabzi Mandi in force, and threatened to advance on the mound battery; while a constant skirmish of musketry went on close to our ridge batteries. The mutineers were checked in their advance, but a first attempt made by portions of the 1st and 2nd Bengal European Fusiliers to drive them from the strong posts they had occupied in Sabzi Mandi failed; Colonel Welchman, 1st Bengal European Fusiliers, who gallantly led the attack, was dangerously wounded, and Lieutenant Jackson, 2nd Bengal European Fusiliers, killed. The heat was excessive, and many of our men fell from the effects of the sun. The fire, however, never ceased, and it became evident that a great effort must be made to drive the mutineers off. To do this, it was necessary to bring up every available man, and the detachment of the 2nd Bengal European Fusiliers and the 4th Sikh Infantry, who had just marched in twenty-two miles, had again to be turned out under a burning sun. To Brigadier Showers was confided the direction of the attack to be made simultaneously from Hindu Rao's ridge and from the low ground in its rear. It was entirely successful, and the enemy withdrawing their guns, retired into the city, having suffered severe punishment. From that moment we kept an advanced piquet in the Sabzi Mandi of 180 Europeans, divided between a *serai* on one side and a Hindu temple on the other side of the Grand Trunk Road, and both of which were immediately strengthened and rendered defensible by the engineers. These posts were only between two hundred and three hundred yards from the right battery at Hindu Rao's ridge, the piquets from which communicated with them, and eventually a line of breastworks running up the ridge connected these piquets with the right battery. Our position was thus rendered much more secure, and the enemy were unable to pass up the Trunk Road to attack our right rear.

In this action we had one officer (Lieutenant Jackson, 2nd Bengal European Fusiliers), 38 men, and four horses killed; three officers (Colonel Welchman,

1st Bengal European Fusiliers, severely; Captain Jones, 60th Rifles, severely; and Lieutenant Murray, Guide Corps, severely), 118 men, and eleven horses wounded, and one horse missing.

The detail with two light guns on piquet at Hindu Rao's (nine-pounders of Major Scott's battery), under the command of Lieutenant Minto Elliot, were in a most exposed position throughout the affair, and suffered from the fire of heavy artillery in front and flank; one gun was disabled, and no less than fourteen of the horses were put *hors de combat*.

Hardly a day passed over now without the troops having to be turned out for some real or threatened attack, but nothing of importance took place until the 27th June, when, early in the morning, a party of mutineers advanced on the Metcalfe piquet, and being easily there repelled, an attack was made on the ridge batteries and the Sabzi Mandi piquets, which was also repulsed. Our loss on this occasion was 13 men killed, one officer (Lieutenant Harris, 2nd Bengal European Fusiliers, severely) and 48 men wounded.

At this period reinforcements began to arrive, and between the 26th June and the 3rd July the following troops joined :—

Two guns of the 1st (European) Troop, 1st Brigade; and two guns of the 5th (Native) Troop, 1st Brigade, Horse Artillery.

A detachment of European reserve artillery from Lahore.

Detachments of newly-raised Sikh Sappers and artillery.

The head-quarters of Her Majesty's 8th Regiment.

The head-quarters of Her Majesty's 61st Regiment.

A squadron of the 5th Punjab Cavalry.

The 1st Punjab Infantry (Rifles).

So that the effective force before Delhi now amounted in round numbers to nearly 6600 men of all arms.

We were also enabled to send a considerable number

of sick and wounded to Umballa, a smaller number having been previously sent *viâ* Bhagpat to Meerut.

On the 30th June another attack was made on the Sabzi Mandi piquet and Hindu Rao's, and was repulsed with a loss on our part of 8 men killed; Lieutenants Yorke, 4th Sikhs (mortally), and Packe of the 4th Sikhs (severely), and 36 men wounded.

In the course of the day it was reported that the enemy were again about to construct a battery near the *Idgah,* so Brigadier Showers was sent in that direction on a reconnaissance with six horse artillery guns under Major Olpherts, a troop of the Carabineers, a troop of the 9th Lancers, a wing of Her Majesty's 75th Regiment, and the 1st Fusiliers. The *sarai* in which the battery was supposed to be in course of construction was empty, but in an adjoining house was found a quantity of saltpetre, together with a number of entrenching tools and sand bags, which were destroyed or brought away.

When the reinforcements arrived, it was again proposed that the place should be taken by a *coup de main,* and a project was drawn out by which one column was to effect an entrance by blowing in the iron grating of the canal near the Kabul Gate, another column to enter the Kashmir Gate after it had been blown in, a third column to escalade the Kashmir Bastion, and a detachment creeping round by the river side to endeavour to effect an entrance in that direction. It seemed pretty clear that success was doubtful in these attacks, unless the surprise was complete, and we had no reason to reckon upon any want of vigilance on the part of the insurgents, who were not by any means *shut up* or unable to send out patrols and piquets. As, moreover, for the four assaulting parties and the reserve not more than 3000[1] infantry (if so many) could be used, it does not seem matter for regret that this attack never took place.

[1] The numbers composing these on 14th September were slightly over 5000, but at the end of June the enemy had not received many of their most important reinforcements, and our troops had not suf-

On the 1st and 2nd July, the Rohilkand mutineers arrived at Delhi, marching across the bridge of boats within full view of the spectators from our camp posted on the ridge. They were a formidable reinforcement, consisting of the whole of No. 15 Horse Battery, two 6-pounder post guns from Shajehanpore, the 8th Irregular Cavalry, and the 18th, 28th, 29th and 68th Native Infantry.

And here I would observe that I have not attempted to give the dates or to allude in any way to all the numerous arrivals of insurgent troops at Delhi: some came in brigades, some in single regiments, and some in detachments. I have referred, however, to all the larger bodies, and the only remaining reinforcements of a strength greater than a regiment that subsequently reached Delhi were the Jhansi troops, consisting of half of No. 18 Light Field Battery, a wing of the 12th Native Infantry, and the 14th Irregular Cavalry; and late in July the Neemuch Brigade, consisting of a Native troop of horse artillery, a wing of the 1st Light Cavalry, the 72nd Native Infantry, 7th Infantry Regiment of the Gwalior Contingent, and the cavalry and infantry of the Kotah contingent. The other arrivals, though on a small scale, were constant, and by the middle of August the very lowest estimate of the numbers of the insurgents was 30,000 men. Their guns, as we know, were as numerous as even they could have desired, and their ammunition appeared inexhaustible.

Our force was insufficient to invest even one-third of the land side of the place, and access to the left bank of the Jumna was at all times perfectly secure by the bridge of boats, which was under the close fire of their ordnance in the Salimgarh, and fully 2500 yards from our nearest gun. We were, therefore, powerless to prevent a constant stream of reinforcements and supplies from pouring into the city, and were thank-

fered from weeks of sickness. See what Lord Roberts says as to the effects of sickness, and the record of the sick-list on pp. 154 and 162. —H. C. F.

ful that we had been so far enabled to keep open our rear, and freely to communicate with the Punjab, whence all our resources were drawn. Had the numerous cavalry of the insurgents been directed with judgment and boldness, it is not too much to say that we could have been put to the most serious straits.

On the afternoon of the 3rd July, large bodies of the insurgents moved into the suburbs and gardens on our right, and all our troops were turned out. At night, the enemy were still in force outside the city, and then moving rapidly upon Alipur, one march in our rear, with a force of five or six thousand men and several guns, compelled our cavalry post there of a squadron of the 5th Punjab Cavalry, under Lieutenant Younghusband, to fall back towards Rai. The fire of their guns was heard in camp, and soon after 2 A.M. a force marched to endeavour to overtake or to intercept the mutineers. It was commanded by Major Coke, and consisted of four guns of Captain Money's troop of horse artillery and two guns of the native troop, Major Scott's horse battery, a squadron of the Carabineers, a squadron of the 9th Lancers, the Guide Cavalry, the wing of Her Majesty's 61st Regiment, and the 1st Punjab Rifles, in all about 300 cavalry, 800 infantry and twelve guns, which was about as strong a detachment as could be spared.

At first it was impossible to ascertain whether the mutineers, after plundering Alipur, had gone straight on towards Rai and Larsauli, or were returning to Delhi, and grave fears were felt that they might be pushing on for Karnal, or at least to intercept treasure which was between Karnal and Delhi, and under a Native escort.

About sunrise, however, it became known that they had re-crossed the canal near Alipur, and were returning towards Delhi along the high and dry ground running nearly parallel with the canal, and at a distance from it of a mile or more. Major Coke at once moved to take them in flank, but had to proceed over a swampy cross-country road for a mile and a half to the Painbári bridge of the canal, and then had more than a mile of swampy fields to pass over. The artillery came first into action, and were immediately replied to by the insurgents' guns, which had been moved into a village when they perceived our approach, their infantry and cavalry at the same time facing towards us. The infantry, however, save some posted in the village, soon commenced moving off again, their cavalry shortly did the same, and their artillery fire slackening, it was evident that their guns also were being withdrawn. Our guns again advanced, though with much difficulty, and the infantry and cavalry were told to hurry on, the Guide Cavalry on our left being desired to push forward and get on the line of the enemy's retreat. The troops, however, were floundering in mud, and progressed but slowly, and all the insurgents' guns were carried off. An ammunition waggon and an artillery store-cart were, however, secured, and all the plunder taken from Alipur was recaptured. A quantity of small-arm ammunition also fell into our hands, and the insurgents had probably some eighty men killed. On his return towards camp, Major Coke rested his infantry and some of his cavalry at the canal bank, and while here was attacked by some fresh troops from Delhi, including a body of about 800 cavalry. The firing was sharp, and cavalry and artillery were sent from camp to Major Coke's support. The attack, however, had been virtually repulsed before these supports arrived, and all returned to camp, the Europeans having suffered much from the intense heat of the sun.

In this affair a body of eighty horse raised at Kohat by a Chief, a personal friend of Major Coke, behaved with gallantry, but the Mir, its leader, was unfortunately killed while pursuing some of the fugitive insurgent infantry.

Our losses on this occasion amounted to three men and seven horses killed; twenty-three men and seven horses wounded, exclusive of casualties in the Kohat Horse.

On the following morning (5th July), Sir Henry Barnard was attacked with cholera, and expired early in the afternoon, greatly regretted by the whole force, and most so by those who knew him best. Brave, kind-hearted, and hospitable, it is doubtful if he had an enemy. Cholera then as ever was present in the camp, and the death of any one excited no surprise; but no doubt Sir Henry Barnard's attack was due, in a great degree, to his unsparing exposure of himself to the sun at all hours of the day, and to great mental anxiety. His indeed had been a most trying position. Arriving for the first time in India, on assuming command of the Sirhind Division in April, he found the whole of the Native troops, to whose characters and peculiarities he was of course an utter stranger, in a most discontented and unsatisfactory state, and a few weeks placed him at the head of a weak force called upon to take Delhi and crush the great strength of the mutineers there concentrated. Had he not felt anxiety he would not have been human, and he[1] as truly died of causes purely arising out of the mutiny as any soldier who fell in battle when opposed to the insurgent sepoys. [*On his death Major-General Reed assumed command of the force.*]

To hinder as far as possible attempts to get round our rear, arrangements were made for blowing up all

[1] In the resolution of the Governor-General in Council, dated 4th December 1857, publishing the various despatches of engagements, in which the Delhi Force was concerned, the services of Sir Henry Barnard were thus commemorated :—

"During a portion of the time over which siege operations extended, dating from the first arrival of the army under the walls of Delhi, the command was held by Major-General Sir Henry Barnard. But this gallant officer was not permitted to witness the final success of the undertaking confided to him, and of which his own brilliant victory at Badli-ki-Sarai was the worthy commencement. Struck down by sickness, he died at his post, giving his last energies to the discharge of his trust; and the Governor-General in Council cannot close this notice of the Campaign of Delhi without offering a tribute of sincere respect to the courage, constancy and devotion to duty which marked the command of Sir Henry Barnard."—H. C. F.

the canal bridges for several miles parallel with the Trunk Road, save that at Painbári, which we retained for our own use, watching it with videttes from our cavalry piquet at the village of Azadpur, two miles in rear of camp.

The Pulchaddar aqueduct, a work of great solidity, which brought the canal water into the city across the Najafgarh Jhil cut, and by which horsemen could pass to our rear, was also blown up. By this latter measure no water could enter the city through the canal, a matter of little moment, however, to the inhabitants of a town situated on the banks of a river, and in which there are many wells.

It was also determined to destroy the Bassi Bridge over the Najafgarh Jhil cut, about eight miles from camp, to render approach to our rear still more difficult, and this was effected on the morning of the 8th July, without opposition, by a party of Sappers under escort of a large detachment of all arms, commanded by Brigadier Longfield, of Her Majesty's 8th Regiment.

On the following morning (9th July) the enemy showed outside the city in great force; our main piquet was reinforced, and the troops remained accoutred in their tents ready to turn out, while an unceasing cannonade was kept up from the city walls and from field artillery outside.

About ten o'clock the insurgents appeared to be increasing in numbers in the suburbs on our right, when suddenly a body of cavalry emerged from cover on the extreme right of our right flank and charged into camp.

As previously mentioned, there was a mound on our right on which was placed a battery of three 18-pounders with an infantry piquet, all facing the Sabzi Mandi suburb. To the right of the mound on the low ground was a piquet of two horse artillery guns and a troop of dragoons, the guns being this day furnished by Major Tombs' troop and commanded by Lieutenant Hills, the cavalry from the Carabineers, and commanded by Lieutenant Stillman. Still further to the right, at a *fakir's* enclosure, was a Native officer's piquet of the 9th Irregulars, from which two videttes were thrown forward some two hundred yards on to the Trunk Road. These videttes could see down the road towards Delhi as far as our piquet at the *sarai*, perhaps seven or eight hundred yards, and up the road to the canal cut, about two hundred yards. Across the road were rather dense gardens.

The place at which the videttes were posted was not visible from camp, and some horsemen in white advancing attracted but little notice, their dress being the same as that of the 9th Irregulars, from which corps the *fakir's* piquet was taken.

Some alarm, however, arose, and the two horse artillery guns at the piquet were got ready, but the leading cavalry insurgents, beckoning men in their rear, dashed on at speed, and the troop of Carabineers, all very young, most of them untrained soldiers, and only thirty-two in number of all ranks, turned and broke, save the officer and two or three men, who nobly stood. Lieutenant Hills, commanding the guns, seeing the cavalry come on unopposed, alone charged the head of their horsemen to give his guns time to unlimber, and cut down one or two of the sawars, while the main body of horsemen, riding over and past the guns, followed up the Carabineers, and a confused mass of horsemen came streaming in at the right of camp.

Major Tombs, whose tent was on the right, had heard the first alarm, and calling for his horse to be brought after him, walked towards the piquet as the cavalry came on. He was just in time to see his gallant subaltern down on the ground, with one of the enemy's sawars about to kill him. From a distance of thirty yards he fired with his revolver and dropped Hills' opponent.

Hills got up and engaged a man on foot, who was cut down by Tombs after Hills had received a severe cut on the head.

Meanwhile great confusion had been caused by the inroad of the sawars, most of whom made for the guns of the native troop of horse artillery which was on the right of camp, calling on the men to join them. The native horse artillerymen, however, behaved admirably, and called out to Major Olpherts' European troop, which was then unlimbered close by, to fire *through them* at the mutineers. The latter however managed to secure and carry off some horses, and several followers were cut down in camp. Captain Fagan, of the artillery, rushing out of his tent, got together a few men and followed up some of the sawars, who were then endeavouring to get away, and killed fifteen of them. More were killed by some men of the 1st Brigade, and all were driven out of camp, some escaping by a bridge over the canal cut in our rear. It is estimated that not more than one hundred sawars were engaged in this enterprise, and about thirty-five were killed, including a native officer.

All this time the cannonade from the city and from many field guns outside raged fast and furious, and a heavy fire of musketry was kept up upon our batteries and on the Sabzi Mandi piquets from the enclosures and gardens of the suburbs.

A column was therefore formed to dislodge them, consisting of Major Scott's horse battery, the available men of the wings of the 8th and 61st Foot and the 4th Sikh Infantry, in all about 700 infantry and six guns, reinforced *en route* by the head-quarters and two companies of the 60th Rifles, under Lieutenant-Colonel J. Jones; the infantry brigade being commanded by Brigadier W. Jones, and Brigadier-General Chamberlain directing the whole. As this column swept up through the Sabzi Mandi, Major Reid was instructed to move down and co-operate with such infantry as could be spared from the main piquet. The insurgents were cleared out of the gardens without difficulty, though the denseness of the vegetation rendered the mere operation of passing through them a work of time.

At some of the *sarais*, however, a very obstinate resistance was made, and the insurgents were not dislodged without considerable loss. Eventually everything was effected that was desired; our success being greatly aided by the admirable and steady practice of Major Scott's battery under a heavy fire, eleven men being put *hors de combat* out of its small complement.

By sunset the engagement was over, and the troops returned to camp drenched through with rain, which for several hours had fallen at intervals with great violence.

Our loss this day was 1 officer and 40 men killed, 8 officers and 163 men wounded, and 11 men missing: horses, 8 wounded and 18 missing. The officer killed was Ensign Mountsteven, Her Majesty's 8th Regiment; and the following were wounded:— Lieutenant Hills, Horse Artillery, severely; Captain Daniell, Her Majesty's 8th Regiment, severely; Captain Burnside, Her Majesty's 61st Regiment, Major of Brigade, slightly; Lieutenant Griffiths, Her Majesty's 61st Regiment, severely; Ensign Andros, Her Majesty's 61st Regiment, slightly; Captain Kemp, 5th Regiment Native Infantry, attached to the 2nd Bengal European Fusiliers (in command Sabzi Mandi piquet), severely; Lieutenant Eckford, 69th Regiment Native Infantry, attached to the Sirmoor Battalion, slightly; Lieutenant Pullan, 36th Regiment Native Infantry, attached to the 4th Sikh Infantry, severely.

The enemy must have lost near 500 men, most of whom were killed on the spot.

The exact circumstances of the inroad of the cavalry into camp were never correctly ascertained, but there seems little reason to doubt that there was some treachery on the part of the piquet of the 9th Irregulars, and the insurgent cavalry evidently reckoned upon assistance in our camp, particularly from the native troop of horse artillery, who however behaved nobly.

In the account of the action of Badli-ki-Sarai, allusion has been made to the want of confidence reposed in the portions of the 4th and 9th Irregulars with the force. Some men had behaved well, but it was evident that the general feeling in camp was that there was bad blood amongst them. Indeed, our Sikhs and Punjabis spoke plainly on the subject. The other wing of the 9th and a wing of the 17th Irregular cavalry had now come to Delhi, and it was determined to send both corps back to the Punjab. This was accordingly carried out. The head-quarters of the 4th Irregulars remained, barely a hundred men. Not a single desertion, I believe, took place from this portion of the 4th throughout the siege, but they were for the latter part of the time deprived of their horses and swords and employed solely as orderlies.

A selected squadron of the 1st Punjab Cavalry, composed wholly of Sikhs and Punjabis, now came to Delhi, and the whole cavalry force then and until the end of the siege, save that 200 Mooltan Horse joined with General Nicholson in August, consisted of six weak squadrons of dragoons, five squadrons of Punjab and Guide Cavalry, and Captain Hodson's Corps of Sikh Horse in process of raising. Of the native portion one squadron was always detached to Alipur, the first march towards Karnal.

The Native troop of horse artillery previously referred to had its guns taken away at a later date, simply to remove temptation and because some of the young soldiers had deserted. Not one old soldier of the troop deserted during the siege, and throughout they were constantly employed and behaved very well in the mortar batteries. When Delhi was taken they were given back their guns and horses. Their horses and arms were also then restored to the head-quarters of the 4th Irregular Cavalry.

On the 14th July the mutineers again came out in great force, and attacked our batteries on Hindu Rao's ridge from an early period in the day, and for many hours kept up an incessant fire of artillery and musketry. As the fire from the ridge failed to drive them off, a column under Brigadier Showers moved into the Sabzi Mandi about 3 P.M., and after a sharp struggle forced them to withdraw their field artillery and to retire into the city. Our men pressed them so closely as to suffer from the grape fired from the city walls, but we found on this as on subsequent occasions that the grape thrown from large guns and howitzers ranged freely up to 1000 or 1100 yards, and then inflicted mortal wounds. Our troops, however, on the 14th July pursued to within 600 yards.

The column under Brigadier Showers consisted of six horse artillery guns under Major Turner and Captain Money, the 1st Fusiliers under Major Jacob, and Major Coke's corps of Punjab Rifles,[1] with a few of the Guide Cavalry and Hodson's Horse and the Kohat *risalah*. Brigadier-General Chamberlain accompanied the column, and on passing the foot of Hindu Rao's ridge it was joined by Major Reid with all the available men from his position.

Our loss this day was 15 men and 2 horses killed; 16 officers, 177 men, and 7 horses wounded; and 2 men missing.

The officers wounded were—

Brigadier-General Chamberlain, Acting Adjutant-General, severely.
Lieutenant Roberts, Officiating Deputy Assistant Quartermaster-General, slightly.

Engineers.

Lieutenant Walker, Bombay, severely.
Lieutenant Geneste, and 2nd-Lieutenant Carnegie, slightly.

Horse Artillery.

Lieutenant Thomson, severely.

Her Majesty's 75th Regiment.

Lieutenants Rivers and Faithfull, slightly.

[1] The 1st Punjab Infantry.

1st Bengal European Fusiliers.

Lieutenant Daniell, severely.

Sirmoor Battalion.

Lieutenant Tulloch, severely.
Lieutenants Ross and Chester, slightly.

Guide Corps.

Lieutenants Shebbeare, Hawes, and De Brett, slightly.

1st Punjab Infantry.

Lieutenant Pollock, severely.

The enemy were lying thick in many places, and their loss was estimated at 1000. For hours carts were seen taking the corpses into the city. An old temple called by the European soldiers "The Sammy House," some way down the slope of the ridge towards the city, and within 900 yards of the Mori Bastion, which had been for some time held by us, was the scene of hard fighting. Occupied by a party of Guide Infantry, it defied all efforts to take it, and next morning eighty dead bodies of mutineers were counted round it.

On the 17th July Major-General Reed, whose health, from the first most feeble, had now entirely failed him, proceeded on sick leave to Simla. He made over command of the force to Brigadier A. Wilson, of the Artillery, conferring on him the rank of Brigadier-General in anticipation of the sanction of Government, for, as a Colonel, Brigadier Wilson was not the senior officer with the troops before Delhi.

On the 18th July the insurgents again made a sharp and prolonged attack upon the ridge batteries and Sabzi Mandi. About 1 P.M. a column was sent to dislodge them under the command of Lieutenant-Colonel Jones, 60th Royal Rifles, consisting of portions of Her Majesty's 8th, 61st and 75th Regiments, the Sikh Infantry and Guide Cavalry, with four horse artillery guns.

This duty was completely performed, and the enemy dislodged with some loss from the positions they had taken up.

Our casualties during the day amounted to one officer and twelve men killed, three officers and sixty-six men wounded, and two men missing, with seven horses wounded.

Lieutenant Crozier, 75th Regiment, was killed, and the following officers were wounded:—

Artillery.

Lieutenant Chichester, slightly.

Engineers.

Lieutenant Jones, dangerously, since dead.

Her Majesty's 61st Regiment.

Lieutenant Pattoun, severely.

This was the last real contest in the Sabzi Mandi, for by this time the incessant exertions of the engineers had cleared away the old *sarais*, walls and gardens for some distance round the posts held by our piquets in that suburb, while the breastworks connecting these piquets with the crest of the Hindu Rao ridge were completed and perfected.

Hereafter these piquets were never exposed to more than a distant and comparatively harmless fire.

While the engineers were engaged in this work, the ridge defences were not neglected, and gradually became most formidable. In favourable positions field guns from the captured ordnance were placed, and though the duty on the foot artillery was very hard, it was found possible to man all the guns with the aid of the newly-raised Sikh artillery sent from the Punjab. The "Sammy House," before alluded to, on the city slope of the ridge, or nearest post to the walls, was greatly strengthened, and cover provided for the men occupying it—a very necessary measure, exposed as it was to the fire of the Burn [1] and Mori Bastions, and within grape range of the latter, while infantry could come up unperceived to within a short distance.

On the 20th July it was reported that a battery was being constructed in the gardens on our right from a distance at which heavy guns could have thrown shot into camp. A reconnaissance, therefore, was made by a column under Lieutenant-Colonel Seaton, 35th Native Light Infantry, attached to the first brigade. The detachment consisted of four horse artillery guns, a troop of the Guide Cavalry, 150 of Her Majesty's 75th Regiment, 400 of the 1st Bengal European Fusiliers, and 200 of the Guide Infantry. No traces of an enemy or of any earthworks were found; but on retiring towards camp some of the insurgents emerging from the suburb of Trevelyanganj, followed up our troops. The Guide Infantry, who formed the rear guard, however, turned about, and with a cheer drove them completely away.

The casualties this day were only one man killed, three officers, eleven men and two horses wounded.

The officers wounded were—

Artillery.

Lieutenant Dickins, dangerously (since dead).

1st Punjab Infantry.

Lieutenant Travers, slightly.

Her Majesty's 24th Regiment.

Captain Greensill, Assistant Field Engineer.[2]

On the morning of the 23rd July large numbers

[1] Named after Colonel William Burn, who, in conjunction with Colonel (afterwards General Sir David) Ochterlony, defended Delhi when besieged by Holkar in 1804 (*see* p. 55).

[2] Accidentally wounded while on duty at the Metcalfe piquet, and died on the following morning.

of insurgents emerged from the Kashmir Gate, and, occupying Ludlow Castle and its neighbourhood, brought up some field guns, which fired occasionally at the Metcalfe piquet, but principally at the ridge, and particularly at the Mosque piquet. Fire was opened in reply from the two field guns at the latter piquet, and from two more that came up in support, and from such of the guns at Hindu Rao's as could be brought to bear. By constantly moving about their guns, and aided by the cover of walls and trees, the enemy were enabled to continue their fire, and were doing damage, so Brigadier Showers was ordered to move out from our left and, coming through a gorge, to advance on their flank while their attention was taken up by the fire from the ridge. The troops detailed for this duty consisted of six horse artillery guns under Major Turner, 408 rank and file of Her Majesty's 8th and 61st Regiments, and the 1st Bengal European Fusiliers, 360 of Major Coke's Rifles, and a detachment of the Guide Cavalry.

Two hundred and fifty men of the Metcalfe House piquets, under Lieutenant-Colonel Drought, 60th Regiment, Native Infantry, field officer of the day, were also to advance and co-operate on the left, while the main column moved up the high road, leading to the Kashmir Gate.

The mutineers apparently did not perceive the advance of these troops until they were within a few hundred yards, and after two rounds their guns went off into the city. Some skirmishing, however, took place with their infantry in the gardens and compounds before they were all driven off, after which our troops returned to camp.

Our loss was one officer and eleven men killed, five officers, thirty-four men and two horses wounded and one man missing.

Captain Law, 10th Native Infantry, attached to the 1st Punjab Infantry, was killed, and the following officers were wounded :—

Lieut. Col. T. Seaton, 35th Native (Light) Infantry, attached to the 1st Brigade, severely.
Lieut.-Col. R. Drought, 60th Native Infantry, attached to the 2nd Brigade, severely.

Horse Artillery.

Captain Money, severely.
Lieutenant A. Bunny, slightly.

Her Majesty's 8th Regiment.

Lieutenant Pogson, slightly.

Subsequent to the 23rd of July, for several days nothing occurred save the usual artillery fire on both sides, and the skirmishing at our advance breastwork, but on the 31st a force of several thousand men, with ten field guns and three mortars, moved out of the city and along the Rohtak road, with the intention of making a temporary bridge (for which purpose they took timber) across the Najafgarh Jhil cut and getting to our rear—a move which, if successfully carried out, would have caused us much inconvenience. However, their proceedings were closely watched, and a movable column was held in readiness to march at once against them under Major Coke, should they get over the water cut, after which they had to cross a flooded country almost impassable for guns for some miles, and then to pass the canal itself (which latter, however, would not have been much of an obstacle, but little water coming down at this time, owing to some obstruction or accident above) before they could come on the Trunk Road, the only part of the country where troops could, at this season, move with ease.

The Kumaon Battalion, about 400 strong, were this day at Rai, two marches off, with a large store of ammunition and treasure; so instructions were sent to the commanding officer to march straight in that night, and Major Coke's column went out to Alipur to form an additional escort for the last march. The whole convoy reached camp in the morning, in the midst of drenching rain, and Major Coke's column was again held in readiness to move at an instant's notice.

In the afternoon the mutineers had nearly completed a bridge at Bassi, when a flood came down and swept it away, the timber work being carried past our camp. The force immediately broke up and returned towards Delhi, a large body of infantry moving from the city to meet them at the same time. When the two bodies met, they turned through the Kishanganj suburb, and attacked the right of our position on the ridge. This was about sunset, and all night long the roar of musketry and artillery was incessant. Constantly they came close up to our breastworks, but were always repulsed by the fire of our infantry, aided, when practicable, by grape. Our light mortars too played with effect upon the masses below the ridge, but it was not till 10 A.M. of the 2nd August that their efforts began to cease, and they did not altogether retire until 4 P.M. Our men were admirably steady; and being well protected by breastworks, and never showing, save when the enemy came close up, our loss was trifling, notwithstanding that for many consecutive hours a perfect storm of bullets raged, and the fire of shot and shell both from the city and the Kishanganj was incessant. One officer (Lieutenant Travers, 1st Punjab Infantry) and nine men were killed, and 36 wounded. The enemy's loss seemed to be immense; 127 dead bodies were counted in front of a breastwork to the right of the "Sammy House," and many more were lying in other places. During the darkness too, no doubt, many bodies were carried off.

A few days after this, the insurgents commenced a series of efforts to drive us from the Metcalfe piquet, and constantly plied it with shot and shell from guns brought out of the Kashmir Gate and posted a few hundred yards in advance of the city walls at Ludlow Castle, or in the Kudsia Bagh, while a number of infantry skirmishers, many of whom were riflemen, kept up a nearly constant fire from the jungle in the front, occasionally advancing with shouts, but always being repulsed by our fire when they came near. The losses at the piquet were not many, good cover having been provided, but the approach to it for reliefs, etc., was extremely perilous.

It was determined to put a stop, if possible, to these annoyances, and the following troops were placed at the disposal of Brigadier Showers for the purpose :—

Six horse artillery guns under Captain Remmington; a squadron of the 9th Lancers, under Captain Anson; the Guide Cavalry, under Captain Sanford; one hundred men (75th Foot) from the Metcalfe piquet, under Captain Freer, of Her Majesty's 27th Regiment; the 1st Bengal Fusiliers (350 strong), under Major Jacob; Major Coke's Rifles (250 men), with 100 men each of Her Majesty's 8th, under Captain Robertson, and of the 2nd Fusiliers, under Captain Harris; Kumaon Battalion, under Lieutenant Thomson; and 4th Sikh Infantry, under Captain Chambers.

The insurgents were completely surprised about dawn of the 12th August, some 250 killed (of whom several were artillerymen), and four guns (a 24-pr. howitzer, two 9-pounders and a 6-pounder) captured.

Brigadier Showers himself was severely wounded, as also was Major Coke when in the act of seizing one of the enemy's guns. Lieutenant-Colonel Greathead, 8th Foot, was sent to take command on Brigadier Showers becoming disabled, and superintended the return of the troops.

Besides the two above-named officers, the following were wounded :—Lieutenant Sherriff, 2nd Bengal European Fusiliers, mortally, since dead; Lieutenant Innes, 60th Native Infantry, orderly officer; Lieutenant Lindsay, Horse Artillery; Lieutenant Maunsell, Engineer; Captain Greville and Lieutenant Owen, 1st Fusiliers, all slightly; with 19 men and one horse killed, 85 men and eight horses wounded, and five men missing. Of the casualties, thirty-four were in the 1st Bengal European Fusiliers and thirty-three in the 1st Punjab Infantry (Coke's corps).

By the insurgents placing guns on the opposite side of the river, the Metcalfe piquet after this suffered some annoyance from the enemy, and the camp of the 1st Punjab Infantry had to be shifted; but before any other engagement of importance took place, we had received a most valuable reinforcement in Brigadier-General J. Nicholson's column, consisting of Captain Bourchier's European Horse Battery, Her Majesty's 52nd Light Infantry, the remaining wing of Her Majesty's 61st Regiment, the 2nd Punjab Infantry, and 200 Mooltanee Horse. It was still necessary, however, to wait for the siege-train with a large quantity of ammunition in progress from Ferozepore.

On the 13th or 14th August, a body of the enemy, principally cavalry, left Delhi by the Najafgarh road, with the object, it was presumed, of interrupting our communications with Umballa and the Punjab, or of attacking Hansi or Jhind.

Lieutenant W. S. R. Hodson was, therefore, detached to watch them, and, as far as possible, to frustrate their intentions. He took with him the head-quarters of his own newly-raised corps of horse, 233 sabres, 103 of the Guide Cavalry, and 25 Jhind horsemen, with six European officers.

On the first march (at Kharkhaudah) he managed to surprise and nearly to destroy a party of mutineer irregular cavalry sawars of different regiments, including Risaldar Bisharat Ali, 1st Irregular Cavalry.

The flooded state of the country rendered movement extremely difficult, but Lieutenant Hodson pushed on to Rohtak, on approaching which place he had a skirmish with a body of footmen and a few sawars, headed by Babar Khan, the Chief of the Ranghar tribe. These men were charged, and thirteen of them killed.

The next morning Lieutenant Hodson's party was again attacked by Babar Khan with about

300 horsemen that he had managed to collect, supported by about 900 matchlockmen. The heads of the assailants were immediately charged and driven back, but as a fire was kept up from the enclosures near the town, Lieutenant Hodson retired, and so drew the insurgents out into open country, upon which he again charged, and drove them into the town, fifty of their horsemen being left dead on the ground.

All the disaffected the same night evacuated Rohtak, and Lieutenant Hodson, agreeably to orders, returned to camp on the 22nd August.

The whole of his men behaved admirably; the Guide Cavalry, as usual, with forward gallantry, well aided by Lieutenant Hodson's own new levy and the few horsemen of the Jhind Rajah.

Our casualties were—

Guide Cavalry Detachment.

Eight men and two horses wounded.

Jhind Horse.

Two sawars wounded.

Hodson's Horse.

Lieutenant H. H. Gough (slightly).
Five men and five horses wounded.

The force before Delhi at this time, notwithstanding great sickness, was much stronger than it had ever been previously. The number of effective rank and file was as follows:—

Artillery, European	548
Artillery, Native[1]	477
Sappers and Miners, Native[2]	673
Cavalry, European	485
Cavalry, Native[3]	769
Infantry, European	2703
Infantry, Native	2467

[1] Composed of newly-raised Sikh artillery, gun lascars and drivers.

[2] Principally composed of newly-raised Punjab Sappers and Miners.

[3] Including 241 of Captain Hodson's newly-raised corps.

or in round numbers, 8000 rank and file of all arms.

Besides the above, there were in camp (notwithstanding that several hundred sick and wounded had been sent to Umballa) sick 1535, wounded 304.[1]

In the course of the 24th, a large force of the enemy, with 18 guns, left Delhi and proceeded in the Bahadurgarh direction, with the avowed intention of intercepting our siege-train, known to be in progress from Ferozepore with a very slender escort. Brigadier-General Nicholson was accordingly detached at daybreak on the 25th, to endeavour to overtake and bring this body of the rebels to action. His column was composed of 16 horse artillery guns under Major Tombs, with Captains Remmington and Blunt, 30 Sappers under Lieutenant Geneste, a squadron of the 9th Lancers under Lieutenant Sarel, a squadron of the Guide Cavalry, under Captain Sanford, the squadron of the 2nd Punjab Cavalry, under Lieutenant Nicholson, 200 Mooltanee Horse under Lieutenant Lind, 420 of Her Majesty's 61st Regiment under Lieutenant-Colonel Rainey, the 1st Bengal European Fusiliers (380 men), under Major Jacob, the 1st Punjab Rifles (400), under Lieutenant Lumsden, and the 2nd Punjab Infantry (400), under Captain Green.

The difficulties of the march were very great, the line of route being off the Trunk Road. Before reaching Nangloi, nine miles from camp, two difficult swamps had to be crossed. Here intelligence was received of the enemy's movements, and the troops immediately pushed on towards Najafgarh, at which place they arrived about 4 P.M., and found the enemy posted, occupying a position about a mile and three-quarters in length, extending from the bridge over the Najafgarh canal to the town of Najafgarh. The

[1] A graphic account of the sickness in camp, of its insanitary surroundings and plague of flies, and of the appearance of adjutant birds on the scene, is given by Lord Roberts in his "Forty-One Years in India."—H. C. F.

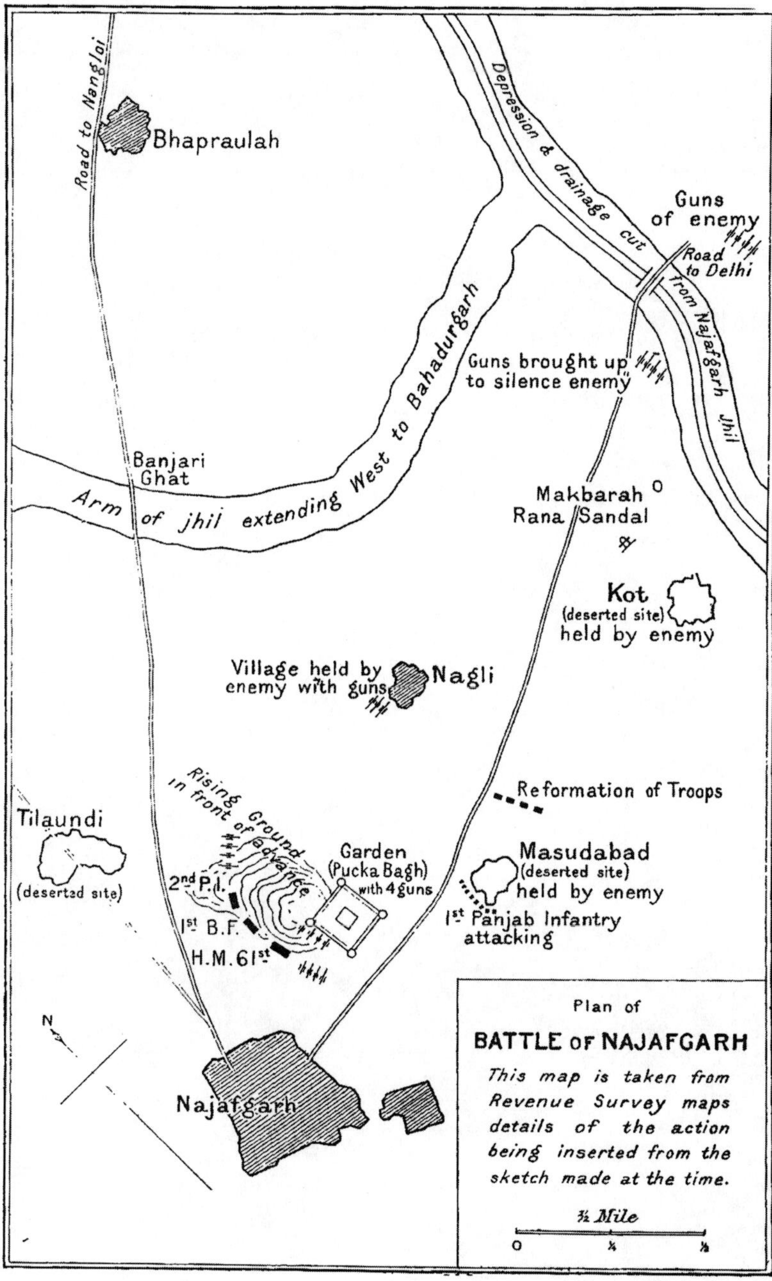
Road to Nanglai
Bhapraulah
Depression & drainage cut from Najafgarh Jhil
Guns of enemy
Road to Delhi
Arm of jhil extending West to Bahadurgarh
Guns brought up to silence enemy
Banjari Ghat
Makbarah Rana Sandal
Kot (deserted site) held by enemy
Village held by enemy with guns
Nagli
Rising Ground in front of advance
Reformation of Troops
Tilaundi (deserted site)
Garden (Pucka Bagh) with 4 guns
Masudabad (deserted site) held by enemy
2nd P.I.
1st B.F.
H.M. 61st
1st Panjab Infantry attacking
N
Najafgarh
Plan of
BATTLE OF NAJAFGARH
This map is taken from Revenue Survey maps details of the action being inserted from the sketch made at the time.
½ Mile
0 ¼ ½

[To face p. 155.

baggage was left behind (before crossing a ford[1] in front of the insurgents' line), protected by the detachment of the 2nd Punjab Cavalry, and 120 Mooltanee Horse.

The strongest point of the insurgents' position was an old (*walled garden*) on their left, in which were four guns, and they had nine more between the (*garden*) and bridge.

By 5 P.M. our troops were across the ford, and advanced to the attack of the (*garden*), with the intention, after its capture, of changing front to the left and sweeping down the enemy's line to the bridge.[2]

One hundred men of each corps were left in reserve, and the 61st Foot, the 1st Fusiliers, and the 2nd Punjab Infantry, were formed up with four guns on the right and ten on the left flank, supported by the squadrons of the 9th Lancers and the Guide Cavalry. After a few rounds from the guns, the infantry charged, carried the position, changed front, and swept down the line, the insurgents flying over the bridge with our guns playing on them. They left thirteen field pieces in our hands.

[1] Known as the Banjari ford. It crosses the arm of the Jhil which extends to Bahadurgarh.—H. C. F.

[2] The localities connected with the battle of Najafgarh may not be altogether clear from the account of it to readers who have not seen the ground, and as the Sketch Map which accompanied General Nicholson's Report was not very exact or complete, I substitute the accompanying map, which shows the details of the sketch upon the groundwork of the Revenue Survey Map of 1872-73. The walled garden (called the sarai in the original report), which had strong corner towers, and is known as the Pakka Bagh, lay beyond rising ground to the north of the road leading east from the town of Najafgarh to the bridge across the Jhil drain, and the position on the old site of Masudabad, attacked by the 1st Punjab Infantry, lay south of it and of the road, near which the main body of troops reformed after carrying the principal position attacked. (According to the old people of the place, who were present in 1857, the 1st Punjab Infantry did not enter the town, which was deserted, but skirted it merely on their way to attack the enemy on the Masudabad site

Meanwhile the 1st Punjab Infantry had cleared the town of Najafgarh.

It being found that a village (*Nagli*) in rear was still held by a party of the enemy who were cut off, the 1st Punjab Rifles were sent to take it, but met with a very obstinate resistance, their gallant young commander being killed, and the 61st Foot had to be sent back in support before the place was taken. Indeed, more properly speaking, it was not taken, but was evacuated by the enemy during the night.

The troops bivouacked on the field without food, having been marching or fighting all day, and during the night the Sappers mined and blew up the Najafgarh bridge.

The column returned to camp on the evening of the 26th, the enemy having quite relinquished their intention of going to our rear, and being in full march for Delhi.

Our casualties were two officers and twenty-three men killed, two officers and sixty-eight men wounded, sixteen horses killed and four wounded. Officers,—Lieutenant Gabbett, 61st Foot, and Lieutenant Lumsden, 1st Punjab Infantry, killed; Lieutenant Elkington, 61st Foot (since dead), and Assistant-Surgeon Ireland, Horse Artillery, both dangerously wounded.

called a "village held by the enemy," on the Sketch Map.) The reformed main body of troops swept down the road to the bridge across the Jhil, the enemy deserting a position which they held at Kot to the south of it, and our guns were pushed to the front to silence theirs on the further side of the canal cut. With our troops in this position, the village of Nagli, which lies slightly north-east of the walled garden, was in the rear on the north side of the road and opposite the 1st Punjab Infantry, which was following up the main body, and which was diverted north to attack the village, and in doing so lost its commanding officer. The people of the village were all hiding in the sugar cane; according to the statement of various survivors, the village was at once taken by our troops, and all the mutineers in it were killed, but the statement in the Narrative is no doubt the correct one.—H. C. F.

The following ordnance was captured on this occasion:—

24-pounder	howitzer		1
12 ,,	howitzers		2
9 ,,	guns		2
6 ,,	,,		4
4 ,,	,,	brass Native guns	2
3 ,,	,,	brass Native guns	2

with a large quantity of ammunition.

General Nicholson's own Report will be read with interest here:—

From Brigadier-General J. NICHOLSON, *Commanding the 4th Infantry Brigade, to Major* R. S. EWART, *Deputy Assistant Adjutant-General, Field Force, dated Camp before Delhi, 28th August* 1857.

Squadron, Her Majesty's 9th Lancers	1
Horse Artillery guns	16
Guide Cavalry	120
2nd Regiment, Punjab Cavalry	80
Wing of Her Majesty's 61st Regiment	420
1st European Bengal Fusiliers	380
1st Regiment, Punjab Infantry	400
2nd Regiment, Punjab Infantry	400
Detachments, Sappers and Miners	30
Mooltanee Horse	200

I have the honour to report, for the information of Major-General Wilson, Commanding before Delhi, that agreeably to his orders, I marched from this at daybreak on the 25th, with the troops noted in the margin, to intercept a force of the enemy said to be moving from Delhi towards Bahadurgarh, with the intention of attacking us in the rear.

On my arrival at the village of Nángloi, about nine miles from this (and to reach which I had to cross two difficult swamps), I learned that the enemy had been at Palam the previous day, and would probably reach Najafgarh in the course of the afternoon; I therefore decided on leaving the Bahadurgarh road, and if possible coming up with and routing the enemy at Najafgarh before nightfall.

I crossed a tolerably deep and broad ford over a branch of the Najafgarh Jhil, near the village of Bápraula, at about 4 P.M., and found the enemy in position on my left and front, extending from the bridge over the Najafgarh canal to the town of Najafgarh itself, a distance of a mile and three-quarters or two miles.[1] Their strongest point was an old (*garden*) on their left centre, in which they had four guns: nine more guns were between this and the bridge.

It was five o'clock before the troops were across the ford and parallel with the position. As the evening was so far advanced, and I had no guides, I laboured under the disadvantage of being compelled to make a very hasty reconnaissance.

The plan which I determined on was to force the left centre (which, as I have said, was the strongest part of the position), and then changing front to the left, to sweep down their line of guns towards the bridge.

I accordingly formed up Her Majesty's 61st Regiment, the 1st Fusiliers, and the 2nd Punjab Infantry (with the exception of 100 men of each corps, whom I had told off on the march as a rear guard and reserve), with four guns on the right and ten on the left flank, supported by the squadron of the 9th Lancers and the Guide Cavalry; and after the artillery had fired a few rounds, I advanced and charged with the infantry.

The enemy was driven out with scarcely any numerical loss to us (though Her Majesty's 61st had a most gallant and promising officer, Lieutenant Gabbett, mortally wounded), and I then changed front to the left, and so turned the whole position in which their guns were. The enemy made little

[1] It is really a little over two miles.—H. C. F.

resistance as we advanced, and were soon in full retreat across the bridge, with our guns playing upon them, thirteen of their field pieces having fallen into our hands.

At the same time that I attacked the (*garden*), I directed Lieutenant Lumsden, Officiating Commandant of Major Coke's corps (the 1st Regiment, Punjab Infantry), to advance and clear the town of Najafgarh on our right. This service was well performed by Lieutenant Lumsden, who after passing through the town brought his right shoulder forward, and followed in rear of the main line.

The enemy's guns were now all in our possession, and I supposed the conflict at an end, when it was reported to me that a few men had concealed themselves in the little village of Nagli, which was at this time a few hundred yards in rear of our line. I immediately sent orders to Lieutenant Lumsden, who was then nearly abreast of the village, to drive them out; but though few in number, they had remained so long that our troops were on all sides of them; and seeing no line of retreat open, they fought with extreme desperation.

Lieutenant Lumsden was, I regret to say, killed, with eleven of his men; twenty-six more were wounded, and I was obliged to send back the 61st Regiment to reinforce the 1st Regiment, Punjab Infantry. This corps also suffered a loss of another gallant officer, Lieutenant Elkington, dangerously wounded, and five men killed and several more were wounded, before the village was in our possession.

The enemy's cavalry, apparently not less than 1000 strong, more than once made a show of charging during the action, but were on each occasion driven back by the fire of our artillery. Our own cavalry I regretted much my inability to employ against them, but I had been obliged to leave the squadron of the 2nd Regiment, Punjab Cavalry, under Lieutenant Nicholson, and 120 of the Mooltanees to look after the baggage, and I had of Lancers, Guides and

Mooltanees not more than 300 left to escort the guns and form a reserve.

I passed the night at the bridge, with the 1st Fusiliers and 2nd Regiment, Punjab Infantry, and a detachment of artillery and Lancers. I had the bridge mined and blown up by the Sappers, and all the waggons and tumbrils which I had not the means of bringing away were also blown up by Major Tombs. Shortly after daybreak, I started on my return to camp, and fearing lest more rain should render the ground (already sufficiently difficult) quite impracticable, I brought the column in the same evening.

It only now remains for me to fulfil the pleasing duty of expressing my extreme satisfaction with the conduct of the troops in these operations. No soldiers ever advanced to the attack of a position with greater gallantry and steadiness than Her Majesty's 61st Regiment, the 1st Fusiliers, and the 2nd Regiment, Punjab Infantry. No infantry was ever more ably assisted by artillery. Major Coke's regiment, under its gallant and lamented officiating commandant, Lieutenant Lumsden, sustained its high reputation.

The troops are likewise entitled to great credit for the cheerfulness with which they bore the hardships they were exposed to; they marched at daybreak, and had to cross two difficult swamps before their arrival at Nangloi, and as it would not have been prudent to take the baggage across the ford at Bapraula, they were obliged, after fourteen hours' marching and fighting, to bivouac on the field without food or covering of any kind.

The officers to whom I am most indebted for their services on this occasion, and whom I would beg to bring prominently to the favourable notice of the Major-General, are Major Tombs, commanding the Artillery (this officer's merits are so well known to the Major-General that it is unnecessary for me to dwell upon them); Major Jacob, commanding the 1st Fusiliers; Captain Green, commanding the 2nd Regiment, Punjab Infantry, and Captains Remmington and Blunt, and Lieutenants Wilson and Sankey of the Artillery. I also received every assistance from my staff and orderly officers, Captain Blane, Her Majesty's 52nd Regiment, my Brigade-Major; Captain Shute, Deputy Assistant Quartermaster-General; Captain Trench, 35th Native Infantry, and Lieutenant Dixon, late 9th Light Cavalry, my orderly officers, and Lieutenant R. C. Low, on the staff of the Major-General Commanding.

Lieutenant Sarel, Her Majesty's 9th Lancers, to whom I entrusted the command of the cavalry with the guns during the action, and of the rear guard on the 26th, performed these duties very much to my satisfaction. The same remarks apply to Captain Gordon, Her Majesty's 61st Regiment, who commanded the reserve during the action and night of the 25th.

Sir Theophilus Metcalfe was good enough to accompany and give me the benefit of his local knowledge; he was also present and very forward in the attack on the (*garden*).

Lieutenant Geneste, of the Engineers, deserves credit for the very complete and successful manner in which he blew up the bridge.

On the morning of the 26th the insurgents in the city turned out in great force, apparently believing that we had few men left in camp during General Nicholson's absence.

The piquets were immediately reinforced, and the enemy commenced an attack on the right of the ridge, and opened fire with field guns from Ludlow Castle on the Mosque. The attack, however, never became very serious, and after suffering severely from our artillery fire, the insurgents retreated into the city.

Our loss in this affair was only eight killed and thirteen wounded.

Towards the end of the month our sick increased a good deal, and on the 31st August 2368 men were in hospital.

Early in September the siege-train, being close at hand, preparations were made for the commencement of active operations for the capture of Delhi, and one of the first things done was to form a trench to the left of the "Sammy House," at the end of which a battery was constructed for four 9-pounders and two 24-pounder howitzers. The object of this battery was to prevent sorties from the Lahore or Kabul Gates passing round the city wall to annoy our breaching batteries, and also to assist in keeping down the fire of the Mori Bastion.

As this battery was within reach of grape from the Mori Bastion, several casualties occurred during its construction, and Lieutenant Warrand of the Engineers lost an arm while on duty there.

By the 6th September all reinforcements that could possibly be expected, together with the siege-train, had arrived. The former consisted of detachments of artillery, and of the 8th Foot and 60th Rifles, the 4th Punjab Rifles, and a wing of the Belúch Battalion, and when the actual siege operations commenced, the number of effective rank and file of all arms, artillery, sappers, cavalry and infantry, and including lascars, drivers, newly-raised Sikh sappers and artillery, and recruits of Punjab corps, was 8748, and there were 2977 in hospital. The strength of British troops was—

Artillery	580
Cavalry	443
Infantry	2294

The European corps were mere skeletons, the strongest only having 409 effective rank and file, while the 52nd Regiment, Light Infantry, which three weeks before had arrived with fully 600 rank and file out of hospital, had now only 242.

The Kashmir Contingent of 2200 men and four

guns had also reached Delhi, and several hundred men of the Jhind Rajah's Contingent (which had previously been most usefully employed in keeping up our communication with Karnal) were, at the Rajah's particular request, brought in to share in the credit of the capture, the Rajah himself accompanying.

For a detail of the actual operations of the siege I annex a copy of an admirable letter that appeared in the *Lahore Chronicle* of the 30th September, 1857, under the signature of "FELIX," who is apparently an officer of Engineers. In the margin I will take the liberty to correct one or two trifling errors, and to add some information.

Letter from "FELIX" *to the Editor of the* Lahore Chronicle.

"Your readers will have understood from the intelligence which has been from time to time published, that, from the period of the arrival of our army before Delhi in June last, up till very lately, the position occupied by our troops has been in effect a purely defensive one. It extended from the piquet at Metcalfe's house, close to the river on the left, along the ridge facing the north side of Delhi as far as the Sabzi Mandi suburb on our right, where this ridge terminates, distance from the city wall averaging from 1200 to 1500 yards.

"We had from the first no choice as to the front of attack, our position on the north being the only one that could secure our communications with the Punjab, whence our supplies and reinforcements were drawn.

"Whether the city might or might not have been carried by a *coup de main*, as was contemplated first in June and afterwards in July, it is needless now to enquire.

"But judging from the resistance we afterwards

experienced in the actual assault, when we had been greatly reinforced in men and guns, it appears to me fortunate that the attempt was not made. The strength of the place was never supposed to consist in the strength of its actual defences, though these were much undervalued; but every city, even without fortifications, is, from its very nature, strongly defensible (unless it can be effectually surrounded or bombarded), and within Delhi the enemy possessed a magazine containing upwards of 200 guns and an almost inexhaustible supply of ammunition, while their numbers were certainly never less than double those of the besiegers. Few will doubt then that the General in command exercised a sound discretion in refusing to allow a handful of troops, unaided by siege-guns, to attack such a place, knowing, as he did, what disastrous results must follow a failure.

"By the beginning of this month, however, we received the siege-train from Ferozepore, and further reinforcements of European and native troops from the Punjab, and it being known that there was no hope of any aid from down country for a considerable time, it was resolved that the siege should be at once commenced and prosecuted with the utmost vigour.

"Our available force amounted in round numbers to 6500 infantry, 1000 cavalry, and 600 artillery, Europeans and natives—the regiments in camp being Her Majesty's 9th Lancers, Her Majesty's 6th Dragoon Guards,[1] the Guide Cavalry, Hodson's Horse, and detachments of the 1st, 2nd, and 5th Punjab Cavalry; Her Majesty's 8th Foot (part of), 52nd Foot, 60th Rifles (part of), 61st Foot, 75th Foot, and the 1st and 2nd Bengal Fusiliers, the Sirmoor and Kumaon Battalions (Gurkhas), the 4th Sikh Infantry, the Guide Infantry, and the 1st, 2nd and 4th Regiments of Punjab Infantry,[2] four

[1] Only four weak troops of the 6th Dragoon Guards.

[2] Also a weak wing of the Beluch Battalion, besides the Jhind and Kashmir Contingents.

troops of Horse Artillery (Tombs', Turner's, Remmington's, and Renny's),[1] two light field batteries (Scott's and Bourchier's), and some companies of foot artillery attached to the siege-guns, which numbered about forty heavy guns and howitzers, and ten heavy and twelve light mortars.

"The means of the engineers were very restricted, not in officers, but in trained men, of whom there were only about 120 regular sappers. Some companies of Mazbi Sikhs had, however, been rapidly raised and partially trained, and a body of coolies had also been collected who worked remarkably well; the park had been at work for some time in collecting material; and 10,000 fascines, 10,000 gabions, and 100,000 sand bags were ready for future operations; field magazines, scaling ladders and spare platforms had also been duly prepared, and great credit is due to Lieutenant Brownlow of the Engineers, in charge of the park, whose activity and intelligence contributed not a little to the eventual success of our operations.

"The north face being the side to be attacked, it was resolved to hold the right in check as far as possible, and to push the main attack on the left: *first*, as the river would completely protect our flank as we advanced; *second*, as there was better cover on that side; *third*, as after the assault the troops would not find themselves immediately in narrow streets, but in comparatively open ground.

"The front to be attacked consisted of the Mori, Kashmir, and Water Bastions, with the curtain walls connecting them. These bastions had been greatly altered and improved by our own engineers many years ago, and presented regular faces and flanks of masonry with properly cut embrasures; but the

[1] Only four guns of Major Tombs' troop were at Delhi. Money's troop (commanded by Captain Blunt subsequent to 23rd July) has been omitted, and Renny's merely consisted of the portion of the Native troop that had been attached to four guns, but deprived of their ordnance.

height of the wall was twenty-four feet above the ground level, of which, however, eight feet was a mere parapet, three feet thick, the remainder being about four times that thickness. Outside the wall was a very wide berm, and then a ditch sixteen feet deep and twenty feet wide at bottom, escarp and counterscarp steep, and the latter unrevetted, and the former revetted with stone, and eight feet in height. A good sloping glacis covered the lower ten feet of the wall from all attempts of distant batteries.

"On the evening of the 7th September, No. I Advanced Battery, in two portions, was traced about 700 yards from the Mori Bastion. The right portion, for five 18-pounders and one eight-inch howitzer, was to silence the Mori and prevent its interfering with the attack on the left; the left portion, for four 24-pounders, was intended to hold the Kashmir Bastion partially in check. The working parties were very little disturbed during the night; the covering parties in front kept the musketry at a distance, and except three well-aimed showers of grape thrown from the Mori, which knocked over some workmen, we received no further annoyance. By the morning the two portions of the battery were finished and armed, though not ready to fire until nearly sunrise; a trench was also made connecting the two portions, and extending a little to the right and left, so as to give communication with a wide and deep ravine, which, extending very nearly up to our left attack, formed a sort of first parallel, and gave good cover to the guard of the trenches, the dhoolies, etc. For some time we were well pounded from the Mori with round shot and grape, but as our guns in the new battery got gradually into play, the enemy's fire grew less and less, and was at length completely overpowered. This battery became known as Brind's, being worked by that officer with great effect till the end of the siege.

"On the evening of the 8th and 9th, No. II Battery was traced and commenced. To our surprise we had been allowed to seize this advanced position at Ludlow Castle, within six hundred yards of the city, without even a fight for it on the previous day. In fact there is little doubt the enemy still thought the attack was to be on the right, where all the fighting had hitherto been, and where all our old batteries were located. Ludlow Castle and the Kudsia Bagh were now occupied by strong detachments, and formed our chief support to the left attack. During the 9th, a sharp fire of musketry, shot and shell, was opened on these positions by the enemy from the jungle in front, and from the Kashmir and Water Bastions, and the Salimgarh, but no great damage was done. During the nights of the 9th and 10th, No. II Battery was completed and partially armed, but not yet unmasked. It was in two portions. One immediately in front of Ludlow Castle, for nine 24-pounders, to open a breach in the curtain between the Kashmir and Water Bastions immediately to the left of the former, and to knock off the parapet to the right and left for some distance, so as to give no cover to musketry. The other portion, some 200 yards to the right, consisting of seven eight-inch howitzers and two 18 pounders, was to aid the first portion, and work with it for the same end. No. III Battery was also commenced on the left, and No. IV Battery, for ten heavy mortars, was completed in the Kudsia Bagh, but not yet unmasked. Major Tombs was in charge of this battery. The light mortars, under Captain Blunt, were afterwards worked from the rear of the Custom House.

"During the nights of the 10th and 11th, No. II Battery was strengthened, armed, and unmasked, and No. III Battery completed. This last was made in the boldest manner within a hundred and eighty yards of the Water Bastion, behind a small ruined house in the Custom House compound, and under such a fire of musketry as few batteries have ever been exposed to; it was for six 18-pounders, which were to open a second breach (*by*) the Water Bastion.

and was worked by Major Scott. The enemy also went to work to-night, and made an advanced trench parallel to our left attack, and about 350 yards from it, from which at daybreak they opened a very hot fire of musketry, which was maintained throughout the rest of the siege; they had previously got some light guns and one heavy gun out into the open on our right, which caused considerable annoyance by their enfilade fire.

"On the 11th our batteries opened fire, a salvo from the nine 24-pounders opening the ball, and showing by the way it brought down the wall in huge fragments what effect it might be expected to produce after a few hours. The Kashmir Bastion attempted to reply, but was quickly silenced, and both portions of No. II went to work in fine style, knocking the bastion and adjacent curtains to pieces. Majors Campbell and Kaye, Captain Johnson and Lieutenant Gray had charge of No. II.[1] No. III, however, did not commence fire till the following day, when the full power of our artillery was shown, and the continuous roar of fifty guns and mortars pouring shot and shell on the devoted city, warned the enemy that his and our time had at length come. Night and day, until the morning of the 14th, was this overwhelming fire continued. But the enemy did not let us have it all our own way. Though unable to work a gun from any of the three bastions that were so fiercely assailed, they yet stuck to their guns in the open, which partially enfiladed our position; they got a gun to bear from a hole broken open in the long curtain wall; they sent rockets from one of their martello towers, and they maintained

[1] Major Campbell commanded the left portion, and Major Kaye the right, but the former officer being wounded on the evening of the 11th, Captain Johnson, Assistant Adjutant-General of Artillery, then serving in that battery, succeeded to the command, and held it to the moment of the assault, when he resumed his place on General Wilson's staff.

a perfect storm of musketry from their advanced trench, and from the city walls.

"On the night of the 13th the engineers stole down and examined the two breaches near the Kashmir and Water Bastions;[1] and both being reported practicable, orders for the assault were at once issued, to take place at daybreak the following morning.

"The arrangements for the storming were as follows:—

"1ST COLUMN[2]

Under Brigadier-General J. Nicholson.

Her Majesty's 75th Regiment. 1st Bengal Fusiliers. 2nd Punjab Infantry.	To storm the breach near the Kashmir Bastion, and escalade the face of the bastion.

"Engineer officers attached—Lieutenants Medley, Lang and Bingham.

"2ND COLUMN[3]

Under Brigadier W. Jones, Commanding Her Majesty's 61st Regiment.

Her Majesty's 8th Regiment. 2nd Bengal Fusiliers. 4th Sikh Infantry.	To storm the breach in the Water Bastion.

"Engineer officers attached—Lieutenants Greathead, Hovenden and Pemberton.

---

[1] Lieutenants Medley and Lang examined the former, Lieutenants Greathead and Home the latter.

[2]	Men.
75th Foot (Lieutenant-Colonel Herbert) .	300
1st Fusiliers (Major Jacob) . . .	250
2nd Punjab Infantry (Captain Green) . .	450
Total	1000

[3]	Men.
Her Majesty's 8th Foot (Lieut.-Col. Greathead)	250
2nd Fusiliers (Captain Boyd) . . .	250
4th Sikh Infantry (Captain Rothney) . .	350
Total	850

"3RD COLUMN [1]

Under Colonel G. Campbell, Commanding Her Majesty's 52nd Regiment.

Her Majesty's 52nd Regiment. Kumaon Battalion. 1st Punjab Infantry.	To assault the Kashmir Gate after it should be blown open.

"Engineer officers attached—Lieutenants Home, Salkeld and Tandy.

"4TH COLUMN [2]

Under Major C. Reid, Commanding the Sirmoor Battalion.

Detachments of European regiments Sirmoor Battalion Guide Infantry Detachment of Dogras	To attack the suburb Kishanganj, and enter the Lahore Gate.

"Engineer officers attached — Lieutenants Maunsell and Tennant.

"5TH COLUMN [3]

Under Brigadier J. Longfield, Her Majesty's 8th Regiment.

Her Majesty's 61st Regiment. 4th Punjab Infantry.	The Reserve.

"Engineer officers attached—Lieutenants Ward and Thackeray.

---

[1]

	Men.
Her Majesty's 52nd Regiment (Major Vigors) .	200
Kumaon Battalion (Captain Ramsay) . .	250
1st Punjab Infantry (Lieutenant Nicholson) .	500
Total	950

[2] The 4th Column consisted of the Sirmoor Battalion and Guides, and such of the piquets (European and Native) as could be spared from Hindu Rao's, altogether 860 men, besides the Kashmir Contingent, actual strength not known.

[3] The Reserve was thus composed—

	Men.
Her Majesty's 61st (Lieutenant-Colonel Deacon)	250
4th Punjab Infantry (Captain Wilde) . .	450
Wing, Beluch Battalion (Lieut.-Col. Farquhar)	300
Jhind auxiliaries (Lieutenant-Colonel Dunsford)	300
Total	1300

Besides 200 of the 60th Rifles under Lieutenant-Colonel Jones, after they had covered the advance of the stormers.

"At 4 A.M. (*on 14th September*)[1] the different columns fell in, and were marched to their respective places, the heads of Nos. 1, 2, and 3 Columns being kept concealed until the moment for the actual assault should arrive.

"The signal was to be the advance of the Rifles to the front to cover the heads of the columns by skirmishing.

"Everything being ready, General Nicholson, whose excellent arrangements elicited the admiration of all, gave the signal, and the Rifles dashed to the front with a cheer, extending along and skirmishing through the low jungle, which at this point extends to within fifty yards of the ditch. At the same moment, the heads of Nos. 1 and 2 Columns from the Kudsia Bagh, and advanced steadily towards the breach(*es*). Our batteries had maintained a tremendous fire up to the moment of the advance of the troops, and not a gun could the enemy bring to bear on the storming columns; but no sooner did these emerge into the open, than a perfect hailstorm of bullets met them from the front and both flanks, and officers and men fell fast on the crest of the glacis. For ten minutes it was impossible[2] to get the ladders down into the ditch to ascend the escarp; but the determination of the British soldier carried all before it, and Pandy declined to meet the charge of the British bayonet. With a shout and a rush the

1 This was a Monday, as the 11th May and 8th June (battle of Badli-ki-Sarai) 1857 had been. It was a curious coincidence, as noticed by the Senior Chaplain with the Force, the Rev. Mr Rotton, that the lesson for 14th September should have been the third chapter of Nahum:—"Woe to the bloody city . . . . The horseman lifteth up both the bright sword and glittering spear, and there is a multitude of slain, and a great number of carcases. . . . The gates of thy land shall be set wide open unto thine enemies; the fire shall devour thy bars."—H. C. F.

2 This hardly applies to No. 2 Column, which the Brigadier commanding reported took possession of the breach and walls without the slightest check.—H. C. F.

breaches were both won, and the enemy fled in confusion.[1]

"Meanwhile the explosion party advanced in front of the 3rd Column straight upon the Kashmir Gate. This little band of heroes (for they were no less) had to advance in broad daylight to the gateway in the very teeth of a hot fire of musketry from above, and through the gateway and on both flanks; the powder bags were coolly laid and adjusted, but Lieutenant Salkeld was by this time *hors de combat* with two bullets in him. Sergeant Carmichael then attempted to fire the hose, but was shot dead. Sergeant Burgess then tried and succeeded, but paid for the daring act with his life. Sergeant Smith, thinking that Burgess too had failed, ran forward, but seeing the train alight had just time to throw himself into the ditch and escape the effects of the explosion. With a loud crash the gateway was blown in, and through it the 3rd Column rushed to the assault, and entered the town just as the other columns had won the breaches. General Wilson has since bestowed the Victoria Cross on Lieutenants Home and Salkeld,[2] on Sergeant Smith, and on a brave man of Her Majesty's 52nd (*Bugler Hawthorne*), who stood by

[1] The exact details of the storm assault at the Kashmir Bastion are given differently by different writers. Captain Brookes, who succeeded to the command of the 75th Regiment when Colonel Herbert was wounded, and to that of the 1st Column when General Nicholson was shot, stated in his report that the 1st Bengal Fusiliers, with General Nicholson at their head, escaladed the left (*i.e.* east) face of the bastion, and that the 75th assaulted the actual breach, and this seems probably the correct account. Colonel Herbert, it will be remembered, had led his regiment to the attack on the Badli-ki-Sarai position, and now led it in the attack on the Kashmir breach.—H. C. F.

[2] Both these gallant officers have since died. Lieutenant Home was blown up on the 1st October by the premature explosion of a mine in destroying the fort of Malagarh. Lieutenant Salkeld, who lost an arm, and had his thigh broken in the storm, died of his wounds after lingering for many days.

Lieutenant Salkeld to the last, and bound up his wounds.[1]

"General Nicholson then formed the troops in the Main Guard inside, and with his Column proceeded to clear the ramparts as far as the Mori Bastion. It was in advancing beyond this (*from the Kabul Gate*)[2] towards the Lahore Gate that he met the wound which has since caused his lamented death—a death which it is not too much to say has dimmed the lustre of even this victory—as it has deprived the country

[1] Lord Roberts, who was sent from Ludlow Castle by General Wilson to bring news of how the attack was progressing inside the city, has given us a memorable sketch of the appearance of the Kashmir Gate after the explosion. He "crept through the wicket, which was the only part blown in, and found the interior of the gateway blocked by an 18-pounder gun, under which were lying the scorched bodies of two or three sepoys who had evidently been killed by the explosion."—H. C. F.

[2] The spot where General Nicholson was wounded, and which is now marked in the city wall by a marble tablet, is scarcely eighty yards from the Kabul Gate, removed some years back, and the Western Jumna Canal, which enters the city on the south side of the gate (p. 92). Lord Roberts records in his Memoirs the touching incident of how he found the wounded General lying deserted in a dhooly outside the Kashmir Gate, and arranged for his being taken on to the camp. It is difficult to understand how, with the force at his disposal, General Wilson hoped to be able to occupy and hold, on the day of assault, the city wall round to the Lahore Gate, and the line of the Chandni Chauk almost down to the palace, with the Jama Masjid as an advanced post, as this would have comprised nearly half of the city exclusive of the palace. It was necessary, no doubt, to occupy the Kabul Gate so as to prevent the enemy issuing from the city and attacking our rear and camp, and it was *this* gate which Colonel Reid has stated he was ordered to enter by (see his letter of 2nd February 1858, in the Rev. Mr Rotton's Narrative of the Siege of Delhi, and the papers quoted at the foot of this note), but otherwise an advance on the palace from the Kashmir Gate would have been made with the left flank, protected all the way by the river wall, and the capture of the palace would have at once caused a retreat of all the rebels, whose only way of escape would then have been by the south, as the Bridge of Boats was commanded, and could have been easily

of one of the ablest men and most gallant soldiers that England anywhere numbers among our ranks.

"The 4th Column, I regret to say, failed; but as it was too far for me to know anything of its real progress, I prefer leaving its story to be told by another instead of sending you a vague and imperfect account. Had this Column succeeded, its possession of the Lahore Gate would have saved much subsequent trouble.

"Mr Editor, I regret that my account must stop here, as, being wounded myself at this stage of the proceedings, I was unable to witness the subsequent capture of the magazine, the Burn Bastion, the palace, and finally of the whole city. Some one else will doubtless conclude my story in a more worthy manner than I have told it.

"Thus terminated the siege of Delhi. Our loss during the actual siege was about 300 men.[1] On the day of the assault it was 61 officers and 1178 men killed

destroyed, from the palace. In Captain Trotter's life of General Nicholson, it is said he was urgent in his advice: "Don't press the enemy too hard, leave them a golden bridge to retire by," but his persistent advance towards the Lahore Gate was hardly in keeping with this.

In a small collection of papers published by him in 1861, Colonel Reid wrote as follows:—

"*September 13th.*—Nicholson has been with me making arrangements about the assault, which we hope will take place at daybreak tomorrow. Nicholson will carry a blue flag with his column, which I shall anxiously look out for when I am making my way into the city. The General approves of my plan of attack. I proposed that my attack on Kishanganj and Trevelyanganj should take place before daylight, but it was decided I should attack at the same time, and that my signal to advance was to be the explosion—the blowing in of the Kashmir Gate.

"The last time I saw the fine fellow (General Nicholson) was on the evening of 13th September, when he came up to make arrangements with me regarding the attack next morning, where we were to meet, etc., that he should open the Kabul Gate for me from the inside after I had taken Kishanganj, Trevelyanganj and Paharipur."—H. C. F.

[1] Actually 327 from date of opening of batteries to moment of assault.

and wounded,[1] being nearly one-third of the whole number engaged. The 1st Fusiliers alone lost nine officers, and other regiments, I believe, in proportion. The engineers suffered heavily; the three officers conducting Nos. 1, 2, and 4 Columns (Lieutenants Medley, Greathead and Maunsell) were all struck down early in the fight, and of 17 officers on duty that day, ten were put *hors de combat*. The loss of the enemy is never likely to be correctly ascertained; but at the end of the operations it is probable that at least 1500 men must have been killed between the 7th and 20th, and a very large number wounded, who were carried away.

"For the complete success that attended the prosecution of the siege, the chief credit is undoubtedly due to Colonel R. Baird Smith, the Chief Engineer, and to Captain A. Taylor, the director of the attack. On this latter officer, in fact, in consequence of the chief engineer being wounded, devolved the entire superintendence of the siege works, and his energy and activity will doubtless meet with their due reward. Throughout the operations he seemed to be omnipresent, and to bear a charmed life, for he escaped without a wound. The plan of attack was bold and skilful, the nature of the enemy we were contending with was exactly appreciated, and our plans shaped accordingly. Pandy can fight well behind cover; but here he was out-manœuvred, his attention being diverted from the real point of attack till the last, and then the cover which might have proved such a serious obstacle to us was seized at the right moment without loss and all its advantages turned against him. With plenty of skilled workmen the siege works might have been more speedily constructed, but with the wretched means at our disposal the wonder is that so much was done with so little loss.

[1] Actually 66 officers and 1104 men. The hospital had been advanced from behind the Ridge to a corner of the Metcalfe estate, and it was here that the wounded in the assault were carried.—H. C. F.

"If the siege of Delhi was not a regular siege in the same sense with that of Bhurtpore or Seringapatam, it may yet bear a fairer comparison with a greater than either—that of Sebastopol. In both the strength of the fortifications was as nothing; it was the proportion of besieged to besiegers, the magnitude of the arsenal inside, and the impossibility of a thorough investment that constituted the real strength of the place; in fact, neither were, properly speaking, sieges, but rather attacks on an army in a strongly intrenched position. (Signed) FELIX."

I must now add a few particulars to the above, and complete the account to the period when we were finally in possession of the whole city.

To enable the whole of the siege batteries to be armed, most of the heavy guns were withdrawn from the Ridge, such only being left as were necessary to render that position secure against attack from the Kishanganj direction. The foot artillery, even without relief, being quite unable to man the heavy guns and mortars, nearly all the officers and men of the horse artillery were sent into the batteries and worked in them until the morning of the assault, when they rejoined their troops. In addition to these, the Carabineers and the 9th Lancers furnished a quota of volunteers, whose intelligence and good-will rendered their services most valuable. Several volunteer officers from the line had been under instruction in the Ridge batteries for some days before the breaching batteries opened, and were afterwards most usefully employed in the latter.

The newly-raised Sikh artillerymen of course took their share of the work; and the manner in which a detail of these men under Lieutenant Sir William Hamilton, Bart., worked two of the guns in Major Scott's battery under a close and constant fire of musketry elicited the admiration of those who saw them.

The men of the two field batteries of the force

were not taken for the siege guns, so that one battery furnished the three divisions of guns for the piquets and the other was in reserve in camp.

From the night of the 7th until the batteries were completed, the exertions of all the engineer officers, sappers and pioneers, were unceasing, and large working and covering parties had to be constantly furnished by the infantry.

On the 8th, after No. I or Brind's Battery had opened, a sortie was made from the city, principally of cavalry, but the only result was that several of the insurgents were killed by the fire of our artillery. From the broken ground below the ridge, however, and from a trench in front of No. I Battery, a constant fire of musketry was kept up, and grape had to be used at the light gun battery near the "Sammy House," commanded by Captain Remmington, to keep the skirmishers at a distance.

The other efforts at annoyance until the period of the assault were those described in the letter of "FELIX," and numerous casualties were occasioned, for not only were 327 fighting men put *hors de combat*, but many followers, such as *bhistis*, magazine lascars, ordnance drivers, etc., were killed and wounded. At the Custom House Battery, within 180 yards of the place, the rattle of musketry was incessant, and the approach to the battery was most hazardous. Captain Fagan of the Artillery, a most valuable and gallant officer, was killed here by a musket shot two or three hours after fire had been opened. Once or twice before the guns of No. II Battery were in full play, sorties were made from the Kashmir Gate, and a constant fire was kept up from trenches in front. A portion of the 1st Punjab Infantry (Rifles) under Lieutenant Nicholson was from the 8th to the 14th engaged in protecting No. II Battery, being posted behind a low wall in advance, with a reserve of the same corps together with some European infantry at Ludlow Castle; and all the batteries were of course guarded by strong parties of infantry.

The guns placed by the enemy in the Teliwara suburb completely enfiladed Nos. I and II Batteries, and were a source of much annoyance. They were so sheltered that our ordnance on the Ridge and at the "Sammy House" Battery were never able altogether to silence them.

From the Salimgarh too a very constant fire of shells was kept up, which dropped about the Custom House Mortar Battery and No. II Battery.

The Kishanganj batteries still continued to play at intervals on the Ridge.

During the actual period of the siege but one attempt was made to annoy our rear. A body of cavalry crossing the canal drove in our piquet of irregular horse at Azadpur; but parties of Punjab and Guide Cavalry speedily turning out pursued and killed twenty-five of the mutineers, including a native officer. Lieutenant Watson, 1st Punjab Cavalry, was wounded on this occasion; one man and two horses were killed, eleven men and thirteen horses wounded.

During the assault the protection of the camp was confided to the convalescents of corps, a portion of the cavalry, and some horse artillery, under Colonel Dennis, Her Majesty's 52nd Regiment, Light Infantry. The infantry piquets all joined their regiments, save a small detachment at the mosque. After the assault and until the total capture of the city no infantry could be sent back to camp; but on the 15th most of the cavalry and the horse artillery had returned, and the Sirmoor Battalion and the Guide Corps being at Hindu Rao's House, the camp with all the sick, wounded, stores, etc., became tolerably secure, and the anxiety which was felt in case it should be attacked in rear by a body of troops (which the enemy might have spared), while we were involved in the city, was allayed.

Brigadier Grant, with the bulk of the cavalry (about 600 sabres) and a troop and a half of horse artillery, was directed to move down when the assault took place to the neighbourhood of No. I Battery, to check any attempt to take our storming columns in flank by sortie from the Lahore and Ajmir Gates; and No. I Battery was to keep up its fire on the Mori until our columns were found to be progressing in that direction.

Taking up the account where "FELIX" leaves off, I will briefly describe what occurred to the several columns.

Nos. 1 and 2, having effected an entrance, proceeded round the walls to their right, overcoming opposition, and taking a small battery and a tower between the Kashmir and Mori Bastions, the Mori itself, and the Kabul Gate. All attempts, however, to take the Burn Bastion and Lahore Gate failed. The troops had to advance up a narrow lane swept down by grape and musketry, and in one of these attempts General Nicholson was mortally wounded. As far as the Kabul Gate our hold was secured, and preparations were immediately made for opening fire from the bastions inwards on the town, sand-bag parapets being constructed across the gorges.

The 3rd Column, under Colonel Campbell, of Her Majesty's 52nd Regiment, Light Infantry, after storming the Kashmir Gate, proceeded through the town towards the Jama Masjid, conducted in the most gallant manner by Sir Theophilus Metcalfe, of the Civil Service, who had volunteered for the duty, for which he was well qualified from local knowledge. By taking the column by a circuitous route but little opposition was met with until the Chandni Chauk was reached,[1] and possession obtained of the *Kotwali*.[2] After this, however, men fell fast, and it was found impossible to carry out the object assigned, viz., the

[1] This column went down the Dariba, the closed gate of this street being pluckily opened by a chaprassi, Mohan Singh, and five men of the 52nd Regiment, and penetrated to within 100 yards of the Jama Masjid. This, however, was too strongly defended to be rushed, and after half an hour, the column was obliged to fall back.—H. F. C.

[2] The police station.

capture of the Jama Masjid. Eventually this column fell back to the neighbourhood of the church and joined the Reserve, a proceeding which met with the full approval of the Major-General Commanding.

The Reserve followed No. 3 Column into the Kashmir Gate, the wing of the Belúch Battalion having been previously detached to the right of No. II Battery, and eventually sent to Hindu Rao's as a support, when the serious nature of the struggle in Kishanganj became known.

The College Gardens were cleared of the insurgents by the Reserve, and held by the 4th Punjab Rifles and some of Her Majesty's 61st Regiment. The Water Bastion, Kashmir Gate, Skinner's house, and the house of Ahmad Ali Khan, a large commanding building, were also held by this column. Upon the retirement of No. 3 Column, the Kumaon Battalion were placed in Skinner's house, Her Majesty's 52nd Regiment at the church, and the 1st Punjab Infantry in the houses at the end of the two streets that led into the open space around the church from the interior of the city. Guns too were posted at the head of these streets, which stopped an attempt that was made to follow up No. 3 Column.

No. 4 Column, under Major Reid, advanced from the Sabzi Mandi towards Kishanganj, the Kashmir Contingent co-operating in two divisions, the main body under Major R. Lawrence acting as a reserve, and a detachment under Captain Dwyer attacking the *Idgah* upon the right. The latter was so sharply attacked by the insurgents, who were in great force, that after losing a great number of men and four guns, it was completely defeated and fell back to camp.

Major Reid's Column met with the most strenuous opposition, greatly increased doubtless by the failure of the detachment of the Kashmir Contingent *on the right.*

Captain Muter, 60th Rifles, who succeeded to the command of the advance after Major Reid's fall, the next senior officer to Major Reid (Major Lawrence) being in command of the Reserve, and therefore some way in the rear, judiciously withdrew the advanced troops to the Sabzi Mandi. When Major Lawrence became aware of Major Reid's fall, he, as in duty bound, assumed command of the whole column, and made all subsequent dispositions.

Major Lawrence maintained the defence of the ground in the neighbourhood of the canal, until the necessity for it ceased.

Their retirement was much aided by a fire of shrapnel shells opened by Lieutenant H. J. Evans from the light guns at the battery called the "Crow's Nest." One party of the Guide Infantry, however, were surrounded in an enclosure and could not get away. Their rescue was eventually effected in a spirited manner by the wing of the Belúch Battalion, which as before stated had been detached to this quarter.

Meanwhile Brigadier Grant with his cavalry and guns had most effectually prevented any annoyance to the flanks of the assaulting columns, but his troops had suffered severely from the fire of the Teliwara guns and the Burn Bastion, three of the former of which were, however, spiked by our artillery.

The heavy fire brought on the cavalry caused Major-General Wilson to send up Captain Bourchier's battery in aid of the horse artillery guns under Major Tombs, which had as usual been most efficiently commanded, but had sustained heavy loss.

The duty assigned to the cavalry having been completed, they were withdrawn to the neighbourhood of Ludlow Castle, with piquets towards the ridge.

The Belúch Battalion also being no longer required outside, moved into the city and joined the Reserve.

During the 15th several mortars were got into position to shell the town and palace. A battery commanding Salimgarh and part of the palace was opened from the College gardens, and some houses were taken in advance of our first positions. A breach was made also from the College in the Magazine defences. The enemy all this time kept up a cannonade on our position in the city from Salimgarh; from the Magazine a constant musketry fire was maintained on the College compound, and more or less skirmishing went on at all our advanced posts. This occasioned, however, little loss, as directly we occupied a house sand-bag defences were put up wherever requisite.

At dawn on the 16th the Magazine was stormed[1] and taken with slight loss to us by Her Majesty's 61st Regiment, part of the 4th Punjab Infantry, and the wing of the Belúch Battalion.

Kishanganj this morning was evacuated by the enemy and five heavy guns left, of which possession was taken by a party sent forward from Hindu Rao's. We were now for the first time enabled to see the immense strength of the insurgent position here and in Teliwara, and which they had spared no labour to improve.

During the 17th and 18th our right and left positions at the Kabul Gate and Magazine were brought into direct communication by a line of posts, in rear of which everything was our own. Pushing still forward, the Bank, Major Abbott's house, and the dwelling of Khan Mahomed Khan were taken, so that our posts were now close to the palace and Chandni Chauk. These advances were not made without opposition, both from field artillery and musketry, but being conducted with great judgment, our loss was trifling.

All our mortars (most of them from the Magazine) now played constantly upon the palace and the quarters of the town occupied by the enemy, and must have materially contributed to the subsequent evacuation of the palace. Indeed, it became evident that the insurgents were gradually escaping from the place

[1] 171 guns were recovered in the Magazine, and 35 were captured in position in various places.—H. C. F.

at the opposite side. Few went over the bridge, as our guns commanded it.

On the evening of the 19th, the Burn Bastion was surprised and captured by a party from the Kabul Gate, and early next morning the Lahore Gate and Garstin Bastion were likewise taken and held. The cavalry, also, going round by the *Idgah* found the camp of a large force of the mutineers outside the Delhi Gate evacuated; and Lieutenant Hodson pushing in, secured it, his sawars killing a number of wounded or sick sepoys. Quantities of clothing, ammunition, and plunder were taken in this camp, everything showing that the insurgents had fled with precipitation. Some cavalry entering by the Delhi Gate took possession of the Jama Masjid, and were speedily supported by infantry and guns.

While this was going on a column had been formed to take the palace, which appeared deserted, save that occasionally a musket shot was fired from over the gateway at our troops at the head of the Chandni Chauk. Powder bags were brought up and the gateway blown in. Only two or three fanatics were found inside, and a number of wounded sepoys, who soon fell victims to the bayonets of our men.[1]

The whole city was now entirely in our hands; and the troops were posted at the various gateways, bastions, &c., headquarters being established in the

[1] The first troops to enter the fort and palace were the 4th Punjab Infantry under Lieutenant M'Queen—now Sir John M'Queen, K.C.B. It had been intended to breach the fort wall by artillery; but Lieutenant M'Queen, having made a reconnaissance on his own account from the piquets stationed in houses in front of the fort, discovered that there were only eight or ten gunners at the gate outwork, with two guns trained to fire on the gateway. It was accordingly determined to blow the gate in, and this was done again by Captain Home, and the 4th Punjab Infantry at once rushed in, broke the chain which held the inner gate by firing muskets close to it, and charged down the vaulted passage into the palace. A single sentry remained in this passage, and fired at Lieutenant M'Queen when at a distance of only a few yards from

palace, which was held by Her Majesty's 60th Rifles and the Kumaon Battalion.

The town was nearly empty of inhabitants, many of whom indeed (principally women and children of *bunniahs*) had been passed out by our guards subsequent to the assault. Now and then sepoys or fanatical Mahomedans, wounded or hiding, were discovered by parties of our troops, dragged out and shot.

On the 21st,[1] Lieutenant Hodson, with the valuable aid of the head of our Intelligence Department (Maulavi Rajab Ali), captured the king a few miles from Delhi. He was brought in and placed under a European guard, and now awaits a trial, which has been ordered.

On the following day two of the king's sons and a grandson, all deeply implicated in the atrocities committed in May, were also captured through Lieutenant Hodson's exertions. They were shot,[2]

him, but fortunately the bullet went through that officer's helmet only. The fort was found deserted, though a few individuals were discovered here and there, and were shot. Shortly after the palace had been captured from this side, Lieutenant Aikman, V.C., also of the 4th Punjab Infantry, entered it through the Salimgarh, again meeting a solitary sentry only.

[1] On this date a royal salute was fired in honour of the capture of Delhi, and on Sunday, 27th September, a thanksgiving service was held in the Diwan-i-Khas.—H. C. F.

[2] Regarding this much-debated incident, I will only say that while Lieutenant Hodson's action in insisting upon the surrender of their arms by the mob with the princes at Humayun's Tomb, so as to allow the safe removal of the latter meanwhile, was one of the most marked displays of cool daring exhibited in the whole of the Mutiny campaign, it seems scarcely credible that there was any grave fear of an attempt to rescue the captives. When after sending off the arms, Hodson and MacDowell, second in command, galloped after and up to the escort of *ten* men only with the prisoners, they overtook them between the Jail and the Delhi Gate of the city, which must have been held by a guard of our troops; and considering that the city was mainly deserted on the 22nd September (see above), and that all the

and their bodies exposed for twenty-four hours in front of the *kotwali*.

On the morning of the 24th a strong movable column, under the command of Lieutenant-Colonel Greathead, Her Majesty's 8th Regiment, moved into the Doab, to clear it and to endeavour to open communication with General Havelock at Cawnpore; and the connection of the writer with the Delhi force ceased. (*On the same morning Brigadier-General Nicholson, who had died the previous day, was buried in the new cemetery in front of the Kashmir Gate*).

It is impossible, however, to conclude without alluding to the trials and constancy of the troops employed in this arduous siege. Called on at the hottest season of the year to take the field, imperfectly equipped, and with the extent of difficulties to be faced very imperfectly known, all felt that a crisis had arrived to meet which every man's cheerful, willing and heartfelt energies must be put forth to the utmost; and how well this was done those who were with the army know and never can forget. For the first five weeks every effort was required, not indeed to take Delhi, but to hold our own position, and day after day for hours together every soldier was under arms under a burning sun and constantly exposed to fire. Notwithstanding the daily casualties in action, the numerous deaths by cholera, the discouraging reports relative to the fidelity of some of the native portions of our own force, the distressing accounts from all parts of the

followers of the king's party, who had not retreated from it, were necessarily in custody, or hiding, there must have been less chance of a rescue at the spot where the princes were shot than there had been at any point on the road between it and Humayun's Tomb, along which *ten* sawars had escorted them without any attempt at rescue. The number of men with Lieutenant Hodson at the time was about ninety, a few being behind with the carts carrying the surrendered arms; and, according to MacDowell's account, ten of these sufficed to keep the mob back, while the princes were first ordered to get out of their cart, and were then ordered back into it, and were finally shot in it by Hodson.—H. C. F.

country, the constant arrival of large reinforcements of mutineers, and the apparent impossibility of aid ever reaching in sufficient strength to enable us to take the place, the courage and confidence of the army never flagged; and, besides enduring a constant and often deadly cannonade for more than three months, in thirty different combats, our troops invariably were successful, always against long odds, and often opposed to ten times their numbers, who had all the advantages of ground and superior artillery.

At last the actual siege commenced. Batteries were at once thrown up in open ground within grape range of the walls, and though the loss in doing this was comparatively small, owing to some apparent misconception on the part of the enemy, the design was one of the boldest ever conceived. The establishment of Major Scott's battery within 180 yards of the walls, to arm which heavy guns had to be dragged from the rear under a constant fire of musketry, was an operation that can rarely have been equalled in war.

Finally, these soldiers worn with disease, tired with incessant duty, and sadly reduced in numbers, in open day stormed a place defended by vastly superior force, many crossing a ditch twenty-four feet deep, and clambering up a breach in face of a deadly fire, and having done this had at once to commence a series of fresh operations for the reduction of the town, which after six days' constant toil or skirmishing were attended with complete success.

All behaved nobly, but it may be permitted me to allude somewhat to those corps most constantly engaged from the beginning, the 60th Rifles, the Sirmoor Battalion and the Guides. Probably not one day throughout the siege passed without a casualty in one of these corps; placed in the very front of our position, they were ever under fire. Their courage, their high qualifications as skirmishers, their cheerfulness, their steadiness, were beyond commendation. Their losses in action show the nature of the service.

The Rifles commenced with 440 of all ranks; a

few days before the storm they received a reinforcement of nearly 200 men; their total casualties were 389.

The Sirmoor Battalion commenced 450 strong, and once was joined by a draft of 90 men. Its total casualties amounted to 319.

The Guides commenced with about 550 (cavalry and infantry), and the casualties were 303.

The incessant labours of the artillery as well as of the engineer department deserve especial mention; 365 casualties in the former and 293 in the latter branch are proof of the exposure to which they were subjected. There can be no brighter passage in the history of the Bengal Artillery than that which will tell of their exertions before Delhi, whether in the heavy batteries or in the various engagements in which field artillery alone took part. The duties of the engineer officers were most laborious, and involved constant exposure, more than two-thirds being killed or wounded; and the remnant of the old Corps of Sappers and Miners (the only trained Sappers present) behaved with the most perfect fidelity, and on numerous occasions with exemplary gallantry, notwithstanding that the bulk of their comrades were opposed to them. The returns annexed will show how heavily all corps suffered, even those who joined towards the close; and there was no regiment that could not boast of brilliant feats. Europeans and natives alike were animated by one spirit, and happy was the Government which at such a time numbered these troops amongst the ranks of its army.

There is but one point left to which to allude,—the strength of Delhi. Absurd accounts of the weakness of the place were circulated in India and in England. "FELIX" shows where its principal strength lay. Suffice it that a wall twelve feet thick, with a ditch in front of considerable width and about twenty-four feet deep, with an admirable glacis covering the wall for a full third of its height, bastions in capital order (each holding ten, twelve or fourteen pieces of heavy artillery), so as to form good flanking defences around a city seven miles in extent, with the river on one face, constitute a formidable position. When added to this it is borne in mind that at the very lowest estimate there were never fewer than double as many defenders as assailants, and more generally four times as many; that there could be no investment even in name; that upwards of three hundred guns, of which a large proportion were of heavy calibre, were actually captured in front of or in the place; and that the defenders' supply of ammunition was plentiful to the last, it will be allowed that the General whose task it was to take Delhi had no ordinary enterprise on hand.

Honour to him for his resolution, which persevered to the end, and which led to the success that probably more than anything else will be found to have contributed to the restoration of British authority wherever it has been shaken in India.

How Sir John Lawrence supported and reinforced the army, at the risk of denuding the country under his Government of troops that might be most urgently required, how vigorously he aided the operations in every way, has already been acknowledged by the Government of India. To him the Army of Delhi, as well as the British nation, owe a deep debt of gratitude, and which by the former certainly will not be forgotten.[1]

[1] In 1857 Delhi, and what was known as the old Delhi territory, comprising the present districts of Gurgaon, Delhi, Rohtak and Hissar, and two-thirds of Karnal, were under the Lieutenant-Governor of the north-west provinces. When Sir John Lawrence wrote to Mr Colvin, urging the vital importance of the early recapture of Delhi, he was informed in reply that the Lieutenant-Governor had made his arrangements, and that Mr Greathead, the Commissioner with the Army, was apprised of them. One cannot help thinking that if Delhi had been from the first under the great Chief Commissioner, who was intimately acquainted with it, more vigorous steps would have been taken to repress the troublesome population of the country, and to cut the rebels off from their supplies and other resources.—H. C. F.

Annexed is a return of casualties in action. I should have wished to have added a return of casualties by sickness, and a correct plan of Delhi with our positions and those of the insurgents. These I have been unable to obtain at present owing to my having quitted Delhi with the pursuing column; but doubtless both hereafter will be forthcoming in an official form.

(Signed) H. W. NORMAN, *Lieut.*,
Asst. Adjt.-Genl. of the Army.

CAMP OF MOVABLE COLUMN,
CAWNPORE, *the 28th October* 1857.

List of Officers killed, died of wounds, or wounded at or near Delhi, from the 30th May 1857 to the final capture of the palace on the 20th September 1857.

[KILLED OR DIED OF WOUNDS.]

Staff.

Brigadier-General J. Nicholson, commanding the 4th Infantry Brigade.
Colonel C. Chester, Adjutant-General of the Army.
Captain C. W. Russell, 54th Native Infantry, Orderly Officer.
Captain J. W. Delamain, 56th Native Infantry, Orderly Officer.

Artillery.

Captain R. C. H. B. Fagan.[1]
Lieutenant E. H. Hildebrand.[1]
Lieutenant H. G. Perkins.[1]
Lieutenant T. E. Dickens.[1]

Engineers.

Lieutenant P. Salkeld.
2nd-Lieutenant F. L. Tandy.
2nd-Lieutenant E. Jones.
Captain T. M. Greensill, 24th Foot, Assistant Field Engineer.
Assistant-Surgeon S. Moore, 6th Dragoon Guards.

Her Majesty's 8th (the King's) Regiment.

Lieutenant W. W. Pogson.[1]
Lieutenant W. R. Webb.[1]
Lieutenant W. H. Mountsteven.

Her Majesty's 9th Lancers.

Captain (Brevet Lieutenant-Colonel) R. A. Yule.

---

[1] Previously slightly wounded.
[2] Previously severely wounded.
[3] Severely wounded.
[4] Slightly wounded.
[5] Twice slightly wounded.
[6] Dangerously wounded.
[7] Very severely wounded.
[8] Once very severely, once very slightly wounded.
[9] Once severely, twice slightly wounded.
[10] Once severely, once slightly wounded.
[11] Previously twice slightly wounded.

Her Majesty's 52nd Light Infantry.

Lieutenant J. H. Bradshaw.

Her Majesty's 60th Royal Rifles.

Captain F. Andrews. | Ensign W. H. Napier.

Her Majesty's 61st Regiment.

Lieutenant T. Gabbett. | Ensign E. S. B. Elkington.

Her Majesty's 75th Regiment.

Captain E. W. J. Knox. | Lieutenant A. Harrison.
Lieutenant J. R. S. FitzGerald. | Lieutenant E. V. Briscoe.
Lieutenant W. Crozier.

Corps of Guides.

Lieutenant Quintin Battye, 56th Native Infantry, Commandant of Cavalry.

Belúch Battalion.

Lieutenant C. B. Bannerman, 1st Bombay Native Infantry.

1st Punjab Infantry.

Lieutenant E. J. Travers, 32nd Native Infantry, 2nd-in-command.

Lieutenant W. H. Lumsden, 68th Native Infantry, Adjutant.

2nd Bengal European Fusiliers.

Lieutenant S. H. Jackson. | 2nd-Lieutenant D. F. Sherriff.

3rd Native Infantry.

Lieutenant J. Yorke, attached to the 4th Regiment, Sikh Infantry.

Lieutenant R. W. Alexander.

10th Native Infantry.

Lieut. (Bt.-Capt.) W. G. Law, attached to 1st Punjab Infantry.

11th Native Infantry.

Ensign E. A. Lisle-Phillipps, attached to Her Majesty's 60th Rifles.[11]

For references, see p. 190.

17th Native Infantry.

Lieut. R. P. Homfray, doing duty with the 4th Punjab Infantry.

20th Native Infantry.

Lieut. M. A. Humphrys, attached to Her Majesty's 60th Rifles.

26th Native Infantry.

Ensign J. T. Davidson, attached to the 2nd Punjab Infantry.

33rd Native Infantry.

Lieutenant J. H. Browne, attached to the Kumaon Battalion.

38th Native Infantry.

Lieutenant C. H. Fitzroy Gambier, attached to the 2nd Bengal European Fusiliers.

42nd Native Infantry.

Lieutenant A. W. Murray, attached to the Corps of Guides.[2]

45th Native Infantry.

Ensign O. C. Walter, attached to the 2nd Bengal European Fusiliers.

54th Native Infantry.

Ensign C. E. Wheatley, attached to the Sirmoor Battalion.

55th Native Infantry.

Captain G. G. M'Barnet, attached to 1st Bengal European Fusiliers.

65th Native Infantry.

Lieut. E. Speke, attached to the 1st Bengal European Fusiliers.

WOUNDED.

Staff.

Brigr.-Genl. N. B. Chamberlain, 16th Native Infantry, acting Adjutant-General of the Army.[3]

Colonel A. M. Becher, 61st Native Infantry, Quartermaster-General of the Army.[3]

For references, see p. 190.

Lieutenant F. S. Roberts, Bengal Artillery, officiating Deputy Assistant Quartermaster-General.[4]

Brigadier St G. D. Showers, 2nd Bengal European Fusiliers, commanding the 1st Infantry Brigade.[3]

Captain H. E. H. Burnside, 61st Foot, Brigade Major, 3rd Infantry Brigade.[5]

Lieutenant F. C. Innes, 60th Native Infantry, Orderly Officer.[4]

Sirmoor Battalion.

Major C. Reid, 10th Native Infantry, Commandant.[3]

1st Punjab Infantry.

Major J. Coke, 10th Native Infantry, Commandant.[3]

Lieutenant C. J. Nicholson, 31st Native Infantry, acting Commandant.[3]

Local Ensign C. Prior, attached.[4]

2nd Punjab Infantry.

Captain G. W. G. Green, 2nd European Bengal Fusiliers, Commandant.[4]

Lieutenant T. Frankland, 48th Madras Native Infantry, 2nd-in-command.[3]

Corps of Guides.

Captain H. Daly, 1st Bombay European Fusiliers, Commandant.[3]

Lieutenant C. W. Hawes, 43rd Native Infantry, Adjutant.[4]

Lieutenant T. G. Kennedy, 62nd Native Infantry, officiating Commandant of Cavalry.[3]

Kumaon Battalion.

Captain H. F. M. Boisragon, 1st European Bengal Fusiliers, 2nd-in-Command.[3]

Bengal Engineers.

Lieutenant-Colonel R. Baird Smith, Chief Engineer.[4]

Lieutenant G. T. Chesney, Brigade-Major of Engineers.[3]

For references, see p. 190.

Lieutenant W. W. H. Greathead.[7]
Lieutenant F. R. Maunsell.[3]
Lieutenant J. G. Medley.[3]
Lieutenant E. Walker.[4]
Lieutenant W. E. Warrand.[6]
Lieutenant H. A. Brownlow.[6]
Lieutenant M. G. Geneste.[4]
Lieutenant J. St J. Hovenden.
Lieutenant Æ. Perkins.[4]
2nd-Lieut. J. U. Champain.[4]
2nd-Lieut. R. C. B. Pemberton.[4]
2nd-Lieut. P. Murray.[4]
2nd-Lieut. H. A. L. Carnegie.[4]

Bombay Engineers.

Lieutenant J. T. Walker.[3]

Artillery.

* Brigadier H. Garbett.[4]
Captain (Bt. Major) J. H. Campbell.[3]
† Captain (Bt. Lieut.-Col.) M. Mackenzie.[3]
Captain E. K. Money.[5]
Captain J. Young.[4]
Captain (Bt. Maj.) H. Tombs.[5]
Captain T. E. Kennion.[3]
Captain A. Light.[4]
Lieutenant A. Bunny.[4]
Lieutenant H. P. Bishop.[4]
Lieutenant G. Baillie.[4]
Lieutenant A. Gillespie.[4]
Lieutenant E. L. Earle.[4]
Lieutenant A. H. Lindsay.[4]
Lieutenant C. Hunter.[4]
2nd-Lieut. J. Hills.[3]
2nd-Lieut. M. Elliot.[3]
2nd-Lieut. P. Thompson.[3]
2nd-Lieut. A. H. Davidson.[3]
2nd-Lieut. E. Fraser.[4]
2nd-Lieut. R. T. Hare.[4]
2nd-Lieut. H. Chichester.[4]
Asst.-Surgeon W. W. Ireland, M.D.[6]
Lieutenant and Riding-Master S. Budd.[4]

Punjab Sappers.

Local Ensign L. Gustavinski.[5]
Local Ensign C. Anderson.[4]

Her Majesty's 6th Dragoon Guards.

Captain C. P. Rosser.[6]
Lieut. A. A. de Bourbel.[3]

Her Majesty's 8th Regiment.

Major (Bt. Lieut.-Col.) J. C. Brooke.[3]
Captain E. G. Daniell.[3]
Capt. (Bt. Maj.) R. S. Baynes.[6]
Lieut. (Bt. Capt.) D. Beere.[3]
Lieut. (Bt. Capt.) E. N. Sandilands.[5]
Lieutenant G. F. Walker.[3]
Lieutenant W. F. Metge.[4]

---

* Died at Simla on the 14th January, 1858, from the effects of the wound he received before Delhi.

† Died of his wounds, 5th October 1857, at Simla.

For references, see p. 190.

Her Majesty's 27th Regiment.

Captain R. Freer, attached to Her Majesty's 75th Regiment.[4]

Her Majesty's 52nd Light Infantry.

Colonel G. Campbell.[4]
Captain J. A. Bayley.[3]
Lieutenant W. Atkinson.[4]
Ensign T. Simpson.[4]

Her Majesty's 60th Royal Rifles.

Captain H. F. Williams.[3]
Captain C. Jones.[3]
Captain G. C. H. Waters.[10]
Lieutenant H. P. Eaton.[6]
Lieutenant J. S. D. M'Gill.[4]
Lieutenant J. D. Dundas.[4]
Lieutenant H. G. Deedes.[4]
Lieutenant P. J. Curtis.[3]
Ensign W. G. Turle.[3]
Ensign A. S. Heathcote.[4]
Surgeon J. H. K. Innes.

Her Majesty's 61st Regiment.

Captain W. E. D. Deacon.[3]
Lieutenant T. M. Moore.[4]
Lieutenant W. H. W. Pattoun.[3]
Lieutenant A. C. Young.[3]
Lieutenant C. J. Griffiths.[3]
Lieutenant T. B. Hutton.[4]
Ensign E. B. Andros.[4]

Her Majesty's 75th Regiment.

Lieut.-Col. C. Herbert.[5]
Captain T. C. Dunbar.[4]
Captain A. Chancellor.[4]
Captain R. Dawson.[6]
Lieut. and Adj. R. Barter.[3]
Lieut. C. R. Rivers.[4]
Lieut. E. Armstrong.[4]
Lieut. G. C. N. Faithfull.[4]
Lieut. C. M. Pym.[4]
Ensign R. Wadeson.[3]
Paymaster D. F. Chambers.[4]
Asst.-Surgeon S. A. Lithgow.[4]

Her Majesty's 84th Regiment.

Captain the Hon'ble A. H. A. Anson, attached to Her Majesty's 9th Lancers.[4]

1st Bengal European Fusiliers.

Colonel J. Welchman.[6]
Major G. O. Jacob.[1]
Captain S. Greville.[9]
Captain E. Brown.[6]
Lieut. H. M. Wemyss.[10]
Lieut. J. W. Daniell.[3]
Lieut. E. A. C. Lambert.[4]
Lieut. A. G. Owen.[10]
2nd-Lieutenant N. Ellis.[4]

For references, see p. 190.

2nd Bengal European Fusiliers.

Lieutenant A. Elderton.[5] | Lieutenant J. T. Harris.[3]
Lieutenant C. R. Blair.[6]

3rd Light Cavalry.

Lieutenant H. H. Gough, attached to Hodson's Horse.[4]

6th Light Cavalry.

Lieutenant B. Cuppage, attached to Her Majesty's 9th Lancers.[4]

3rd Native Infantry.

Captain J. P. Caulfeild, attached to 1st Bengal European Fusiliers.[4]

Ensign O. I. Chalmers, attached to the Corps of Guides.[4]

4th Native Infantry.

Lieutenant C. F. Packe, attached to the 4th Sikh Infantry.[5]

5th Native Infantry.

Captain D. Kemp, attached to 2nd Bengal European Fusiliers.[8]

7th Native Infantry.

Lieutenant D. B. Lockhart, attached to the Sirmoor Battalion.[3]

9th Native Infantry.

Lieutenant S. Ross, attached to the Sirmoor Battalion.[4]

11th Native Infantry.

Lieutenant T. M. Shelley, attached to 1st Punjab Infantry.[4]

16th Native Infantry.

Captain W. Graydon, attached to the 1st Bengal European Fusiliers.[5]

20th Native Infantry.

Lieutenant A. Tulloch, attached to the Sirmoor Battalion.[10]

35th Native Infantry.

Lieutenant-Colonel T. Seaton, C.B., attached to the 1st Infantry Brigade.[3]

Lieutenant H. T. Pollock, attached to 1st Punjab Infantry.[7]

For references see p. 190.

36th Native Infantry.

Lieutenant H. D. E. W. Chester, attached to the Sirmoor Battalion.[4]

Lieutenant A. Pullan, attached to the 4th Sikh Infantry.[3]

49th Native Infantry.

Lieutenant A. B. Temple, attached to the Kumaon Battalion.[4]

55th Native Infantry.

Lieutenant E. H. Woodcock, attached to 1st Bengal European Fusiliers.[3]

57th Native Infantry.

Lieutenant F. H. Jenkins, attached to the 4th Sikh Infantry.[3]

Lieutenant E. E. B. Bond, attached to the Corps of Guides.[3]

Lieutenant H. De Brett, attached to the Corps of Guides.

58th Native Infantry.

Ensign T. Dayrell, attached to Her Majesty's 75th Regiment.[3]

60th Native Infantry.

Lieutenant-Colonel R. Drought, attached to the 2nd Infantry Brigade.[3]

Captain J. C. Hay, attached to 2nd Bengal European Fusiliers.[6]

Lieutenant R. H. Shebbeare, attached to the Corps of Guides.[5]

Lieutenant T. N. Walker, attached to 2nd Bengal European Fusiliers.[5]

69th Native Infantry.

Lieutenant A. H. Eckford, attached to the Sirmoor Battalion.[4]

28th Bombay Native Infantry.

Lieutenant J. Watson, attached to the 1st Punjab Cavalry.[4]

(Signed) H. W. NORMAN, *Lieut.*,
Assistant Adjutant-General of Army.

PALACE OF DELHI,
The 23rd September 1857.

For references, see p. 190.

Return of Killed, Wounded, and Missing of the Delhi
in the neighbourhood of Delhi, on 30th May 1857,

Corps.	Effective strength of all ranks on 11th Sept. 1857.	Killed.									
		Officers.		Non-Commissioned Officers.		Drummers, etc.		Rank and File.			
		European.	Native.	European.	Native.	European.	Native.	European.	Native.	Total.	Horses.
Staff	...	4	...	...	...	...	...	...	...	4	8
Artillery, including drivers, gun-lascars, and newly-raised Sikh Artillery	1350	4	1	4	1	...	...	39	25	74	55
Engineers and Sappers and Miners (including five companies newly raised Punjab Sappers) . .	722	3	2	3	3	...	...	1	31	43	...
Her Majesty's 9th Lancers .	391	1	...	1	..	...	...	25	...	27	39
Her Majesty's 6th Dragoon Guards (four troops) . . .	123	1	...	5	...	...	...	13	...	19	16
Detachment, 4th Irregular Cavalry (disarmed and dismounted) .	78	...	...	...	...	...	...	...	...	...	...
Detachment, 1st Punjab Cavalry .	147	...	...	...	...	...	...	...	1	1	1
Detachment, 2nd Punjab Cavalry	114	...	...	...	...	...	...	...	...	...	1
Detachment, 5th Punjab Cavalry .	107	...	...	...	...	...	...	...	...	...	1
Hodson's Irregular Horse .	462	...	...	...	...	...	...	...	...	...	2
Her Majesty's 8th Regiment	322	3	...	5	...	...	...	19	...	27	...
Her Majesty's 52nd Light Infantry .	302	1	...	1	...	...	...	17	...	19	...
Her Majesty's 60th Rifles .	390	4	...	2	...	1	...	106	...	113	...
Her Majesty's 61st Regiment .	402	2	...	2	...	...	..	28	...	32	...
Her Majesty's 75th Regiment	459	5	...	4	...	1	...	74	...	84	...
1st European Fusiliers	427	3	...	10	...	2	...	83	...	98	...
2nd European Fusiliers .	370	4	...	7	...	1	...	71	...	83	...
Sirmoor Battalion . .	212	1	...	...	3	...	...	...	82	86	...
Kumaon Battalion . .	312	1	...	...	2	...	...	...	18	21	...
Guide Corps (Cavalry and Infantry: 302 Infantry, 283 Cavalry) .	585	2	5	...	13	...	2	...	50	72	16
4th Sikh Infantry (including recruits)	414	1	2	...	3	...	...	...	40	46	...
1st Punjab Infantry (including recruits) . . .	664	3	3	...	5	...	...	...	66	77	...
2nd Punjab Infantry (including recruits) . .	650	1	1	...	3	...	...	...	38	43	...
4th Punjab Infantry (including recruits) . .	541	1	...	...	1	...	...	...	8	10	...
Wing Beluch Battalion .	322	1	...	...	...	...	...	...	7	8	...
Pioneers (unarmed and undisciplined) . .	No return	...	...	1	1	...	...	...	23	25	...
Grand Total .	9866	46	14	45	35	5	2	476	389	1012	139

ABS

	Officers.	Native Officers.	Non-Commissioned Officers.
Killed	46	14	80
Wounded	140	49	207
Missing	...	...	1
Total ...	186	63	288

Memorandum.—Those officers who died of wounds during the siege are included as killed, but those returned as killed of other ranks were all killed at the time, there being no documents available to show what number of wounded soldiers died in consequence of their injuries.

2163 Officers and men were killed, wounded, and missing, prior to 8th September, on which date the batteries for the reduction of the place were opened.

327 Officers and men were killed, wounded, and missing, from above date until morning of assault.

1170 Officers and men were killed, wounded and missing, in the assault of 14th September.

177 Officers and men were killed, wounded, and missing, from 15th September until final capture of the City on the 20th idem.

Total 3837

Field Force, from the commencement of the Operations up to the capture of the City on the 20th September.

Wounded.										Missing.										Total of Killed, Wounded, and Missing.	
Officers.		Non-Commissioned Officers.		Drummers, etc.		Rank and File.				Officers.		Non-Commissioned Officers.		Drummers, etc.		Rank and File.					
European.	Native.	European.	Native.	European.	Native.	European.	Native.	Total	Horses.	European.	Native.	European.	Native.	European.	Native.	European.	Native.	Total.	Horses.	Officers and Men.	Horses.
9	...	...	...	...	...	...	...	9	2	...	...	...	...	...	...	...	...	...	...	13	10
23	1	13	2	4	...	199	47	289	62	...	...	...	...	...	...	...	2	2	4	365	121
19	1	6	10	...	...	...	50	86	...	...	...	...	...	...	...	...	9	9	...	138	...
2	...	3	...	...	...	61	...	66	46	...	...	...	...	...	...	...	...	...	36	93	121
2	...	3	...	...	...	6	...	11	11	...	...	...	...	...	...	...	...	...	...	30	27
...	...	...	1	...	...	...	2	3	3	...	...	...	...	...	...	...	...	...	...	3	3
1	...	...	...	...	...	...	5	6	12	...	...	...	...	...	...	...	...	...	3	7	16
...	...	...	...	...	...	...	3	3	2	...	...	...	...	...	...	...	...	...	...	3	3
...	1	..	...	...	...	...	3	4	4	...	...	...	...	...	...	...	...	...	...	4	5
1	5	...	...	...	...	...	5	11	11	...	...	...	...	...	...	...	...	...	1	11	14
7	...	9	...	...	...	120	...	136	...	...	...	...	...	...	...	...	...	...	...	163	...
4	...	8	...	...	...	65	...	77	...	...	...	...	...	...	...	5	...	5	...	101	...
10	...	17	...	...	..	249	...	276	...	...	...	...	...	...	...	...	...	...	...	389	...
7	...	7	...	...	..	105	...	119	...	...	...	...	1	...	...	4	...	5	...	156	...
14	...	7	...	...	...	177	...	198	...	...	...	...	...	...	...	3	...	3	...	285	...
11	...	23	...	1	...	186	...	221	...	...	...	...	...	...	...	...	...	...	...	319	...
6	...	11	...	...	...	145	...	162	...	...	...	...	...	...	...	...	...	...	...	245	...
6	8	...	8	...	1	...	210	233	..	...	...	...	...	...	...	...	...	...	...	319	...
2	3	...	3	...	..	...	30	38	...	...	...	...	...	...	...	...	5	5	...	64	...
6	10	...	43	...	4	...	168	231	33	...	...	...	...	...	...	...	...	...	9	303	58
3	7	...	8	...	...	...	98	116	..	...	...	...	...	...	...	...	...	...	...	162	...
5	5	...	7	...	...	...	134	151	...	...	...	...	...	...	...	...	...	...	...	228	...
2	4	...	7	...	. .	...	96	109	...	...	...	...	...	...	...	...	...	...	...	152	...
...	2	...	5	...	...	...	54	61	...	...	...	...	...	...	...	...	...	...	...	71	...
...	1	...	5	...	...	...	43	49	...	...	...	...	...	...	...	...	1	1	...	58	...
...	1	1	...	...	...	...	128	130	...	...	...	...	...	...	...	...	...	...	...	155	...
140	49	108	99	5	5	1313	1076	2795	186	...	...	...	1	...	...	12	17	30	53	3837	378

(Signed) H. W. NORMAN, *Lieut.*,
Asst. Adjt.-Genl. of the Army.

TRACT.

Drummers.	Rank and File.	Total.	Horses.	Europeans.	Natives.	Total.
7	865	1012	139	572	440	1012
10	2389	2795	186	1566	1229	2795
...	29	30	53	13	17	30
17	3283	3837	378	2151	1686	3837

N.B.—Since this return was compiled it has been ascertained that a mistake took place in the return furnished by the 8th Foot of casualties at the assault, seventeen more men having been killed than were actually entered. Owing to the numerous casualties in corps during the siege, it is probable that some were omitted to be returned, and that the loss in several regiments exceeds that above shown.

PALACE OF DELHI,
The 23rd September 1857.

(Signed) H. W. NORMAN, *Lieut.*,
Asst. Adjt.-Genl. of the Army.

So ends the record of the Siege of Delhi, a record worthy of the endurance and courage which it commemorates. Colonel Baird Smith's original report will doubtless prove no less interesting than Lieutenant Norman's narrative.

From Lieutenant-Colonel R. BAIRD SMITH, *Chief Engineer, Delhi Field Force, to the Assistant Adjutant-General, Delhi Field Force, dated Head-Quarters, Delhi, 17th September* 1857.

I have the honour to submit herewith, for the information of the Major-General Commanding, the following report of the operations carried on by the Engineer Brigade under my command during the siege and capture of Delhi.

To make these more intelligible, I may first detail very briefly the leading and characteristic features of the place.

The eastern face of the city rests on the Jumna, and during the season of the year when our operations were carried on, the stream may be described as washing the base of the walls. All access to a besieger on the river front is, therefore, impracticable. The defences here consist of an irregular wall with occasional bastions and towers, and about one-half of the length of the river face is occupied by the palace of the King of Delhi and its outwork, the old Moghal fort of Salimgarh.

The river may be described as the chord of a rough arc formed by the remaining defences of the place. These consist of a succession of bastioned fronts, the connecting curtains being very long, and the outworks limited to one crown-work at the Ajmir Gate, and Martello towers, mounting a single gun, at such points as require some additional flanking fire to that given by the bastions themselves. The bastions are small, mounting generally three guns in each face, two in each flank, and one in embrasure at the salient. They are provided with masonry parapets about twelve feet in thickness, and have a relief of about sixteen feet above the plane of site. The curtain consists of a simple masonry wall or rampart sixteen feet in height, eleven feet thick at top, and fourteen or fifteen feet at bottom. This main wall carries a parapet, loopholed for musketry, eight feet in height and three feet in thickness. The whole of the land front is covered by a berm of variable width, ranging from sixteen to thirty feet, and having a scarp wall eight feet high; exterior to this is a dry ditch of about twenty-five feet in width, and from sixteen to twenty feet in depth. The counter-scarp is simply an earthen slope, easy to descend. The glacis is a very short one, extending only fifty or sixty yards from the counter-scarp; using general terms, it covers from the besieger's view from one-half to one-third of the height of the walls of the place.

These details will, I trust, be sufficient to give a general conception of the nature of the defences of Delhi; they are, in a word, modernised forms of the ancient works that existed when the city fell before Lord Lake's army in 1803. They extend about seven miles in circumference, and include an area of about three square miles.

The ground occupied by the besieging force presents some features deserving of notice here, as having exercised a most important influence on the plan and progress of the works of attack. On the western side of Delhi there appear the last outlying spurs of the Aravalli Mountains, represented here by a low ridge which disappears at its intersection with the Jumna, about two miles above the place. The drainage from the eastern slope of the Ridge finds its way to the river along the northern and north-western faces of the city, and has formed there a succession of parallel or connected ravines of considerable depth. By taking advantage of these hollow ways, admirable cover was constantly obtained for the troops, and the labour of the siege most materially reduced. The whole of the exterior of the place presents an extraordinary mass of old buildings of all kinds, of thick brushwood and occasional clumps of forest trees, giving great facilities for cover, which, during the siege operations at least, proved to be, on the whole, more favourable to us than to the enemy.

In anticipation of the siege, means had been taken to store the engineer park with all the materials and tools likely to be required during the operations. The siege-train placing the artillery means in an equally satisfactory state of efficiency, ground was broken as soon after its arrival as possible, being on the night of the 7th September 1857.

The project of attack submitted by me to the Major-General Commanding, and honoured with his sanction, provided for a concentrated rapid and vigorous attack on the front of the place included between the Water (or Moira[1]) and Kashmir Bastions, provision being made at the same time for silencing all important flanking fire, whether of artillery or musketry, that could be brought to bear on the lines of advance to be taken by the assaulting columns. Due care was also taken to protect the exposed right flank of the trenches from sorties. The left was secured by being rested on the river, and by the occupation of the Kudsia Bagh, a very strong post in front.

The best information procurable indicated that, on the front of attack, the fire of from twenty-five to thirty pieces might have to be subdued.[2]

[1] This is wrongly printed, and was no doubt wrongly copied as Mori, instead of Moira, so called from Lord Moira, subsequently the Marquis of Wellesley.—H. C. F.

[2] Of the artillery men on these guns Major Reid wrote a few days before 14th September: "I never saw such plucky gunners in my life. Fight it out they will, and every gunner will be killed at his guns."—H. C. F.

To effect this, 54 siege guns were available, and were distributed as follows:—

Siege Battery No. I, for ten pieces, of which six were to be directed against the defences of the Shah (or Mori) Bastion, with the object of ruining it[1] and preventing its flank fire from bearing on the advance of the assaulting columns. The remaining four were directed against the Kashmir Bastion, with the object of diverting its fire from the covering and working parties engaged on No. II Battery.

13-pounders	5
8-inch howitzer	1
Total ...	6

Distance 700 yards.

Four 24-pounders.

Siege Battery No. II, for 18 pieces, designed to breach the curtain to the right of the Kashmir Bastion, to destroy the defences of the bastion itself, and to strip off the parapet for about 200 yards on each side of the breach, and thus deprive infantry of all cover.

24-pounders	8
18-pounders	3
8-inch howitzers	7
Total ...	18

Distance 600 yards.

Siege Battery No. III, for eight heavy guns and twelve Cohorn mortars, designed to destroy the defences of the (Moira or) Water Bastion, and to maintain a heavy fire of shells on both the Water and Kashmir Bastions. In the original project the site of this battery was about 330 yards from the Water Bastion; but subsequent examination making it doubtful whether the position was an effective one, Captain Taylor pushed a reconnaissance in advance to the Custom House, or within a hundred and sixty yards, and finding there

18-pounders	8
Cohorns	12
Total ...	20

Distance 160 yards.

[1] There is a slip in the original here, where reference is made to the Shah and Mori Bastions. There was only one bastion at the north-west corner of the city, known as the Shah or Mori Bastion.—H. C. F.

an excellent site for a breaching battery, reported the circumstance to me. I obtained at once the Major-General's sanction to this bold advance, and it is satisfactory to be able to say that Battery No. III was constructed with remarkably few casualties, and proved one of the most efficient of the series. It was, however, limited to six breaching guns, and in the demolition of the light parapets was aided by 9-pounders.

10-inch mortars	4
8-inch mortars	6
Total ...	10

Battery No. IV, for ten heavy mortars, to shell the whole of the ground between the Water and Kashmir Bastions, and the localities in the neighbourhood where the enemy would be likely to find a shelter.

9-pounders	4
24-pounders	2
Total ...	6

On the extreme right, four heavy guns were left in position, and on an advanced plateau on the Ridge a battery[1] for six field guns was constructed, by which the only route open to the enemy's sorties would be swept by grape. Although the enemy gave some annoyance with light guns in this direction, he was unable to make a single effective sortie.

At different times, between the 7th and 11th, these batteries opened fire with an efficiency and vigour which excited the unqualified admiration of all who had the good fortune to witness it. Every object contemplated in the attack was accomplished with a success even beyond my expectations, and I trust I may be permitted to say that while there are many noble passages in the history of the Bengal Artillery, none will be nobler than that which will tell of its work on this occasion.

On the night of the 13th, the breaches in the curtain between the Water and Kashmir Bastions were examined personally by Lieutenants Greathead,

[1] This was the Sammy House Battery.—H. C. F.

Medley, and Lang, of the Engineers, who reported both in excellent condition for assault. No. I Siege Battery had effectually disposed of the Mori Bastion; No. II had completely destroyed the musketry cover near the main breach; No. III had done the same near the Water Bastion breach, and it was evident that the place was ripe for the assault. On reporting the circumstance to the Major-General, he issued instant orders, naming the next morning, or that of the 14th, for this critical operation.

The details of the assault will be best laid before the Major-General by the brigadiers commanding the different columns. I will therefore only state here that the following distribution of the Engineer officers was made—

1ST COLUMN

Under Brigadier-General J. Nicholson.

Captain A. Taylor.	Lieutenant Bingham.
Lieutenant Medley.	Lieutenant Lang.

Ensign Chalmers.

2ND COLUMN

Under Brigadier W. Jones, Commanding Her Majesty's 61st Regiment.

Lieutenant Greathead.	Lieutenant Murray.
Lieutenant Hovenden.	Ensign Gustavinski.

3RD COLUMN

Under Brigadier G. Campbell, Commanding Her Majesty's 52nd Regiment.

Lieutenant Home.	Lieutenant Tandy.
Lieutenant Salkeld.	Ensign Nuthall.

4TH COLUMN

Under Major C. Reid, Commanding the Sirmoor Battalion.

Lieutenant Maunsell.	Lieutenant Tennant.

RESERVE COLUMN

Under Brigadier J. Longfield, Her Majesty's 8th Regiment.

Lieutenant Ward.	Lieutenant Thackeray.

These officers accompanied the columns to which they were attached during the assault, and I grieve to say that a large proportion fell wounded, more or less dangerously, under the heavy fire of the enemy.

It only remains for me, in closing this report, to bring under the favourable notice of the Major-General Commanding the officers of the brigade whose merits have been conspicuous.

To my second-in-command, Captain Taylor, Director of the Trenches, I have been indebted for the most constant, cordial, and valuable assistance throughout the whole period of the operations. Gifted with rare soundness of professional judgment, his advice has been sought by me under all circumstances of difficulty or doubt, and I find that I cannot express too strongly to the Major-General my sense of the valuable services this officer has rendered.

To Captain Chesney (very severely wounded), Brigade-Major of Engineers, I have also hearty acknowledgments to make for the uniform efficiency, zeal, and intelligence with which he has conducted the duty of his office.

Lieutenants Greathead and Maunsell, Directing Field Engineers on the left and right attacks, respectively, have earned my warm approbation by the manner in which they performed duties involving great labour and exposure. Both guided columns of attack, and both, I grieve to add, were severely wounded while doing so.

The gallantry with which the explosion party under Lieutenants Home and Salkeld performed the desperate duty of blowing in the Kashmir Gate in broad daylight, and in the face of the enemy, will, I feel assured, be held to justify me in making special mention of it. The party was composed, in addition to the two officers named, of the following:—

Sappers and Miners.

Sergeant John Smith.
Sergeant Andrew Blair Carmichael.
Corporal F. Burgess *alias* Joshua Burgess Grierson.
Fourteen Native Sappers and Miners.
Ten Punjab Sappers and Miners.

Her Majesty's 52nd Regiment.

Bugler Robert Hawthorne.

Covered by the fire of Her Majesty's 60th Rifles, this party advanced at the double towards the Kashmir Gate; Lieutenant Home, with Sergeants John Smith and Carmichael and Havildar Madho, all of the Sappers, leading and carrying the powder bags, followed by Lieutenant Salkeld, Corporal Burgess, and a section of the remainder of the party. The advanced party reached the gateway unhurt, and found that part of the drawbridge had been destroyed; but passing across the precarious footing supplied by the remaining beams, they proceeded to lodge their powder against the gate. The wicket was open, and through it the enemy kept up a heavy fire upon them. Sergeant Carmichael was killed while laying his powder, Havildar Madho being at the same time wounded. The powder being laid, the advanced party slipped down into the ditch to allow the firing party under Lieutenant Salkeld to perform its duty. While endeavouring to fire the charge, Lieutenant Salkeld was shot through the leg and arm, and handed over the slow match to Corporal Burgess, who fell mortally wounded just as he had successfully performed his duty. Havildar Tilok Singh, of the Sappers and Miners, was wounded, and Ram Het, sepoy of the same corps, was killed during this part of the operation.

The demolition having been most successful, Lieutenant Home happily unwounded, caused the bugler to sound the regimental call of the 52nd Regiment, as the signal for the advance of the column. Fearing that amid the noise of the assault the sound might not be heard, he had the call repeated three times, when the troops advanced, and carried the gateway with entire success.

I feel assured that a simple statement of the facts of this devoted and glorious deed will suffice to stamp it as one of the noblest on record in military history. Its perfect success contributed most materially to the brilliant results of the day, and Lieutenants Home and Salkeld, with their gallant subordinates, European and native, will, I doubt not, receive the reward which valour before the enemy so distinguished as theirs has entitled them to.

Lieutenant Home mentions with special approbation the cool courage of Sergeant John Smith, and while sincerely regretting their loss, he states that the gallantry shown by Sergeant Carmichael and Corporal Burgess could not have been surpassed. Bugler Hawthorne's conduct has also been particularly commended. This brave man, after performing his own dangerous duty, humanely attached himself to Lieutenant Salkeld, bound up his wounds under a heavy musketry fire, and ultimately had him removed without further injury, and I beg to commend him most cordially to the favourable notice of the Major-General.

The following native officers and sepoys of the Sappers and Miners are reported by Lieutenant Home to have shown the most determined bravery and coolness throughout the whole operations:—Havildar Madho, who accompanied the advance under Lieutant Home; Subadar Tola, Jemadar Bisram, Havildars Tilok Singh and Ramtaroy, and Sepoy Sahib Sing, who were with the firing or reserve parties. The remarkable courage shown by the Native officers and men in assisting their wounded European comrades deserves to be mentioned as showing the excellent feeling between them.

Lieutenant Medley (wounded) was appointed to

guide the 1st Division of the 1st Column to the main breach, which he had personally examined the night before, and, though shot through the arm, continued with the column until it was established in the Kabul Gate. Lieutenant Lang was appointed to similar duties with the 2nd Division, and both officers have earned my best thanks by the gallant and efficient manner in which they did their work. Lieutenant Hovenden (wounded) conducted the ladder party of the 2nd Column, and here, as on all occasions, showed the intelligence and gallantry which have made his services so valuable during the siege.

I beg also to bring under the notice of the Major-General the good service on this occasion of Lieutenant Henry Bingham, an old and most meritorious officer, whose gallantry in action on previous instances had led the Government to confer upon him the commission of Lieutenant. He commanded a party of the Corps of Sappers and Miners in the assault of the main breach with his accustomed bravery, and I respectfully recommend him for favourable consideration.

To Lieutenant H. A. Brownlow (dangerously wounded), who had charge of the Engineer Park, I have to offer my most cordial acknowledgments for his incessant exertions to expedite the works. This officer was dangerously wounded while carrying to the 3rd Column materials and tools which it was supposed to be in need of.

I have only further to bring under the notice of the Major-General Commanding the admirable conduct of the remaining officers and men of the brigade. None could have displayed a higher and better spirit than they have done, and whether in the trenches, in the assault, or during the occupation, they have been forward and zealous in every duty. I may be allowed to refer especially to the gallantry and devotion of the Sappers and Miners under their Acting Commandant, Lieutenant Maunsell—a remnant of the Corps which mutinied in May last. Throughout the whole operations these men have shown a distinguished bravery and fidelity to their salt, and it has been my agreeable duty to bring, from time to time, special instances of these qualities to the notice of the Major-General. The Punjab Sappers and Miners, under their Commandant, Lieutenant Gulliver (of whose valuable services I was deprived during the siege by his severe illness), and their Acting Commandant, Lieutenant Home, have done excellent service, and give the best possible promise of being an efficient and soldier-like corps.

The Pioneers, under Lieutenant Bingham, have proved to be a most useful and fearless body of men. Though designed for works only, and being unarmed and only rudely organised for the occasion, they have shown perfect readiness to work under fire, and have taken their turn in the most exposed and dangerous positions it has been necessary to occupy.

I take the liberty of mentioning here that since I joined this camp I have received most valuable aid in military arrangements from my Assistant (in the Civil Department) Mr Harry Martin.

I deeply regret the heavy list of casualties which accompanies this report. In Lieutenant Tandy the corps has lost one of its most gallant and promising young officers; but I earnestly hope that the Government will be only temporarily deprived of the services of the wounded, all of whom, I am happy to report, are doing well.

Of the achievements of the force which took Delhi, it is unnecessary for a later and weaker pen to write. What those best able to judge recorded at the time was as follows. General Wilson in his despatch of 22nd September, wrote thus of the men under his command:—

For four months of the most trying season of the year this force, originally very weak in numbers, has been exposed to the repeated and determined attacks of an enemy far outnumbering it, and supported by a numerous and powerful artillery. The duties imposed upon all have been laborious, harassing, and incessant, and, notwithstanding heavy losses, both in action and from disease, have been at all times zealously and cheerfully performed.

And this is what the great Chief of the Army, Sir Colin Campbell, a man sparing in words of commendation, like his greater master, the Duke of Wellington, wrote :—

It is impossible to be too lavish of praise for the untiring energy, invincible fortitude, and splendid gallantry by which this force has been distinguished, from the General in command to the private soldier in the ranks. All have done their duty most nobly ; and the steadfast courage of the men has enabled the General to carry out his enterprise, in spite of scanty means and a deadly season.

And this is what Field-Marshal Lord Roberts, writing forty years later of the siege at which he served, in which he was wounded, and for which (as well as another future Commander-in-Chief in India, Captain (afterwards Sir) Donald M. H. Stewart) he was mentioned in despatches as "an active and gallant officer" attached to the Artillery Brigade in the capacity of Deputy-Assistant-Quartermaster-General, was able to deliberately record :—

Like Norman, when writing his Narrative of the Siege, I feel I cannot conclude my brief account of it without paying my small tribute of praise and admiration to the troops who bore themselves so nobly from the beginning to the end. Their behaviour throughout was beyond all praise, their constancy was unwearied, their gallantry most conspicuous; in thirty-two different fights they were victorious over long odds, being often exposed to an enemy ten times their number, who, moreover, had the advantage of ground and superior Artillery: they fought and worked as if each one felt that on his individual exertions alone depended the issue of the day; they willingly, nay, cheerfully, endured such trials as few armies have ever been exposed to for so long a time. For three months, day after day, and for the greater part of the day, every man had to be constantly under arms, exposed to a scorching Indian sun, which was almost as destructive as, and much harder to bear than, the enemy's never-ceasing fire. They saw their comrades struck down by cholera, sunstroke, and dysentery, more dispiriting a thousand times than the daily casualties in action. They beheld their enemies reinforced while their own numbers rapidly decreased. Yet they never lost heart, and at last, when it became evident that no hope of further reinforcements could be entertained, and that if Delhi were to be taken at all it must be taken at once, they advanced to the assault with as high a courage and as complete a confidence in the result, as if they were attacking in the first flush and exultation of troops at the commencement of a campaign, instead of being the remnant of a force worn out, by twelve long weeks of privation and suffering, by hope deferred (which truly "maketh the heart sick"), and by weary waiting for the help which never came. Batteries were thrown up within easy range of the walls, than which a more heroic [1] piece of work was never performed; and, finally, these gallant few, of whom England should in very truth be everlastingly proud, stormed in the face of day a strong fortress defended by 30,000 desperate men, provided with everything necessary to defy assault.

[1] Well may this be said. The distances of the Batteries I, II, and III, from the guns of the enemy were, as given by Colonel Baird Smith, 700 yards, 600 yards, and 160 yards, and as a matter of fact, the distance of the first two is really somewhat less.—H. C. F.

The list of killed and wounded bears witness to the gallantry of all arms of the service. The effective force at Delhi never amounted to 10,000 men. Of these 992 were killed and 2845 wounded, besides hundreds who died of disease and exposure. Where all behaved nobly, it is difficult to particularise; but it will not, I hope, be considered invidious if I specially draw attention to the four corps most constantly engaged: the 60th Rifles, the Sirmoor Battalion of Gurkhas, the Guides,[1] and the 1st Punjab Infantry. Placed in the very front of the position, they were incessantly under fire, and their losses in action testify to the nature of the service they performed. The 60th Rifles left Meerut with 440 of all ranks; a few days before the assault they received a reinforcement of nearly 200, making a total of 640; their casualties were 389. The Sirmoor battalion began with 450 men, and were joined by a draft of 90, making a total of 540; their loss in killed and wounded amounted to 319. The strength of the Guides when they joined was 550 Cavalry and Infantry, and their casualties were 303. The 1st Punjab Infantry arrived in Delhi with three British officers and 664 Natives of all ranks. Two of the British officers were killed, and the third severely wounded, and of the Natives, eight officers and 200 men were killed and wounded; while out of the British officers attached to the regiment during the siege one was killed and four wounded. Further, it is a great pleasure to me to dwell on the splendid service done by the Artillery and Engineers. The former, out of their small number, had 365 killed or

[1] Of these three regiments, the Chief of Sir Colin Campbell's staff wrote in a despatch of 23rd September 1857, as follows:—"Such are the pride and pleasure that the Commander-in-Chief experienced in perusing your account of the devoted courage displayed by all ranks (of the force employed at the Hindu Rao piquet under Major Reid's command) during the prolonged attacks so successfully resisted, that he only wishes it was in his power to bring to the notice of the Government, both of Her Majesty's and the Honourable Company the name of every man—officer or soldier—engaged."—H. C. F.

disabled, and the latter two-thirds of their officers and 293 of their men.

And these are the burning words in which Lord Canning, Governor-General, and shortly afterwards First Viceroy of India, recorded for all time the memory of the exploits of the Delhi Field Force, and never was noble encomium more nobly deserved.

General Order by the Right Hon'ble the Governor-General of India in Council, No. 1227, *dated Fort William, 2nd October* 1857.

The Right Hon'ble the Governor-General of India in Council has received by a telegraphic message the gratifying announcement that Delhi is entirely in the hands of Major-General Wilson's army.

Delhi, the focus of the treason and revolt which for four months have harassed Hindustan, and the stronghold in which the mutinous army of Bengal has sought to concentrate its power, has been wrested from the rebels.

The King is a close prisoner in the palace. The head-quarters of Major-General Wilson are established in the Diwan-i-Khas. A strong column is in pursuit of the fugitives.

Whatever may be the motives and passions by which the mutinous soldiery and those who are leagued with them have been instigated to faithlessness, rebellion, and crimes at which the heart sickens, it is certain that they have found encouragement in the delusive belief that India was weakly guarded by England, and that before the Government could gather together its strength against them, their ends would be gained. They are now undeceived.

Before a single soldier of the many thousands who

are hastening from England to uphold the supremacy of the British power has set foot on these shores, the rebel force, where it was strongest and most united, and where it had the command of unbounded military appliances, has been destroyed or scattered by an army collected within the limits of the North-Western Provinces and the Punjab alone.

The work has been done before the support of those battalions which have been collected in Bengal from the forces of the Queen in China and Her Majesty's Eastern colonies could reach Major-General Wilson's army; and it is by the courage and endurance of that gallant army alone, by the skill, sound judgment, and steady resolution of its brave commander, and by the aid of some Native Chiefs true to their allegiance, that, under the blessing of God, the head of rebellion has been crushed, and the cause of loyalty, humanity, and rightful authority vindicated.

The Governor-General in Council hopes that the receipt of despatches from Major-General Wilson will soon place it in his power to make known the details of the operations against Delhi, and to record fully and publicly the thanks and commendation which are due to the officers and men by whose guidance, courage, and exertions those operations have been brought to a successful issue.

But the Governor-General in Council will not postpone till then his grateful acknowledgment of the services which have been rendered to the Empire at this juncture by the Chief Commissioner of the Punjab.

To Sir John Lawrence it is owing that the army before Delhi, long ago cut off from all direct support from the Lower Provinces, has been constantly recruited and strengthened so effectually as to enable its commander not only to hold his position unshaken, but to achieve complete success.

To Sir John Lawrence's unceasing vigilance, and to his energetic and judicious employment of the trustworthy forces at his own disposal, it is due that Major-

General Wilson's army has not been harassed or threatened on the side of the Punjab, and that the authority of the Government in the Punjab itself has been sustained and generally respected.

The Governor-General in Council seizes with pleasure the earliest opportunity of testifying his high appreciation of these great and timely services.

A month later the Governor-General was able to acknowledge the general services of the Delhi Field Force in the individual services of a long roll of distinguished officers, and this is how he did so:—

General Orders by the Right Hon'ble the Governor-General of India in Council, No. 1383, *dated Fort William,* 5*th November* 1857.

The Right Hon'ble the Governor - General in Council has received a despatch from Major-General Wilson, in continuation of that which was published in the Notification No. 1257 of the 8th ultimo, and completing the narrative of the capture of Delhi.

The reports and returns which accompany this despatch establish the arduous nature of a contest carried on against an enemy vastly superior in numbers, holding a strong position, furnished with unlimited appliances, and aided by the most exhausting and sickly season of the year.

They set forth the indomitable courage and perseverance, the heroic self-devotion and fortitude, the steady discipline and stern resolve of English soldiers.

There is no mistaking the earnestness of purpose with which the struggle has been maintained by Major-General Wilson's army. Every heart was in the cause; and whilst their numbers were, according to all ordinary rule, fearfully unequal to the task, every man has given his aid wherever and in whatever manner it could most avail to hasten retribution upon a treacherous and murderous foe.

In the name of outraged humanity, in memory of innocent blood ruthlessly shed, and in acknowledgment of the first signal vengeance inflicted upon the foulest treason, the Governor-General in Council records his gratitude to Major-General Wilson and the brave army of Delhi. He does so in the sure conviction that a like tribute awaits them, not in England only, but wherever, within the limits of civilisation, the news of their well-earned triumph shall reach.

Major-General Wilson has testified to the earnest and efficient support which he has received from every branch of the force under his command.

To Major F. Gaitskell, who, on Brigadier Garbett being disabled by a wound, assumed the command of the artillery in the field, and to the officers and men of that arm, to Lieutenant-Colonel C. Hogge, Director of the Artillery Depot, who volunteered his services as Commissary of Ordnance with the siege-train, to Captain J. Young and to the other officers of that branch, the Governor-General in Council tenders his cordial thanks for their exertions during the whole siege.

To Lieutenant-Colonel R. Baird Smith, for the able and successful conduct of the siege operations, under the discouragement of sickness and pain, the best thanks of the Governor-General in Council are eminently due. This distinguished officer was admirably seconded by Captain A. Taylor and the officers and men of the Engineer Brigade.

To Brigadier J. Hope Grant, Commanding the Cavalry Brigade, and to Brigadiers J. Longfield and W. Jones, commanding the Brigades of Infantry, the Governor-General in Council offers his warm acknowledgments of their excellent service; as also to Colonel Campbell, Commanding Her Majesty's 52nd

Regiment, Light Infantry; to Major C. Reid, Sirmoor Battalion; to Colonel Jones, Commanding the 1st Battalion, Her Majesty's 60th Rifles; and to Colonel J. L. Dennis of Her Majesty's 52nd Regiment, Light Infantry, to whose care the charge of the camp was confided during the operations against the town. The manner in which these officers have discharged their duties is highly appreciated by the Government.

It is a matter of the deepest regret to the Governor-General in Council that the mortal wounds received by Brigadier-General Nicholson in the assault, to the success of which he so eminently contributed, have taken from the army of India one of its brightest ornaments, and have deprived the State of services which it can ill afford to lose. The services rendered by Lieutenant-Colonel H. P. Burn, attached as field officer to the 1st Brigade of Infantry, and by Captain Seymour J. Blane, Her Majesty's 52nd Regiment Light Infantry, Brigade-Major to Brigadier-General Nicholson, have earned the approbation of the Government.

The Governor-General in Council cordially acknowledges the admirable manner in which the staff of the field force and the general staff of the army have performed their arduous duties, and to Brigadier-General Chamberlain, Adjutant-General of the Army; to Captain H. W. Norman, Assistant Adjutant-General; to Major R. S. Ewart, Deputy Assistant Adjutant General; to Captain E. B. Johnston, Assistant Adjutant-General of Artillery; to the officers of the Quartermaster-General's Department, Captain D. C. Shute and Captain H. M. Garstin; as also to Captain W. S. R. Hodson, who has performed good service with his newly-raised regiment of Irregular Horse, and at the same time conducted with great ability the duties of the Intelligence Department; to Lieutenant F. S. Roberts, attached to the artillery brigade as Deputy Assistant Quartermaster-General; to Lieutenant-Colonel Keith Young and the officers of the Judge Advocate-General's Department; as well as to Captain C. H. Barchard, Captain J. R. Turnbull, Captain R. H. D. Lowe, Lieutenant R. C. Low, and to Major H. A. Ouvry, attached to the personal staff of Major General Wilson, the Governor-General in Council offers his best thanks for the zealous assistance which they have afforded to their commander and to the State.

The Governor-General in Council has much pleasure in recognising the valuable aid rendered to the force by the officers of the Civil Service who have been attached to it, and His Lordship in Council desires to record his approbation of the services of Mr Hervey Greathead, whose untimely death is a heavy public loss, of Mr C. B. Saunders and of Mr R. M. Clifford, who made themselves most useful to the Major-General in action, and of Sir Theophilus Metcalfe, whose gallantry in conducting the assaulting column under Colonel Campbell through the city was conspicuous.

While tendering his thanks to the officers whose conduct on the occasion of the final assault of the city has been brought under his notice, the Governor-General in Council is anxious not to overlook the gallantry displayed on other occasions by several officers who were debarred by wounds or sickness from joining in the operations of that day. The distinguished services of Brigadier St G. D. Showers, of Colonel A. M. Becher, Quartermaster-General of the Army, of Lieutenant-Colonel Seaton, 35th Regiment, Native Infantry, of Lieutenant-Colonel Murray Mackenzie, Major J. Coke, and Captain H. Daly, Commanding the Guides, deserves the recognition, and have gained the approval, of Government.

Lieutenant-Colonel W. B. Thomson, Deputy Commissary-General, and the other officers serving in the Commissariat Department, are entitled to the thanks of the Governor-General in Council for the efficiency with which their duties were performed.

The arrangements made by Superintending Surgeon E. Tritton for the care and comfort of the numerous patients in hospital have been most satisfactory, and the Governor-General in Council has pleasure in offering to that officer, as well as to the regimental and staff officers of the Medical Department by whom he was supported, this acknowledgment of their good service.

The Governor-General in Council desires to express to the non-commissioned officers and men of Her Majesty's 9th Lancers and Carabineers the great satisfaction with which he has received the report of the cheerful and effective assistance rendered by them to their comrades of the artillery in working the batteries.

To all the troops, European and Native, to the officers, non-commissioned officers, and men serving with the Field Force, His Lordship in Council offers his hearty thanks for the gallantry, perseverance, skill, and discipline which they have displayed throughout the service on which they have been employed.

Where so much has been done to command admiration, it is difficult fairly to select acts for particular notice. But the Governor-General in Council feels that no injustice will be done to any man if he offers a tribute of admiration and thanks to the brave soldiers who, under Lieutenants Home and Salkeld, accomplished the desperate task of blowing open the Kashmir Gate.

From first to last, from the first advance of the devoted little band against the ramparts, throughout the perilous operation so successfully achieved, to the last act of Bugler Hawthorne in tending his officer's wounds under a heavy fire—this deed was one of deliberate and sustained courage, as noble as any that has ever graced the annals of war. It will be the care of the Governor-General in Council that the brave men, Englishmen and Natives, who survive to share the glory of it shall not go unrewarded, and that the memory of those who fell shall be honoured.

It is a satisfaction to the Governor-General in

Council to find that, in estimating upon a late occasion the eminent services rendered by the Chief Commissioner of the Punjab to the State during the siege of Delhi, and in expressing his earnest thanks for them, he has spoken the sentiments of the individual best able to appreciate those services at their true value. To the indefatigable exertions of Sir John Lawrence, Major-General Wilson frankly attributes his own success.

There remains to the Governor-General in Council the pleasing duty of noticing the part taken in the contest before Delhi by some of the neighbouring Native Chiefs.

The loyal and constant co-operation of the Maharajah of Patiala and his troops ; the steady support of the Rajah of Jhind, whose forces shared in the assault : and the assistance given to the British arms by Jan Fishan Khan and Sirdar Mir Khan Sahib well call for the marked thanks of the Governor-General in Council.

These true-hearted Chiefs, faithful to their engagements, have shown trust in the power, honour, and friendship of the British Government, and they will not repent it.

The Governor-General in Council will also have the gratification of thanking Maharajah Ranbir Singh of Kashmir for the timely support given by the Jummoo Contingent, placed by His Highness under the command of Captain Richard C. Lawrence. The conduct of the ruler of Kashmir has been that of a sincere ally.

CHAPTER IV

THE SOUTH SIDE OF MODERN DELHI AS FAR AS THE MAUSOLEUM OF THE EMPEROR HUMAYUN, THE DARGAH OF SHEKH NIZAM-UD-DIN-AULIA, AND THE TOMB OF NAWAB SAFDAR JANG.

FIVE HUNDRED yards beyond the Delhi Gate of the city a road to the left leads through mounds of old ruins to the Kotila, or Citadel of Firoz Shah, built on the Jumna about 1350-70, and containing the Lat and Jama Masjid, known by the name of that Sultan. The fortress of Firozabad was also designated the Kushk-i-Firoz Shah.

The Lat is one of the two stone pillars of Asoka (300 B.C.), removed from Topra, seven miles south-west of Jagadhri, in the Amballah district, and from Meerut, and erected by Firoz Shah in his palaces at Delhi. The following interesting account of how this was done is taken from the chronicles of his reign by Zia-ud-din-Barni :—

"After thinking over the best means of lowering the column, orders were issued commanding the attendance of all the people dwelling in the neighbourhood, within and without the Doab, and all soldiers, both horse and foot. They were ordered to bring all implements and materials suitable for the work. Directions were issued for bringing parcels

Lat of Asoka in Kotila of Firoz Shah.

[To face p. 223.

of the cotton of the Simbal (silk cotton tree). Quantities of this silk cotton were placed round the column, and when the earth at its base was removed, it fell gently over on the bed prepared for it. The cotton was then removed by degrees, and after some days the pillar lay safe upon the ground. When the foundations of the pillar were examined, a large square stone was found as a base, which also was taken out. The pillar was then encased from top to bottom in reeds, and raw skins, so that no damage might accrue to it. A carriage, with forty-two wheels, was constructed, and ropes were attached to each wheel. Thousands of men hauled at every rope, and after great labor and difficulty the pillar was raised on to the carriage. A strong rope was fastened to each wheel, and 200 men pulled at each of these ropes. By the simultaneous exertions of so many thousand men the carriage was moved, and was brought to the banks of the Jumna. Here the Sultan came to meet it. A number of large boats had been collected, some of which could carry 5000 and 7000 maunds of grain, and the least of them 2000 maunds. The column was very ingeniously transferred to these boats, and was then conducted to Fírozábád, where it was landed and conveyed into the Kushk with infinite labor and skill."

"At this time the author of this book was twelve years of age, and a pupil of the respected Mír Khán. When the pillar was brought to the palace, a building was commenced for its reception near the **Jam'a Masjid**, and the most skilful architects and workmen were employed. It was constructed of stone and chunam (mortar), and consisted of several stages. When a stage was finished the column was raised on to it, another stage was then built, and the pillar was again raised, and so on in succession until it reached the intended height. On arriving at this stage, other contrivances had to be devised to place it in an erect position. Ropes of great thickness were obtained, and windlasses were placed on each of the six stages of the base. The ends of the ropes were fastened to the top of the pillar, and the other end passed over the windlasses, which were firmly secured with many fastenings. The wheels were then turned, and the column was raised about half a *gaz*. Logs of wood and bags of cotton were then placed under it to prevent it sinking again. In this way by degrees, and in the course of several days, the column was raised to the perpendicular. Large beams were then placed round it as supports, until quite a cage of scaffolding was formed. It was thus secured in an upright position, straight as an arrow, without the smallest deviation from the perpendicular. The square stone, before spoken of, was placed under the pillar. After it was raised, some ornamental friezes of black and white stone were placed round its capital, and over these there was raised a gilded copper cupola called in Hindi *kalas*. The height of the obelisk was thirty-two gaz; eight gaz were sunk in its pedestal, and twenty-four gaz were visible. On the base of the obelisk there were engraved several lines of writing in Hindi characters. Many Brahmans and Hindu devotees were invited to read them, but no one was able. It is said that certain infidel Hindus interpreted them, stating that no one should be able to remove the obelisk from its place till there should arise in the latter days a Muhammadan king, named Sultan Fíroz."

The height of the pillar, above the platform, is thirty-seven feet, the circumference at the base being nine and one-third feet, and at the top six and a half feet. The four inscriptions of Asoka are wonderfully sharp and clear; they are among the oldest existing records of India, dating from the third century before the Christian era. Added to them, in much more modern characters, is a double inscription, one two and a half feet above, and one just below the Buddhist record, of the Chauhan Prince Visala Deva and of the date of 1164 A.D.

From the platform of the pillar a fine view is obtained of the ruins of the Firozabad Citadel, of the Purana Kila, and Humayun's Mausoleum, and of the remains of still older cities and buildings right up to the Kutab Minar. The Lat is noticed in the works of many visitors to Delhi, and attracted the special admiration of the great Prince, the Lord Timur.

The City of **Firozabad** extended, as has been seen, as far west as the Kalan Masjid (p. 65), now enclosed by the walls of Shahjahanabad, and probably spread two miles north and south—the chronicler says it reached from Kasbah Indrapat to Kushk-i-Shikar—(p. 222), and was thus a larger city than its later rival. In the streets of it desperate fighting of large forces took place after the death of Firoz Shah and his immediate successors. The citadel, as subsequently in the case of the Purana Kila and Shahjahanabad, was placed on the banks of the Jumna, and it is the lofty ruins of this that we see immediately adjoining the Lat to the south and south-west. Corresponding to the Lat platform is the Jama Masjid of Firoz Shah, which must once have been a fine structure; like other mosques of the same date (see p. 324), it consisted of arcades of several rows of arches round an open central court; on the edge of this the large slabs on which the outer double columns of the arcades rested can still be seen. In the centre of the open quadrangle was a sunken octagonal structure, perhaps somewhat like the mausoleum of

Sultan Ghari (p. 284), round which the record of the reign of Firoz Shah, and, in particular, of the public works executed by him, was engraved (see pp. 273-277). The mosque was visited by Sultan Timur, on the last day of 1398, for the purpose of devotions on his way from carnage and rapine in Old Delhi to carnage and rapine in Meerut and Amballah, and a meteoric disappearance from Hindustan in the manner of his appearance. In the mosque, or in the buildings adjoining it, was murdered the Emperor Alamgir II., in 1761, having been enticed to his fate by the report of the residence on the spot of a peculiarly holy fakir.

It is well worth while to walk through the ruins of the Kotila, and rejoin one's carriage nearer the point where the road to the Lat leaves the main road. The walls of most of the houses of Firozabad finally disappeared when building materials were needed for Shahjahanabad; but a few buildings still remain, the most notable being a picturesque mosque, known as the Chausath Khambhe, or Sixty-four Pillars, at the back of the jail. Near the above point on the left hand is a handsome gateway of stone and red sandstone, known as the **Lal Darwazah**. This was undoubtedly the north gate of the Delhi of Sher Shah (1540 A.D.): there is a corresponding gate on the south side, opposite the south-west corner of the Purana Kila. The latter, however, can hardly have been in the actual southern wall of the city, having regard to its position in relation to the citadel, and was probably the entrance to some royal bazar under the citadel.

The Purana Kila of Sher Shah.

[To face p. 227.

A little south of the Lal Darwazah and on the right is the Caravan Sarai of Farid Khan, converted into a jail. This nobleman was one of the principal Amirs of the court of Jehangir, and Governor of the Punjab, and it was owing to his action that this emperor was promptly proclaimed successor of his father, and the rebellion of Prince Khusru was almost as promptly subdued. Farid Khan, who received the title of Murtaza Khan, founded Faridabad, a well-known, flourishing little town, built in the land of the very ancient Tilpat, some twelve miles south of Delhi, and restored the Salimgarh, and probably built the bridge to it (p. 40). He is buried in the cemetery at Sarai Shahji, about 400 yards due east of the Begampur Mosque (p. 251), with an extremely beautiful inscribed stone at the head of his grave.

Yet a similar distance down the road on the left side are a fine mosque and ruined palace built by a still greater nobleman of the Moghal Court, Mahabat Khan, the bold Rajput, captor of the Emperor Jehangir, who afterwards went into rebellion with Prince Shahjehan. This nobleman became a Shiah towards the end of his life, and is buried in the Karbala, lying to the south-east of the tomb of Safdar Jang.

On leaving this, the extremely picturesque walls of the Purana Kila come into full view, and after passing along the north-west side of these, and, on the right, the second city gate above noticed, a road turns to the left and leads to the bridge in front of the south gateway of the Fortress. Opposite the point of junction of the two roads is a fine enclosure with a handsome portal of red sandstone, and a large mosque, known as the Khair-ul-Manazil (the Auspicious of Houses), or Lal Chauk (Red Enclosure). This was built in 1561 A.D. by Máham Anagah, the foster-mother of the Emperor Akbar, and mother of Adham Khan (p. 242); from it a few years later an attempt was made by an archer to assassinate the Emperor.

The **Purana Kila** was constructed on the site of the historical Indrapat—one of the five villages[1] over which the war celebrated in the "Ramayana" was waged—by the Emperor's Sher Shah and Humayun. The historian who describes its phenomenally rapid completion, under the designation of Din Panah, to the latter before his expulsion by the former, was probably more courtly than truthful, and it is practically certain that the present walls and gates and the buildings which they surround are the work of the Pathan Usurper and his successors. The lofty south gate will probably be considered as effective as any of the buildings of Delhi previous to 1640 A.D.—the decoration on it is very pleasing. From the gate a lane leads northwards to the back of the **Mosque of Sher Shah**, and the Sher Mandal near it. The facade of the former is quite the most striking bit of coloured decoration at Delhi, and has been satisfactorily restored. The red sandstone used in it is of an unusually deep tone, and very beautiful. The brackets under the balconies are an early type of those which are so marked in the red sandstone palace of Akbar or Jehangir in the Agra Fort. The interior is extremely

[1] These five were Panipat, Sonpat, Baghpat, Indrapat, and Tilpat.

Mosque of Sher Shah in the Purana Kila.

[To face p. 228.

fine, the patterns in the pendentives below the dome being very effective.

The **Sher Mandal** is interesting as the building on the steps of which the Emperor Humayun slipped when rising from evening prayer, and met with his death in 1556 A.D. The date of his death is embodied in the anagram: "Humáyun Badshah az bám uftad" ("King Humáyun fell from the roof"), but this does not really give the exact date.

Proceeding down the road from the Purana Kila to Humayun's Tomb, there is seen first on the left a lofty Kos Minara,[1] or milestone, and then on the right the picturesque tombs, known as the Lal Bangala built by the Emperor Shah Alam II., and named after his mother, and on the left again an octagonal tomb, once covered with fine encaustic work, called the Nili Chhatri, or Blue Tomb, of Naubat Khan, an Amir of the Court of Akbar. The channel connecting the Western Jumna and Agra canals runs parallel to the right of the road here, and at three and a quarter miles from the Delhi gate, where a fine tomb, known from the colour of its dome as the Sabz Posh, or Green Top, one route diverges across the canal to the Dargah of Nizam-ud-din-Aulia, and another leads on the left to the **Mausoleum** of **Humayun**, the second great Moghal Emperor. In approaching this, the road

[1] These milestones were placed in the centre of the old royal high roads radiating from Delhi to the Provinces, and many still exist along these. Another very complete one stands opposite the entrance of the Mubarik Bagh (p. 61). According to Sir Henry Elliott, measurements of the distances between nearly twenty of them near Delhi showed they were placed just two and a half miles apart, so that the kos they marked was what is known as the double kos.

passes under the picturesque bright kiosks of the walls of the Bu Halima garden, first admitting of a view of the tomb of Isa Khan (p. 234), and then turns left again at the gate of the garden and the very handsome gateway of Arab Sarai to the portal leading into the garden round the mausoleum. The wings of this are thrown forward, and standing as it does at the top of a fine flight of steps, it forms a worthy approach to the tomb. It was into this portal that Captain Hodson rode on 22nd September 1857, and called upon the retainers of the Delhi Princes to surrender their arms (p. 184).

The trees which formerly hid the mausoleum too much have been cut back, and the building is now fully seen rising finely from a lofty platform under its great dome of white marble. In mere beauty it cannot of course compare with the Taj, but there is an effect of strength about it which becomes the last resting-place of a Moghal warrior whose life was marked by many struggles and vicissitudes, and most people will probably prefer its greater simplicity to either the son's tomb at Sikandra, near Agra, or the grandson's tomb at Shahdara, near Lahore. The ground plan of the tomb is peculiar, as the angles project beyond the central bay on each side, and the freer use of white marble on them adds to the prominence of their position. The decoration of white and grey marble and of fawn-coloured stone on the red sandstone is very effective, and the pierced marble screens in the openings to the interior are among the very finest specimens of this work. The railing on the edge

Mausoleum of the Emperor Humayun. [*To face p.* 230.

of the platform has recently been restored all round it, much to the improvement of the general effect.

The interior is entered from the south side, and the actual vault can also be visited from the lower terrace on this side. The central chamber, which is a very fine and lofty one, contains only the marble tomb of the Emperor. His faithful wife, known as Haji Begam, who built the tomb and Arab Sarai, is buried in the north-east corner of the building. The other corner rooms also contain graves, which are nameless, but are known to include those of the unfortunate Dara Shekoh, of two of the brothers of Shah Alam Bahadur Shah, who fought against him for the Empire, and three sons of these, and of the Emperors Jahandar Shah and Alamgir II. (d. 1712 and 1761 A.D.) The Emperor Jehangir records in his memoirs that while in pursuit of his son, Prince Khusru, he visited the tomb of his grandfather, and distributed alms at it and at the tomb of Nizam-ud-din-Aulia, to which also he went. He would doubtless have appreciated the scene in which his father is represented with Shah Tahmasp in the hall of the Chihal Situn (Forty Pillars) at Isfahan, of which the account given in the note below will perhaps be found interesting.[1]

[1] Humayun is represented as seated on the ground to the right, clad in gold brocade over a crimson dress, and wearing a small reddish turband, such as Rajputs wear, with a black plume in it. His face is pleasing and intelligent, and he looks scarcely more than thirty years of age. Behind him stand three graceful and well-painted figures, reminding one of those recovered in the damaged frescoes at Fatehpur Sikri, one in blue with a chauri, one in white with the king's sword, and one in red with rose-water. Other graceful attendants stand by these, all wearing "kamar bands," or

On the top of the building, round the drum below the dome, are a number of rooms and pavilions, once occupied by a college attached to the mausoleum, and reminding one of the colony of St Peter's dome. The view from the top is extremely fine, and includes nearly everything of interest round Delhi, except Tughlakabad, hid by rising ground to the south. The fine mass of trees on the further bank of the river marks Patparganj and the site of the battle-field of Delhi in 1803 (p. 70).

In the south-east corner of the garden is a nameless picturesque tomb of red sandstone, with some beautiful pierced grilles in the windows, and outside, in the

waist-belts, and all well drawn and well painted, and showing unmistakable signs of Italian influence. Between the two kings is a green cloth with wine vessels and cups of silver, and fruit upon it. On the left side is seated Shah Tahmasp, in a red dress over cloth of gold, girt by a black belt supporting the black scabbard of his sword; he wears a white gold-barred turband, wound round a high kulah, or pointed cap. Behind him are attendants with matchlocks and sword and hawks and golden dishes. In front of him are seated a body of Persian nobles in bright robes, each with his flagon, and in the right foreground of the picture are musicians with tambourine, flageolet, guitar, zither, and panpipes. Between these groups are two dancing girls performing elaborate body posturings, one clad in golden striped, and one in dull robes, and both with very long tresses behind, surmounted by large bosses of silver; the former is about to refresh herself with a cup of wine.

Shah Tahmasp was the second of the Safavean kings of Persia, and reigned from 1526 to 1571. It was to him that Queen Elizabeth commended Mr Anthony Jenkinson, addressing him as "The Right Mightie and Right Victorious Prince, the great Sophie, Emperor of the Persians, Medes, Parthians, Hiroeans, Carmanians, Margians, of the people on this side and beyond the river Tygris, and of all men and nations between the Caspian Sea and the Gulfe of Persia," a commendation which availed the English merchant nothing, for he was ignominiously repulsed from the king's presence.

same direction, is the Nili Burj. This tomb, with its beautiful dark blue dome, is that of Fahim Khan, and was, it is believed, erected to his memory about 1625 A.D., by the Khan-i-Khanan, in whose cause he fought and fell. The large tomb of this chief, son of the great Turk noble Bairam Khan, who won back the Moghal Empire for Humayun at Sirhind and for Akbar at Panipat, and rebelled against the latter, is also seen from the top of the mausoleum. It must once have been an extremely beautiful structure, but it was stripped of most of its marble by the Nawab Wazir of Oudh, Asaf-ud-daulah, and is now only a grand ruin of red sandstone—the centre bays of the sides are particularly fine. The gate which led to the enclosure of this tomb stands on the east side of the Grand Trunk Road, and both can be reached by proceeding half a mile down this from the Sabz Posh Tomb. Khan Khanan himself was Governor of Gujrat and the Punjab, and fought one of the most desperate battles waged with the Bijapur power. A few hundred yards beyond these is the old Moghal bridge, known as the Barah Palah, or Twelve-Arched, which is decidedly picturesque, as viewed from down stream, and well deserves a visit. This bridge was crossed by Mr William Finch in his journey from Agra to Lahore. "The city of Delly" (that is, the Delly of Sher Shah, whom Finch calls Salim), he writes, "lies in a delightful plain, compassed with curious gardens and monuments. It is a matter of two cose (kos) in length from gate to gate, and has the fate of a great many other noble cities of India, to lie partly in ruines. . . . . The ruines of old Delly (*i.e.* Kila Rai Pithora, Jahanpanah, Siri, and Tughlakabad) lie a little distance from here, separated by an arm of the Gemini (Jumna), over which is a bridge of eleven or twelve arches. . . . . Particularly there appears amongst these ruines the carkase of that ancient building called the castle, that had to the number of 52 gates (this is Tughlakabad, p. 291), a thing of surprising glory and stateliness in its time, but now worn out and disfigured to the last degree.

Mr Finch noted quite correctly that there were four Old Delhis, one of Sher Shah and three built by the Pathan Kings, viz., the original Delhi, with its extensions of Jahanpanah and Siri, Tughlakabad, and Firozabad.

Outside the north-east corner of the garden of Humayun's tomb are the remains of a house and a mosque in the severe middle Pathan style, which, according to credible tradition, formed the residence of Shekh Nizam-ud-din-Aulia.

To the east side of the gateway leading into Arab Sarai are two pleasing buildings, known merely as the Afsarwalla (Afsar means crown, as well as officer) mosque and tomb. The graceful proportions of this gateway, and the handsome balcony above it, are noticeable. Fifty yards inside it a lane leads to the right to the **tomb and mosque of Isa Khan**, which should be visited, especially if those of Khairpur cannot be (p. 244). Isa Khan was a leading noble of the times of Sher Shah and his sons, and was buried here in 1547 A.D. The structures are similar to those of the Syad and Lodi Kings, and were once profusely decorated with encaustic tiles. The octagonal tomb, with its raised outer gallery and pavilions round the dome, is specially picturesque.

Crossing the canal near the Sabz Posh tomb, the village and shrine of Nizam-ud-din are immediately reached on the left. North of the Dargah are a number of buildings of the severer middle Pathan type, including one on the left of the side road to it, known as the Barah Khambhe, or Twelve-Pillared (which seems to have been a tomb chamber with arcades round it, and may have been the original of the Chausath Khambhe, p. 243), and another behind it of red sandstone, known as the Lal Mahal, or Red Palace. This was once a very pretty pavilion of the earlier Pathan style (very possibly it was a building of Ala-ud-din for royal accommodation when the court visited the saint), and, with the interior of the mosque of the Dargah, links that style to the buildings of severer mould on this site. Among these again, at the south-east corner of the village, is a fine roofed mosque, known as the Sanjar mosque, which once had four courts, like that of Khirki (p. 286), each measuring forty-three by thirty-three feet. These are larger than the Khirki quadrangles, but the arcades between the courts being much narrower than these, the total area covered by this mosque is considerably less than in the case of the more southern example. It was built by Khan Jahan (p. 65) in 1372 A.D., and is well deserving of a visit, though much of it is now filled up with mud houses. To the east of the mosque is a fine tomb, also of the middle Pathan period, known locally as that of the Talanga Nawab. The first Khan Jahan was originally a Hindu follower of the Talingana, or Warangal chief, who was brought to Delhi after his capture, and this tomb is no doubt connected with the latter or some descendant of his.

The **Dargah** or shrine of **Shekh Nizam-ud-din-Aulia**, whose full title was Shekh-ul-Islam Nizam-ul-hak-wa-ud-din, is with the other Chisti shrines at Ajmir, the Kutab, and Pakpattan, one of the principal places of Muhammadan reverence in all India. This saint was the last of the four, and successor to Shekh Farid-ud-din of Pakpattan, known as Shakar Ganj.

No story in the annals of ancient Delhi is more widely told than that of the quarrel of those, frequent mediæval opponents, the King and the Priest, for do not the desolation of Tughlakabad and the bitter water of the shrine tank bear witness to it to this day. In its full form the tale runs that the Emperor Tughlak Shah impressed the workmen of the saint to finish his new fortress and city. The saint thereupon prosecuted his labours on the tank by means of oil light, whereupon a royal mandate forbade the sale of oil to him. The prayers of the saint then prevailed, so far that the workmen were miraculously supplied with light from the water of the tank, which enabled them still to work upon it at night. In his wrath, the Emperor cursed the water of the tank, and it became bitter, and the saint in retaliation cursed the city of Tughlakabad (p. 288). What is more certain, is that Tughlak Shah did meet his death through the treachery of his son, assisted by the Shekh, who, while the king was approaching Delhi, and was known to be uttering threats against him, kept on saying tranquilly to his disciples: "Dilli hanoz dur ast" ("Delhi is still distant"), a saying which has passed into a proverb in India. If, as tradition runs, the Shekh also had knowledge of the death of Jelal-ud-din-Khilji, which seemed at the time supernatural, it may be shrewdly suspected that he was also in league with a parricidal nephew on that occasion. He was, no doubt, one of the leading politicians of his day, and as such was probably as unscrupulous as his compeers and opponents, but there seems to be no ground whatever for attributing the origin of Thagism to him, and,

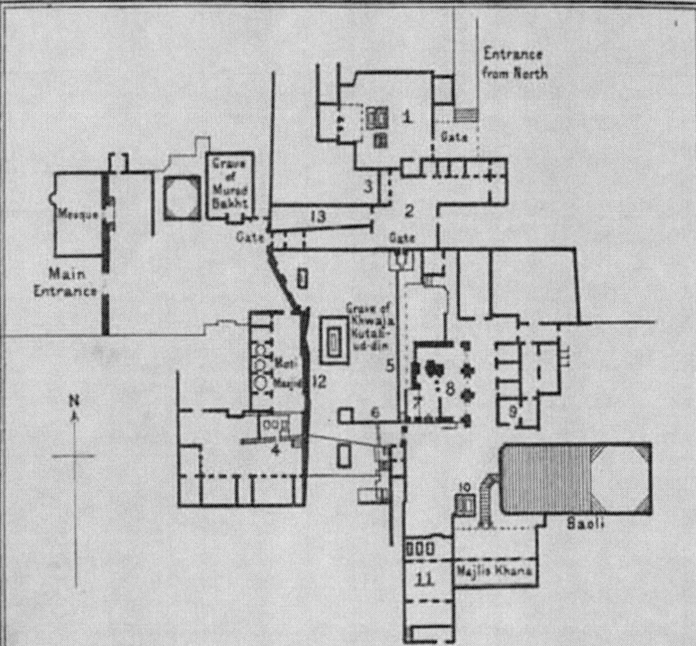

Plan of Dargah (shrine) of
KHWAJA KUTAB-UD-DIN BAKHTIAR KÁKI AT MAHRAULI

1. Grave enclosure of Nawabs of Jhajjar.
2. Main Courtyard
3. Mosque
4. Tombs of Akbar Shah II, Shah Alam & Bahadur Shah.
5. Pierced marble enclosure.
6. Gate
7. Grave of Maulana Fakhr-ud-din.
8. Mosque of Khwaja Sahib.
9. Grave of Dai Ji.
10. ,, ,, Zabita Khan.
11. ,, enclosure of Nawabs of Loharu.
12. Shrine wall with encaustic work.
13. Graveyard of Mohtamid Khan.

Scale of Feet

50 0 100 200

[*To face p.* 281.

Tank at Shrine of Nizam-ud-din Aulia.

[To face p. 237

as a matter of fact, this must have been Hindu. The saint, who settled at Delhi in the time of the Emperor Balban (p. 296), died at the advanced age of ninety-two, in 1324. According to Abulfazl, he was known as Al Bahháth, the Controversialist, and Mahfil Shikan, the Confounder of Assemblies.

The entrance gate to the Dargah bears the date of 1378 A.D., and, like the inner gate beyond the tank, was built by the Emperor Firoz Shah Tughlak, who next to Ala-ud-din was the greatest of the early benefactors of the place. The plan of the interior given here, the first ever made, will render the following description of the interior intelligible. On either side within the entrance is an old Pathan tomb, and by that, on the right, is a mosque of two storeys, a rare arrangement; south of it again is the marble pavilion and grave of Bai Kokal De, a *prima donna* of the Emperor Shah Jehan, and behind that is an old cupola borne by red sandstone pillars. The gravestone of this lady is a very beautiful one, and should be visited from the gallery at the south end of the tank, to which the paved way, picturesquely covered in at the end, leads along the east side. The tank, or Baoli, into which men and boys dive from the surrounding buildings, is named "Chashma dil kusha," or the "Heart-alluring spring" (this gives the date of 713 H., or 1312 A.D., which does not correspond with the era of Tughlak Shah, who was murdered in 725 H., after a reign of four years); an archway now in the water on the east side of the tank is said to conduct to a cell once occupied by the saint. The inner and third gate beyond that of Firoz Shah on the south side of the tank, which leads to the actual enclosure of the Dargah, is of much later date, but no longer bears any inscription. Beyond it is an extremely fine "imli," or tamarind tree, affording a beautiful shade, and at the side of it is an octagonal marble receptacle, filled with sweets and milk on special occasions, like the great cooking pots at the Ajmir shrine. In the angle behind this gate on the right is a Meeting Hall, or Majlis Khana, said to have been built by the Emperor Aurangzeb. In front of the gate and in the middle of the centre court is the **Tomb** of the saint, with the Jam'át Khana, or mosque, to the west of it. The structure over the tomb has been rebuilt and restored by many pious donors, and but little ancient work is left in it now. A wide verandah runs round the exterior, and light is admitted to the grave chamber by pierced marble screens in the inner walls of this. The ceiling of the verandah was restored at the expense of the late Mr R. Clarke, B.C.S. (p. 12). Round the grave, which is always covered, is a low railing of marble, and above it is a canopy of wood, inlaid with mother-o'-pearl. Two inscriptions on the tomb describe it as the "Kiblahgah-i-khas-o-am," and the Kubba-i-Shekh, or the "Place of prayer to which all, great and small, turn," and the "Dome of the Saint."

The **Jam'at Khana** Mosque, known also as the Khizri Mosque, is an extremely fine building of the ornate earlier Pathan style. It cannot have been the work of the Emperor Firoz Shah, who, however, restored it, and may have rebuilt the side

Tomb of Nizam-ud-din Aulia.

[*To face p.* 238.

rooms; and though called after Khizar Khan,[1] the son of Ala-ud-din-Khilji, it seems probable that it was begun at least by the latter, as the centre bay more closely resembles the Alai Darwazah of that monarch (p. 270) than any other building in Old Delhi, and the son was murdered within a year of the death of his father. The front arches, with their heavily engrailed curves, are particularly handsome and effective, and the carved work of the kiblah niche is unusually elaborate and beautiful. The fine timber doors and the Hindu heads of the doorways also deserve special notice. The golden cup hanging from the dome of the central chamber is said to be the one originally suspended there.

South of the tomb of the Shekh come the graves of many persons of note, and amongst them not a few of royal blood, resting as close as possible to his holy influence. Next to the mosque in the front row is a marble enclosure with the grave of **Jahanara Begam**, daughter of Shah Jehan and companion of his captivity, which she survived sixteen years, outliving her rival sister Roshanara Begam, by ten (p. 61). The grave consists of a marble block hollowed out so as to form a receptacle for earth in which grass is planted: at the north side stands a handsome headstone, with verses supposed to have been written by the Princess: "Let green grass only conceal my grave: grass is the best covering of the grave of the meek." On either side of her are buried the son and daughter of two of

[1] This was the prince, whose loves with the Dewal Rani were celebrated in one of the most famous poems of Amir Khusrau.

the late Moghal Kings—doubtless because the cost of a separate place of burial for them was not forthcoming. In the next enclosure on the east lies **Muhammad Shah** (d. 1748), the unhappy Emperor who saw the capture of Delhi by Nadir Shah, and near the fallen head of her house lies the Moghal princess who was married to Nadir Shah's son, and her baby. The entrance to this enclosure and to that opposite on the further side of the passage is decorated with marble doors, on which extremely beautiful patterns of flowers and leaves have been carved. The conception of these hardly appertains to the region of high art, but the execution is well worthy of notice, as are the beautiful pierced marble screens in the walls of the enclosures. The third contains the grave of **Prince Jehangir,** son of the King Akbar II.: it was under completion when Bishop Heber visited the Dargah. The people of Delhi say that the real cause of the prince's removal to Allahabad was that he actually fired at the British Resident, Mr Seton, in the king's palace, the ball passing through that gentlemen's hat.

Yet another gateway leads from the central court to the well-shaded quadrangle on the south, which contains the Chabutra Yáráni and the tomb of the poet Khusrau, as well as many other graves, among them several of the actual disciples of the saint. The first was the platform where the friends of Nizam-ud-din-Aulia used to sit with him in his lifetime, and was thence called "the Seat of the Friends." The second covers the remains of the first and most

Grave Enclosure with Tomb of Emperor Muhammad Shah at Nizam-ud-din.

[To face p. 240.

renowned of the poets of the modern language of India, **Amir Khusrau,** popularly known as the Sugar-tongued Parrot ("Tuti-i-shakar-makál"), and also called in the inscription on his tomb Adim-ul-misal, or the Peerless, both designations giving the date of his death, 725 H., or 1324 A.D. He was a devoted friend of Shekh Nizam-ud-din, and died at an advanced age soon after his master, whom he refused to survive. Among the adventures of his life he was once captured by the Moghal invaders. The present tomb dates from the early years of the seventeenth century. The grave chamber is surrounded by two galleries, and the light which reaches it is very subdued. The well-known historian, Khondamir, was also buried near by, but the Dargah guardians are unable to point out his grave. Beyond the west wall of the southern court is an extremely pretty grave and mosque of one Dauran Khan; and outside the east wall of the central court—it can also be reached by steps from the gallery along the east side of the tank—is the tomb of **Azam Khan,** or Atgah Khan, commonly known as Taga Khan. This man, whose actual name (this is really rather in the style of Humpty Dumpty in "Alice in Wonderland") was Shams-ud-din-Muhammad, saved the life of the Emperor Humayun on the occasion of his final and irretrievable defeat by Sher Shah, and won alike the further consideration of the Emperor Akbar, the title of Azam Khan, and the Governorship of the Punjab, by defeating Bairam Khan at Jalandhur when the latter went into half-hearted rebellion against his master. His wife was a foster-mother to Akbar, as well as Maham Anagah (p. 228), and no doubt great ealousy arose between the families of the two ladies, which culminated in Adham Khan, son of the latter, murdering Azam Khan in the royal palace at Agra in 1556 A.D. The murderer then proceeded to the door of the private apartments of the palace, and upon the Emperor issuing forth, tried to seize his hands in order to secure his pardon. Akbar, however, freed himself by violence, and laid Adham Khan senseless by a single blow, which the court chronicler assures us was like that of a mace, and his body was then, by the Emperor's orders, twice thrown from the lofty palace terrace into the court below. The corpses both of the murdered man and of his murderer were sent to Delhi, the former to be buried here, and the latter at the Kutab, where his mother, who is said to have died of a broken heart, was soon laid beside him (p. 279). The tomb of Azam Khan must have been one of the most effective and pleasing specimens of polychromatic decoration in the whole of India, and even in its present half-ruined condition will be considered by most people extremely pretty. The red sandstone used in it is of an unusually fine colour, and the marble has assumed an ivory hue. Three graves stand on the marble pavement of the sepulchral chamber, decorated with white and black stars. The enclosure wall on the west side was once brightly decorated with encaustic tiles, of which some traces still remain. Two hundred feet to the south-east of this tomb, and practically opposite the Chabutra Yáráni courtyard, is the last building of special interest at the Dargah — the

Chausath Khambhe, or Sixty-four Pillared Hall. This is the family grave enclosure of the sons of Azam Khan and of his brothers, several of whom, like Adham Khan, were commanders of 5000, which was practically the highest military rank that could be attained in ordinary circumstances under the Moghal Emperors. The building was raised by Mirza Aziz Kokaltash, foster brother of the Emperor Akbar, who died in 1624 A.D., and round him are buried a number of members of the family which was known as the Atgah Khail, or Gang, so widely did it spread and flourish under imperial favour. The grey marble arches of the hall are pleasing, and the effect of the interior is decidedly good, and reminds one in a way of the beautiful grey marble chamber of the Moti Masjid of Agra.

To the east of Nizam-ud-din on the road to Mubarikpur are the remains of a fine bridge of later Pathan style, spanning the same ravine as is bridged near the tomb of Sikandar Shah Lodi, north of the village of Khairpur, and which joins that from Khirki and Chiragh Delhi (p. 287) near this point, and passes under the Barah Palah (p. 233) to the Jumna. Proceeding west from Nizam-ud-din towards the tomb of Safdar Jang, the road passes the first-named village one mile and a half away on the left, and the last-named half-a-mile away on the right. Most persons will perhaps hardly care to walk or ride to Mubarikpur, but every one who can spare an hour should certainly visit the **Khairpur** buildings.

These are four in number. That nearest the road, and between it and the village, is the tomb of

Muhammad Shah, third of the Syad kings (died 1445 A.D.), which is figured in Mr Fergusson's "Eastern Architecture." The building is octagonal, and has an exterior arcade, with sloping angles, similar to those of the tombs of Isa Khan (p. 234) and Mubarik Shah; the decoration of the interior of the dome must once have been unusually beautiful. In the village itself, 200 yards further north, is a striking mosque, approached through a very fine gateway, which, from a distance, looks like a tomb. The interior of the gateway, reached by a high flight of steps, is singularly well proportioned and lofty, and was evidently modelled upon the Alai Darwazah (p. 270). Beyond the gateway is an extremely picturesque courtyard, with a mosque on one side and an Assembly Hall on the other, bearing the date of 1498 A.D. This mosque was once entirely covered by the most beautiful plaster decoration, and still retains much of this. The plaster was relieved by colour in the form of patterns of encaustic tiles, and is quite the most beautiful specimen of this class of ornamentation that exists in India. On the north outskirt of the village is a second tomb without name, on which some tile-work of very bright blue may still be seen; and 400 yards beyond it again is the tomb of Sikandar Shah Lodi, who died in 1517—only nine years before the Moghal conquest of India. This tomb is strikingly situated in a walled enclosure which, like Chiragh Delhi (p. 287), stands on the banks of a deep depression, spanned by a bridge of seven arches, carrying the high road that then connected Firozabad and the north with Siri (p. 253) and Old Delhi. The tomb itself is a fine building, but the situation of it is the most pleasing thing connected with it. The pillar which bears the lamp at the head of the grave was once a column of a Jain temple; and it is curious how Hindu details were beginning to reassert themselves in Muhammadan buildings just before the time of the fresh Muhammadan conquest by the Moghals.

The tomb and mosque of **Mubarik Shah** lie

rather more than a mile south of the high road in the village of Mubarikpur. This king was the second of the little-known Syad dynasty, and was murdered in 1433 A.D. The tomb is octagonal in form, and is surrounded by an arched colonnade; it is the earliest of those built in the later Pathan style (p. 326), and, in consequence, encaustic tile-work is employed on it but sparingly, the freer use of this being a subsequent development. The angles of the tomb have sloping buttress piers, and above the dome, surrounded by octagonal cupolas, is a lantern of red sandstone. Rising above a battlemented wall in the midst of trees, it is very picturesque. Outside the enclosure of the tomb is a mosque with two rows of bays and three large domes. Beyond the village to the east is a group of large tombs of the same age, known as the Tin Burj; the principal of these is, according to tradition, the tomb of Khizr Khan, the first Syad king, but this is hardly probable.

A mile south of Mubarikpur is the Moth-ki Masjid, a fine mosque built in 1488 A.D., by Sikandar Khan Lodi, which served as a model for that of Sher Shah in the Purana Kila and the Jamali Mosque at the Kutab. The gateway leading to the mosque and its Hindu arch are very fine, and the back wall of the mosque, with its open flanking towers, is extremely effective; the decoration of the front may have inspired that of the Mausoleum of Humayun. Half a mile south of the mosque again are the ruins of the citadel of Siri, which now enclose the village of Shahpur (p. 254). Two hundred yards on the way to these ruins is a fine well with an inscription of Sikandar Lodi; and just outside them is a large mosque known as the Muhamdi Masjid, with a single dome. The north-west defences of Jahanpanah, which connected Siri with Old Delhi, are well seen from here (p. 255). Outside these, and 300 yards west of the Siri wall, is an extremely picturesque enclosure, known as that of the Makhdum Sabzawar, which well deserves a visit. The interior, approached by a fine gate in the Hindu style, contains a handsome mosque in the severe Pathan style, but with a red sandstone dripstone, a rest-house, and a tomb covered by a cupola, which still has very beautiful text decoration in plaster inside, and once had fine pierced sandstone grilles all round. The little cemetery is overshaded by fine trees, and is quite one of the prettiest bits near Old Delhi.

At the end of the road from Humayun's tomb and Nizam-ud-din rises the **Mausoleum of Nawab Safdar Jang**, nephew and successor of the first Nawab Wazir of Oudh. Safdar Jang (who was Wazir of Ahmad Shah, and was probably responsible for the final ruin of the Moghal Emperors, as he called in the Jats to his aid, whereupon his rival invited the Mahrattas to Delhi) died in 1753 A.D., and this tomb is therefore one of the last great Muhammadan architectural efforts in India, and for its age it deserves, perhaps, more commendation than is usually accorded to it. Though the general arrangement of the tomb is the same as that of the Mausoleum of the Taj, it was not intended to be a servile copy of the latter; and if the decoration of the corner towers is not successful, the combination of white marble and fawn-coloured sandstone in the centre is very pleasing. The plaster decoration of the interior is perhaps more degraded than anything else about the tomb: the gravestone itself is very handsome if a little florid in style. The view from the top of this tomb also is extremely fine, and well repays the labour of the ascent; to the south it overlooks the battle-field where Timur crushed the army of Muhmud Khan in 1398 (p. 249). The gateway leading to the garden,

Mausoleum of Nawab Safdar Jang.

[To face p. 246.

Observatory of Maharaja Jai Singh.

[*To face p.* 247.

and the red sandstone mosque to the north of it, are effective and pleasing. In this mausoleum, and in the Mausoleum of Ghazi-ud-din Khan (p. 64) we have memorials of the two great Muhammadan ruling houses of Oudh and Hydrabad, which made themselves practically independent in the first half of the eighteenth century.

The tomb of Safdar Jang is situated just six miles from Delhi, and five miles from the Kutab. The only object of special interest between it and the Ajmir Gate of the city is the **Observatory of Raja Jai Singh of Jeypur**, but extremely pretty views are obtained from the road of the Khairpur tombs, of the Mausoleum of Humayun, of the Purana Kila, and of the Jama Masjid of Delhi. The Observatory, termed classically the Semrat Yantar, and known vulgarly as the Jantar Mantar, was constructed in 1724 A.D., but was badly damaged by the Jat marauders within fifty years of its erection. The great equatorial dial still exists, but the marble work of the periphery of the circle on which the degrees were marked, and of the gnomon, has entirely disappeared. This work is shown in Daniell's drawing in 1790, but was perhaps restored in that from the fragments which then remained. The two round buildings with tiers of arches, looking like miniature Roman amphitheatres from the outside, served for the measurement of the ascension and declension of the stars. A palace and stables of the Raja of Jeypur once existed in Madhoganj, the village just east of the Observatory, and this village is still held in jagir by the Jeypur State. Rather less than half a mile east of it is an extremely fine baoli, or reservoir-well, known as Ugar Sen's baoli. A mile from the Observatory the outskirts of the Paharganj suburb of the city are reached, and a mile further the Ajmir Gate (p. 64). The great mounds noticed from the road are the ruins of vast brick kilns utilised to supplement the material taken from Firozabad and the city of Sher Shah when Shahjahanabad was built.

CHAPTER V

ANCIENT DELHI OF THE EARLY HINDU AND MUHAMMADAN PERIODS, INCLUDING KILA RAI PITHORA, THE KUTAB MINAR, MOSQUE, AND DARGAH, AND TUGHLAKABAD.

BEYOND the **Mausoleum of Safdar Jang** the high road leading to the Kutab, which is five miles distant, and is frequently seen through the trees on the right, passes on the left the enclosure of Aliganj with a famous Shiah cemetery, the grave of Najaf Khan (the last champion of the Moghal power against the Mahrattas, who died 1782 A.D.), and the village of Bibipur, with a dense grove of tamarisk. On the left now appears the tomb of **Mubarik Shah** (p. 245), beyond the Tin Burj and a picturesque ruined line of arches marking the cemetery of Darya Khan, and south of them the three domes and high back wall of the **Moth-ki Masjid**, while a mile removed on the right the domes of a lofty and very fine Dargah in the village of Muhammadpur attract the eye. On the plain traversed by the road was fought on 12th December 1398 the battle between the Pathan king, Sultan Mahmud Shah and the Moghal invader, Sultan Timur, which ended in the disastrous defeat of the former. It is a curious coincidence that the Moghal king, still more disastrously defeated by the Persian invader, Nadir Shah, three hundred and forty years later, should have borne the name of Muhammad Shah.

Timur[1] had advanced with his army from Jahannuma (p. 58), and the battle was for a time fiercely contested, the Delhi forces being no doubt inspired by the recollection of previous occasions when the Moghal invaders had been defeated before Delhi. "The soldiers of Sultan Mahmud," the rival Sultan writes, "showed no lack of courage, but bore themselves manfully in the fight, still they could not withstand the successive assaults of my soldiers." The Indian forces are put down at 40,000 foot, 10,000 horse, and 125 war elephants, which Timur's men greatly dreaded. The strength of the Moghal force is not definitely recorded, but as Timur took 10,000 horsemen with him to Bhatnir while sending the main body of his army up the Ghaggar, it probably amounted to some 30,000 to 35,000 men. Timur attacked on both flanks, and the Indian forces finally gave way. Nearly all the war elephants were captured, and were sent as trophies of victory as far as to Herat, Shiraz, Samarkand, Aizarbaijan, and Tabriz. This plain had previously been the field of the battle fought by Tughlak Shah against two *fainéant* princelings — "foolish, ignorant lads," records the chronicler, "who went forth like newly-hatched chickens, just beginning to fly, to fight with a veteran warrior like Malik Ghazi, whose

[1] Timur left Samarkand in the spring of 1398, and Kabul in August, and captured Multan in October of that year. He marched from Multan to Delhi *via* Dipalpur, Bhatnir, Sirsa, Fatahabad, Tohana, Kaithal, and Panipat, which had been deserted by orders from Delhi, and crossed the Jumna below Panipat to Luni (p. 58), and thence crossed back again to the Ridge.

sword had made Khurasan and the land of the Moghals to tremble."

The road next passes Mujahidpur on the right, and Karera hidden inside old walls on the left; opposite the latter are seen two groups of tombs of the later Pathan style, one group near the road with a dome surmounted by a pavilion, a frequent feature in this style, and the other group further back not far from the village of Hauz Khas. On the left the ruined walls of the citadel of **Siri** (p. 254) now come into view, and south of it the lofty **Badi Mandal** and the large dark **Begampur Mosque**, both of which are situated within the limits of Jahanpanah.

The former is a high platform from which a splendid view is obtained, and which may have formed part of the Thousand Column Palace[1] (Kasr-i-Hazar Situn) of Muhammad Tughlak. The latter is the finest of the mosques built by Jahan Khan, and well deserves a visit, although the arcades of the mosque are occupied by a village, in which some English refugees were long concealed in 1857. The building dates from 1387 A.D., and is nearly 300 feet square by exterior measurement, the interior court being 247 feet long by 223 broad from east to west; it is the next largest at Delhi to the Jama Masjid of Shahjehan (p. 44).

Between these buildings and the road, half a mile south of Karera, is a fine **Idgah**, with round towers at the ends in the heavy Pathan style, which beyond all doubt is that at which Timur pitched his camp subsequent to the battle of Delhi. What he writes

[1] It was the visit of Timur's ladies to this, and the insults offered to them, which led ultimately to the massacre at Old Delhi by Timur's troops.

in his Memoirs as to this is as follows, referring to the day after Sultan Mahmud and Mallu Khan had fled :—

"I mounted my horse" (at Hauz Khas) "and rode towards the gate of the maidan" (the gate of Siri or Jehanpanah, opening on to the Maidan, or plain, where the battle had taken place). "I alighted at the Idgah, a lofty and extensive building, and I gave orders for my quarters to be moved there, and for my throne to be set up in the Idgah."

It was here that the Sultan received the submission of the people of Delhi, now deserted by their leaders.

A mile away to the right of the road at the south corner of a line of trees is seen the pale dome of the tomb of the Emperor Firoz Shah, situated at the south-east angle of the **Hauz Khas**, or Hauz Alai, of Ala-ud-din, where Timur first rested and encamped after the battle, and received the congratulations of his Amirs on the victory gained. Of Hauz Khas he writes :—

"This is a reservoir which was constructed by the Emperor Firoz Shah, and is faced all round with cement. Each side of the reservoir is more than a bow-shot long, and there are buildings round it."

The tank is extremely picturesque when viewed from below, although it no longer contains any water. There was once a pavilion in the middle of it, as in the Hauz-i-Shamsi at Mahrauli (p. 284). Along the east side and the east end of the south side are the ruins of a number of galleries and steps in the wall of the tank, and above these rise some fine buildings, the domed tomb of the king (died 1389 A.D.) being the finest of all. The exterior of the tomb is plain, but the interior, of which the sides measure 28 feet, is fine, and a certain amount of the coloured decoration of the dome still remains. The three marble tombs are believed to mark the resting-places of the king, of his son Nasr-ud-din Tughlak Shah, and of a grandson. The tomb was restored by Sikandar Shah Lodi, and was specially repaired by the Punjab Government some years ago. Several of the open stone canopies over graves near the tomb are extremely picturesque.

At the ninth milestone from Delhi the road passes through the defences of **Jehanpanah,** which connected the citadel of Siri, built by Ala-ud-din Khan with the original Delhi round the Kutab. This will be clear from the following extracts from Ibn Batuta, who was at Delhi seventy years before Timur, and from Timur's own Memoirs. The former writes :—

Delhi is a city of great extent, and possesses a numerous population. It consists at present of four neighbouring and contiguous cities.

1. Delhi, properly so called, is the old city built by the idolaters, which was conquered in the year 584 H.

2. Siri, also called Dar-ul-Khilafat, or Seat of the Khilafat.

3. Tughlakabad, so called from the name of its founder, the Sultan Tughlak.

4. Jahan-panah, Refuge of the World, specially designed for the residence of the reigning Sultan of India, Muhammad Shah. He built it, and it was his intention to connect all these four cities together by one and the same wall. He raised a portion of it, but abandoned its completion in consequence of the enormous expense its erection would have entailed.

The wall which surrounds Delhi has no equal. It is eleven cubits thick. Chambers[1] are constructed in it which are occupied by the night watch, and the persons charged with the care of the gates. In some of these chambers there are stores of provisions, and

[1] Compare this description with the walls of Tughlakabad (p. 288).

magazines of munitions of war, and in others are kept mangonels and *ra'adas* ("thunder"—machines employed in sieges). Grain keeps in these chambers without change of the least deterioration. I saw some rice taken out of one of these magazines; it was black in colour, but good to the taste. I also saw some millet taken out. All these provisions had been stored by Sultan Balban ninety years before. Horse and foot can pass inside this wall from one end of the city to the other. Windows to give light have been opened in it on the inside towards the city. The lower part of the wall is built of stone, the upper part of brick. The bastions are numerous and closely placed. The city of Delhi has twenty-eight gates. That of Badaun is the principal.

The chief Kazi of Hind and Sind, Kamal-ud-din Muhammad, son of Burhan-ud-din of Ghazni, *Sadr-i Jahan*, informed me how the city of Delhi was conquered from the infidels in 584 (1188 A.D.). I read the same date inscribed upon the *mihrab* of the great mosque of the city. The same person also informed me that Delhi was taken by the Amir Kutab-ud-din Aibak, who was entitled *Sipah-salar*, meaning General of the armies. He was one of the generals of the venerated Shahab-ud-din Muhammad, son of Sam the Ghorian, king of Ghazni and Khurasan.

Timur's description which follows will be found to agree with this, and both are completely confirmed by the ruins and lines of defences on the ground, as General Cunningham has shown. They are indicated upon the map of the country round Delhi, published with this work.

"When my mind was no longer occupied with the destruction of the people of Delhi, I took a ride round the cities. **Siri** is a round city (*shahr*). Its buildings are lofty. They are surrounded by fortifications (*kala*), built of stone and brick, and they are very strong.

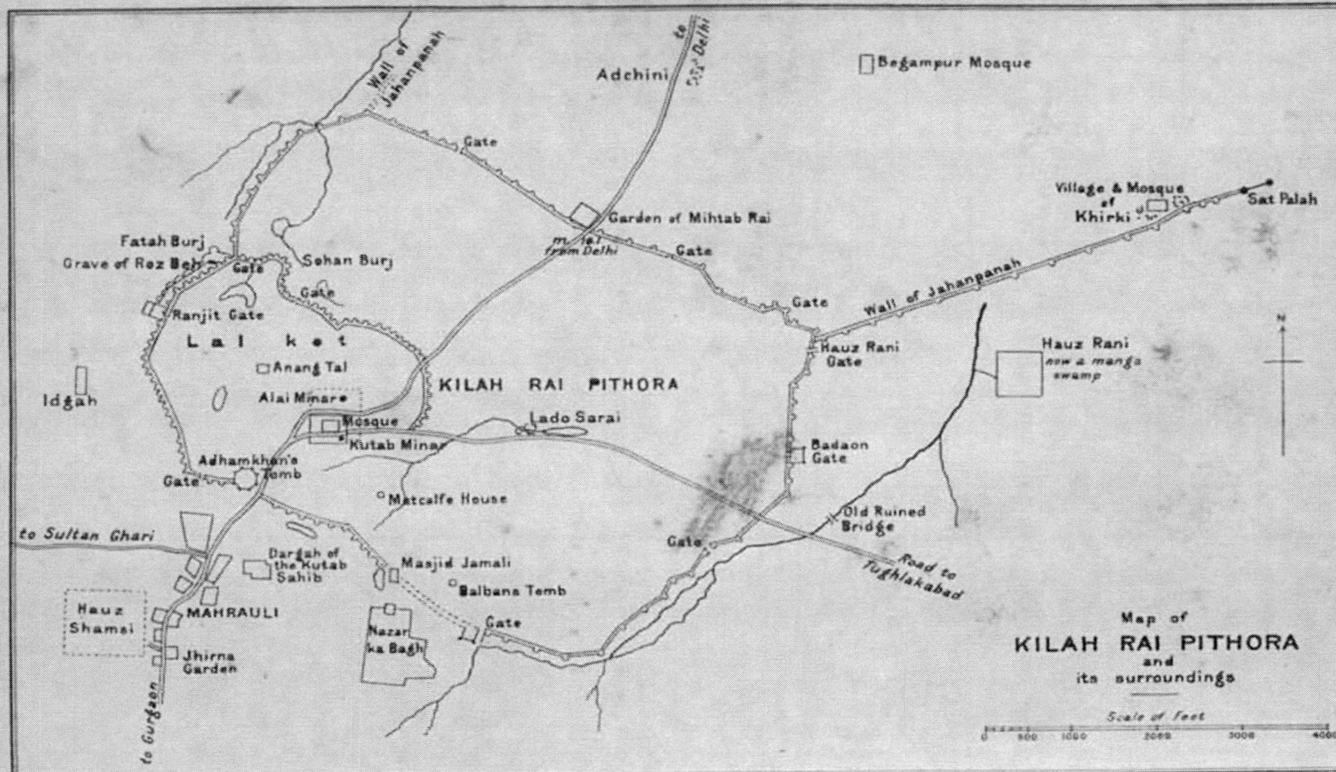
Map of
KILAH RAI PITHORA
and
its surroundings
Scale of Feet
0 500 1000 2000 3000 4000
N
KILAH RAI PITHORA
Lal kot
Wall of Jahanpanah
Gate
Adchini
to Delhi
Begampur Mosque
Village & Mosque of Khirki
Sat Palah
Garden of Mihtab Rai
from Delhi
Fatah Burj
Grave of Rez Beh
Sohan Burj
Ranjit Gate
Anang Tal
Alai Minare
Idgah
Mosque
Kutab Minar
Lado Sarai
Hauz Rani Gate
Hauz Rani
now a mango swamp
Badaon Gate
Old Ruined Bridge
Road to Tughlakabad
Adhamkhan's Tomb
Metcalfe House
to Sultan Ghari
Dargah of the Kutab Sahib
Masjid Jamali
Balbans Tomb
Hauz Shamsi
MAHRAULI
Nazar ka Bagh
Jhirna Garden
to Gurgaon

Old Delhi also has a similar strong fort, but it is larger than that of Siri. From the fort of Siri to that of Old Delhi, which is a considerable distance, there runs a strong wall, built of stone and cement. The part called **Jahanpanah** is situated in the midst of the inhabited city. The fortifications of the three cities have thirty gates. Jahan-panah has thirteen gates, Siri has seven gates. The fortifications of Old Delhi have ten gates, some opening to the exterior and some towards the interior of the city. When I was tired of examining the city I went into the Masjid-i jami,[1] where a congregation was assembled of *saiyids*, lawyers, *shaikhs*, and other of the principal Musalmans, with the inhabitants of their parts of the city, to whom they had been a protection and defence. I called them to my presence, consoled them, treated them with every respect, and bestowed upon them many presents and honours. I appointed an officer to protect their quarter of the city, and guard them against annoyance. Then I remounted and returned to my quarters."

Inside the Jahanpanah defences, which are well seen some 600 yards west of the road, a fine but partly ruined mosque stands up high on the left hand in the village of Kala Sarai; and after proceeding through Adchini with several old buildings and cemeteries (one on the right with the grave of the mother of Shekh Nizam-ud-din-Aulia), the north walls of the Fort of Rai Pithora are reached at a fine garden just beyond the tenth milestone. From the top of the ascent to the higher level inside these are seen the massive southern defences of the citadel of this city,

[1] It does not appear this was the Masjid-i-jama of Old Delhi, *i.e.* the Kutab mosque, or some Mosque in Siri or Jahanpanah, which may have been the Begampur mosque.

the Lal Kot on the right, and on the left the red front of the Jamali Mosque and the huge ruin of the tomb of Sultan Balban to the east of it (p. 278). The road-side trees hide the view of the Kutab Minar. Just half a mile from the outer line of defences the east wall of the citadel is reached, and immediately beyond it the Kutab enclosure. The tomb of Adham Khan, 200 yards beyond this enclosure stands on the south wall of the citadel, and the road ascends to this and then falls to the level of the Mahrauli bazar, built outside the southern line of the defences. It is another curious coincidence that the oldest Hindu citadel at Delhi should have been called the Lal Kot, and the latest Muhammadan fortress, the Lal Kila. Every one who can, should walk along the outside of the west wall of the Lal Kot from Adham Khan's tomb to the picturesque grave of the martyr-warrior Baba Roz Beh in the ditch, and should return through the Fort past the tank of Anang Pal II. by the Ranjit Gate, or, better, by the north-west corner of the wall and the Fatah (Victory) Bastion, from which there is a fine view to the north.

It will be borne in mind that at the Kutab we are in the midst of the memorials of the Muhammadan conquest, not mere invasion, of India, and that these date from 1191 A.D., the year of that conquest, to 1315 A.D., when the Sultan Ala-ud-din Khilji died. Like the Láts of Asoka in the Delhi of Firoz Shah, the iron pillar in the centre of the Kutab Mosque is a transferred memorial of an earlier age, probably the fifth or sixth century A.D., and the carved pillars in the corridor of the original mosque may be of

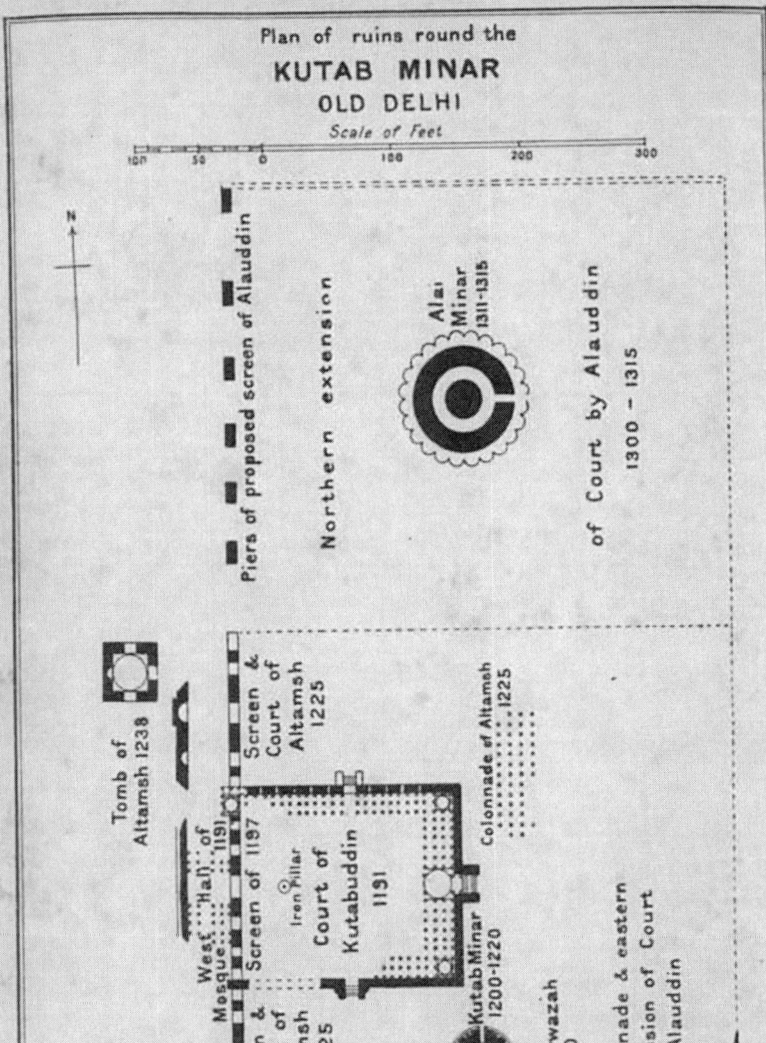

Plan of ruins round the
KUTAB MINAR
OLD DELHI

[To face p. 257.

any date between fifty and two hundred years before 1200 A.D.

The mosque and the buildings round it (of which the disposition will be understood from the annexed plan, taken by kind permission of Messrs Murray from Mr Fergusson's "Eastern Architecture," and completed with various details) are the work of three great kings, who, with the Emperors Balban and Firoz Shah exhaust the rulers of that class previous to the Moghal conquest of India; first, Kutab-ud-din-Aibak (1206 – 1211), who built the innermost court of the mosque, with its corridors and west end, in 1191, and added the screen of arches in front of the west end of the court six years later; secondly, Shams-ud-din Altamsh (1211-1236), who completed the Kutab Minar commenced by his predecessor, added the outer arches of the screen north and south of these of Kutab-ud-din, and built a fresh courtyard, with a cloister of pillars specially prepared for it, extending along the south side as far east as the Kutab Minar, and on the east side still standing opposite the north end of the front of Kutab-ud-din's Mosque, and whose tomb is situated outside the north-west corner of the mosque as enlarged by him; and thirdly, Ala-ud-din Khilji (1295-1315 A.D.) who built the beautiful Alai Darwazah almost under the Kutab Minar, continued the south corridor of Altamsh past this gate, very much further east, and carried it north, so as to include his unfinished minar outside the north-east corner of the mosque as enlarged by Altamsh, made a further extension of the screen of arches to the north, and joined these two extensions along the north side. On the south side the enclosure terminates on the edge of a deep depression below the Alai Darwazah, so no extension of the arches was possible there. Ala-ud-din's tomb stands in the south wall of the enclosure behind the mosque, as first enlarged, and corresponds with that of Altamsh.

The **Mosque of Kutab-ud-din**, known as the **Kuwat-ul-Islam,** or "Might of Islam," is, roughly speaking, 150 feet to the front and back, and half as much again from side to side: the open court-yard in the centre of it is 108 feet by 142 feet. The gates on the east and north sides are still complete, and bear inscriptions relating to the foundation. The gate on the south side has disappeared, together with much of the west end and the whole of the western colonnade of the south wall. Though built entirely of Hindu, or rather Jain materials, every portion of the mosque was rebuilt by the conquerors: the opinions that the plinth of the court and the pillars behind the great screen of arches are *in situ* as erected by the Hindus, are equally erroneous. Originally the exterior of the walls was, no doubt, entirely covered by plaster, as the columns inside were, but this has all disappeared. The view through the east gate is very pleasing, and the view down the vista of columns on either side of the central dome of the east corridor is extremely beautiful. This corridor is practically complete, but only about three-quarters of the north corridor are so, and very little of the south corridor and its plainer columns now remains. The most beautiful

Cloister of Kutab Mosque.

[To face p. 259.

columns are in the north side of the east arcade, and the carving of flower vases, with foliage falling from them, conventional leopards' heads with garlands, ropes with tassels, bells on chains, and many floral designs, deserve to be carefully examined. On the fifth pillar to the north from the centre in the second row from the wall is a relief of a cow and a calf, and in the same line, fifth, on the edge of the courtyard, is, perhaps, the most beautiful of all the pillars. Many half-effaced Jain figures,[1] and not a few undamaged ones, which could be completely concealed by the plaster, will be noticed on the columns.

The galleries in the corner of the arcade should be visited both for the sake of the beautiful ceilings of the domes and the carved scenes with elephants and horses on the beams across the corner of the side compartments of the roof; the numbering on the various stones of the pillars under the south gallery is interesting. The carved scene on the stone above the second window from the front on the outer side of the north wall should also be noticed. It represents, in a mediæval way, the birth of Krishna, the child and its nurse being shown several times over in the same scene. The two scenes are divided by a half open door, and at the end of that towards

[1] Those who have visited the beautiful little Kora Mosque (Χώρα τῶν Ζώντων—it is known to the Turks as Kahriyah Jamisi) in Constantinople, in order to see the very interesting Byzantine mosaics, which are now no longer hidden by whitewash and plaster, will remember that the heads and faces of angel figures on the capitals of the columns in the narthex, and by the baptistery there, have been broken and disfigured in the same way as the heads in the cloister of the Kutab.

the west are represented a cow and a calf, which produces a strong resemblance to the Sacred Manger scene.

The floor of the courtyard is slightly higher than that of the arcades, and drains are cut through the latter to the outside. The iron pillar stands in the centre of the court, as measured from north to south, rather more than half-way up the west half of it; besides the pillar there are several graves in the area, and it is tempting to believe that Kutab-ud-din-Aibak himself may have been buried here after his death from a polo accident at Lahore, though tradition says otherwise.

The great screen of arches which form the most striking feature of the mosque, like that at Ajmir, bears no proportion to the height of the arcades any more than the Kutab Minar does, but this is not really noticeable. It is not necessary to add anything to Mr Fergusson's description of the screen and its beauties:—

"The glory of the mosque is not in these Hindu remains, but in the great range of arches on the western side, extending north and south for about 385 feet, and consisting of three greater and eight smaller arches; the central one 22 feet wide and 53 feet high; the larger side-arches 24 feet 4 inches, and about the same height as the central arch; the smaller arches, which are unfortunately much ruined, are about half these dimensions. Behind this, at the distance of 32 feet, are the foundations of another wall; but only intended, apparently, to be carried as high as the roof of the Hindu pillars it encloses. It seems probable that the Hindu pillars between the two screens were the only part proposed to be

Screen of Arches on west side of the Kutab Mosque. [*To face p.* 260.

roofed, since some of them are built into the back part of the great arches, and all above them is quite plain and smooth, without the least trace of any intention to construct a vault or roof of any sort. . . ."

The arches, built by Hindu architects, are carried up in horizontal courses as far as possible, and are then closed by long slabs.

"The same architects," Mr Fergusson continues, "were employed by their masters to ornament the faces of these arches; and this they did by copying and repeating the ornaments on the pillars and friezes on the opposite sides of the courts, covering the whole with a lace-work of intricate and delicate carving, such as no other mosque, except that at Ajmir, ever received before or since, and which . . . is, without exception, the most exquisite specimen of its class known to exist anywhere."

The details of the ornamentation deserve prolonged examination by the aid of field-glasses. The bands of text in the Tughra character are particularly fine, and the graceful effect of them is much enhanced by the tendril pattern with flowers and bud, which is carried up through the lettering. A similar aid in a very different style of decoration is noticeable in the beautiful bands of texts of encaustic tiles upon a ground of sprays and leaves on the lovely Shahzindah tombs in Samarkand.

The difference in the decoration of the arches of Kutab-ud-din and Altamsh is considerable in detail, but this is not noticeable at a distance. The stone used in the former was of a much paler colour, and the ornamentation of the later arches does not seem to rise so spontaneously or give so aspiring an effect to the facade, a difference which is no doubt accentuated by the panels of diaper work between them.

Of the pillars which carried the roof of the hall of the mosque in front of which the great screen was placed, two groups of twelve and ten alone remain. On one of the columns of the southern group is an inscription with the name of a Mutawali, or Guardian, which appears again beyond the first rounded shaft to the west of the door of the Kutab Minar, thus showing the two structures were of much the same date.

The additions made by the Sultan Altamsh to the original work of Kutab-ud-din, more than doubled the area enclosed by the mosque, and the extensions of Ala-ud-din would again have increased the dimensions to more than twofold, but it seems probable that, like the Alai Minar, these were never wholly completed, in spite of the high-flown admiration of them thus expressed by Amir Khusrau in his "Tarikh-i-Alai":—

"He [the Emperor] determined upon adding to and completing the Masjid-i-Jama of Shamsuddin, by building beyond the three old gates and courts a fourth with lofty pillars . . . and upon the surface of the stones he engraved verses of the Koran in such a manner as could not be done even in wax, ascending so high that you would think the Koran was going up to heaven, and again descending in another line so low, you would think it was coming down from heaven. He then resolved to make a pair to the lofty minar of the Jama Masjid, which minar was then the sole (unique) one of the time, and to raise it so high that it could not be exceeded. He first directed that the area of the square before the masjid should be increased, that there might be ample room for the followers of Islam. He ordered the circumference of the new minar to be made double that of the old one, and that it should be made higher in the same proportion, and he directed that a new casing and cupola should be added to the old one."

The core of the piers of the arches in the further extension of the screen to the north designed by Ala-ud-din still stands, as do the ruins of the gates to the enlarged courtyard on this side; these gates would no doubt have been somewhat similar to the Alai Darwazah. In the middle of this extension to the north would have risen the Alai minaret, of which the stupendous base stands most probably just as the workmen left it on the death of its projector, nearly 600 years ago. It is fortunate, no doubt, that it was never finished, as it would have completely overshadowed and destroyed the effect of the original Kutab Minar, situated at the south-east angle of the original court of the mosque.

Writing of the mosque as a whole, Amir Khusrau says:—

"Masjid-i-o jámá'i feiz-i-Allah;
Zamzama-i-Khutba-i-o tába máh."
("The mosque of it is the depository of the grace of God;
The music of the prayer of it reaches to the sky [moon].")

Ibn Batuta wrote of it: "Its mosque is very large, and in beauty and extent has no equal. Before the taking of Delhi it had been a Hindu temple. In its court there is a pillar which they say is composed of stones from seven quarries."

The Hindus, it may be noted, still sometimes speak of the mosque as the Thakurdawara and Chausath Khambhe, or the Sixty-Pillared. The mosque was repaired by Firoz Shah Tughlak, as was the Kutab Minar—was the scene of a grim massacre by Timur's soldiery,—and was immensely admired by that Sultan, who carried off workmen to construct a similar one in Samarkand, which, however, was never built. A bloody slaughter had already taken place inside the mosque in the reign of Altamsh, when a body of Karmatian heretics, who had taken refuge there, were exterminated by volleys of stones from the roof of the arcades and mailed horsemen riding up the steps into the enclosure.

The **Iron Pillar** in the court of the mosque is one of the most interesting memorials of Hindu supremacy in all India, and dates probably from the sixth century of our era. The inscription upon which this conjecture is based consists of six lines of neat letters: the three couplets merely record the erection of the pillar to Vishnu, by one Chandra Raja. There are also brief inscriptions by the Tuar Anangpal II. and a Chauhan Raja, the former commemorating a re-peopling of Delhi by the prince named in 1052 A.D. The pillar is 23 feet 8 inches high, and rests on a sort of gridiron arrangement under the platform from which it rises. It was long believed, on the authority of those who had made actual excavations, that it extended far below the surface of the ground, whereas the base is only 14 inches deep. The capital was no doubt once surmounted by a Garuda, the eagle vehicle of Vishnu, like the columns in front of the great temples of Jaggarnath at Puri. The Hindu legend connected with the pillar is that it rested on the head

The Iron Pillar and Kutab Minar.

[To face p. 264.

of the great World Serpent, and that a Tuar prince having unadvisedly moved it to see if this was really the case, the curse fell upon him that his kingdom too should be removed.

There is no good reason for doubting that Kutab-ud-din-Aibak began the basement storey of the **Kutab Minar**—the name of the minaret in common parlance is much more probably derived from him than from the saint known as the Kutab Sahib,—any more than there is for doubting that it is entirely of Muhammadan origin, and was primarily intended to serve as a minaret to the mosque of that Sultan. The last is clear, not only from almost contemporary record, but also from the text from the Koran, cap. 62—The Assembly—on the second storey "Oh true believers, when ye are called to prayer on the day of Assembly, listen to the commemoration of God and leave merchandising. . . . The reward of God is better than any sport or merchandise, and God is the best provider."

The lowest storey contains an inscription bearing the name of the first King of Delhi, and two others containing the name of his master, Muhammad-bin-Sam, or Muhammad Ghori; the second and third and fourth storeys bear bands of inscription with the name of Altamsh; and the fifth storey one relating to a restoration in 1368 A.D. by Firoz Shah, who, no doubt, entirely rebuilt the two topmost storeys of their original materials. On the entrance door to the Minar, which is modern, as is the railing of the first gallery, is an inscription of the year 1503 A.D., recording a restoration by Sikandar Shah Lodi, which probably preserved the Minar till 300 years later, when it was thoroughly repaired by the British Government, only just in time apparently, to judge from Major Thorn's narrative of the events of 1803. The value of this restoration must not be lost sight of in the ridicule which has overtaken the officer in charge of the work, a certain Captain Smith, R.E., in connection with the cupola designed by him for the summit, and which still stands in the Kutab grounds. (Colonel Sleeman wrote, not unjustly, of this: "If Captain Smith's storey was anything like the original, the lightning did well to remove it!") One would have been disposed to believe that the original topmost storey was a simple pavilion borne by four, or possibly eight, arches—very likely flat Hindu arches—but this is not borne out by the drawings of the column in Franklin's book and by Daniell, though Ensign Jas. Blunt, who visited Delhi in 1794, says it was "crowned by a majestic cupola of red granite." It would add greatly to the effect of the column if a suitable cupola could be placed upon it.

The height of the Kutab Minar is 238 feet, and of the first gallery 95 feet. The lowest storey has twenty-four flutings alternately round and angular, the second has only rounded flutings, and the third only angular. The line of each fluting is carried up unbroken through each storey, and this adds greatly to the effect of the tower. The parapet of the first gallery appears to have been of a simple crenellated battlement form; the arrow-head pattern in the upper galleries is said to exist also in the Kalaun Mosque of Cairo. The outline of the column

Lowest Band of Ornament, Kutab Minar.

[To face p. 267.

is not at first very pleasing to eyes accustomed to Gothic towers and spires, and from a distant point of view seems perhaps less graceful than when seen from nearer. But of the beauty of the warm colour of the stone, of the splendid bands of texts and ornamentation which encircle it, and of the work on the under sides of the galleries, there can be no question. The lower bands [1] of inscription can be well seen from the top of the south-east corner of the Kuwat-ul-Islam Mosque and the Alai Gate; while charming views of the column as a whole are obtained in framings of the centre arch of the mosque screen and of the last of Altamsh's arches to the south, and other beautiful glimpses from every side will be enjoyed by those who have time to wander round the outskirts of the general enclosure.

For the rest, it is again sufficient to quote what Mr Fergusson writes in this connection:

"It is probably not too much to assert that the Kutab Minar is the most beautiful example of its class known to exist anywhere.[2] The rival which will occur at once to most people is the Campanile at Florence, built by Giotti. That is, it is true, 30 feet taller, but it is crushed by the mass of the Cathedral alongside; and beautiful though it is, it wants that poetry of design

[1] The six bands of inscription in the basement storey contain: first, the designation and title of Kutab-ud-din; second, the titles and praise of Muhammad-bin-Sam; third, a verse from chapter 59 of the Koran; fourth, another recital, as in the second band; fifth, the ninety-seven Arabic names of the Almighty; and sixth, a verse from the Koran, chapter 2. The verse regarding the call to prayer is on the second storey.

[2] Bishop Heber too recorded that the Kutab Minar was the finest tower he had ever seen.

and exquisite finish of detail which marks every moulding of the Minar."

It will interest many to note the plumb line of the tower on a stone in the south side of its basement.

The number of steps to the top of the Kutab is 379. The view from there is very striking, but is practically as extensive from the first gallery. At the foot of the column are seen spread out the mosque and all the buildings which surround it. A little further off lie the encircling lines of the defences of Lal Kot, and Kila Rai Pithora rising highest to the west, and bounded there by the dark wall of the heavy Idgah of Old Delhi. Across the plain north of Rai Pithora's fort may be traced the Jahanpanah embankments, running towards the ruined walls of Siri, which do not, however, show up from here ; the massive dark block of the Begampur Mosque, however, indicates their position. Above Jahanpanah, and to the north-west rises the depressed pale dome of the tomb of the Emperor Firoz Shah in Hauz Khas, and beyond it the bright pointed dome of Safdar Jang's tomb, and almost in a line with it the still brighter domes of the Jama Masjid of Delhi. To the east of Safdar Jang appear the long wall defences of the Purana Kila, with the low white roof of Nizam-ud-din, and the high marble dome of the Emperor Humayun's tomb below them. South of these again is the popular Kalka temple on the rising ground, and below this, and nearly due east of the Kutab, are the fortresses of Tughlakabad and Adilabad, with the low white dome of Tughlak Shah's tomb between them. Nearer and to the north

Interior of Tomb of the Emperor Altamsh.

[To face p. 269

of the road to Tughlakabad are the large groves of trees which mark the Hauz Rani and Khirki, while south of the road and close to the Kutab are the Jamáli Mosque and the lofty ruins of the tomb of the Sultan Balban, and under it on the south the Dargah of the Kutab Sahib, and the houses of Mahrauli half hidden in trees.

The **Tomb of the Sultan Shams-ud-din Altamsh,** behind the north-west corner of the mosque, is a very beautiful building of red sandstone, measuring forty-four feet square on the outside, and thirty feet square in the inside. The interior is profusely decorated with carving, only the lower portions of the wall in the two west angles, and to the right and left of the east door remaining uncarved. These were covered with painting, a fragment of which—possibly a restored portion—may still be seen on the south wall; there are also traces of colour on the beautiful mihrab, or prayer niche, of the west wall. The grave itself is a handsome structure of unusual height and size, with a band of text round the plinth, which is also unusual. That the chamber was intended to be roofed is clear from the remains of the lowest course of a dome on the top of the south wall; but if it was built for her father by Sultan Raziya, as seems probable, it is quite possible that the dome was never completed. Mr Fergusson writes of it:—

Though small, it is one of the richest examples of Hindu art applied to Muhammadan purposes that Old Delhi affords, and is extremely beautiful, though the builders still display a certain degree of ineptness in fitting the details to their new purposes. The effect at present is injured by the want of a roof, which, judging from appearance, was never completed, if ever commenced. In addition to the beauty of its details it is interesting as being the oldest tomb known to exist in India.

The **Alai Darwazah** is not only the most beautiful structure at the Kutab Minar, but is one of the most beautiful specimens of external polychromatic decoration not merely in India, but in the whole world, while the carving of the interior may challenge comparison with any work of the kind. Both exterior and interior merit detailed and leisurely examination.

The effect of the graceful pointed arches in the three external sides of the gate, and in the corner recesses, is extremely pleasing, and the view from the exterior through the southern archway to the round-headed arch of the north side, and the courtyard beyond, is very striking. The decoration of the north arch is curious and unique. The effect of the exterior suffers, from a distant point of view, from the absence of a parapet above the walls; this was unfortunately removed by Captain Smith, as it was greatly ruined. The gate was finished five years before the emperor died, and is specially mentioned by the chronicler of his reign. Of it Mr Fergusson writes:—

It is about a century more modern than the other buildings of the place, and displays the Pathan style at its period of greatest perfection, when the Hindu masons had learned to fit their exquisite style of decoration to the forms of their foreign masters. Its walls are decorated internally, with a diaper pattern of unrivalled excellence, and the mode in which the square is changed into an octagon

Alai Gate—South Side.

[*To face p.* 270.

is more simply elegant and appropriate than any other example I am acquainted with in India. The pendentives accord perfectly with the pointed openings in the four other faces,[1] and are in every respect appropriately constructive. True, there are defects. For instance, they are rather too plain for the elaborate diapering which covers the whole of the lower part of the building, both internally and externally; but ornament might easily have been added, and their plainness accords with the simplicity of the dome, which is indeed by no means worthy of the substructure. Not being pierced with windows, it seems as if the architect assumed that its plainness would not be detected in the gloom that in consequence prevails.

This building, though small—it is only fifty-six feet square externally, and with an internal apartment only thirty-four feet six inches in plan—marks the culminating point of the Pathan style in Delhi. Nothing so complete had been done before,[2] nothing so ornate was attempted by them afterwards. In the provinces wonderful buildings were erected between this period and the Moghal conquest, but in the capital their edifices[3] were more marked by solemn gloom and nakedness than by ornamentation or any of the higher graces of architectural art. Externally, it is a good deal damaged, but its effect is still equal to that of any building of its class in India.

[1] As a matter of fact, the opening on the north side is rounded, and not pointed.

[2] It was no doubt with reference to this and the decoration of the mosque screens and the Kutab Minar that Bishop Heber wrote: "These Pathans built like giants and finished their work like jewellers," though the words occur in immediate connection with the tomb of Adham Khan.

[3] This dictum of Mr Fergusson applies, no doubt, correctly to the buildings of the later severe Pathan style, but hardly, for instance, to the tomb of Tughlak Shah (p. 289), or to those of Mubarik Shah and Sikandar Khan Lodi, or the gateway of the Khairpur Mosque (pp. 244 and 245).

On the east side of the Alai Gate is the sandstone and marble tomb of **Imam Zamin**, one Muhammad Ali, who died in 1539 A.D., and was probably connected with the Kuwat-ul-Islam Mosque. The decoration of this is decidedly effective; that on the dripstone is unusual. It makes an extremely pretty picture, as seen from the south side, in combination with the Alai Darwazah and the trees between the two.

The last building of the group directly connected with the Kutab Mosque and Minar is the **Tomb of Ala-ud-din.** There is no reasonable doubt that this was in the centre of the three ruined rooms which form the south side of the enclosure behind the south end of the great screen of arches of the mosque. The chamber corresponds with the tomb of Altamsh, but is larger, being fifty feet by thirty-two feet. The rooms at either side of this were also probably sepulchral chambers, while those in the wings to the front of it formed part of the college attached to the tomb. Behind the large rooms and part of the west wall is a long gallery which had its own entrance from the south; and in the south-east corner outside are the ruins of a mosque, from which a very fine view of the Kutab Minar and Alai Darwazah is obtained. It is fitting that the grave of this parricide should survive only as a lonely ruin, for the most part "unknown and unnoticed." It was repaired by Firoz Shah, like so many other buildings, and as not a few of these were closely connected with the Kutab, the interesting record of his labours of love may be inserted here.

Among the gifts which God bestowed upon me, His humble servant, was a desire to erect public buildings. So I built many mosques and colleges and monasteries, that the learned and the elders, the devout and the holy, might worship God in these edifices, and aid the kind builder with their prayers. The digging of canals, the planting of trees, and the endowing of buildings with lands are in accordance with the directions of the Law. The learned doctors of the Law of Islam have many troubles; of this there is no doubt. I settled allowances upon them in proportion to their necessary expenses, so that they might regularly receive the income. The details of this are fully set forth in the *Wakf-Nama* (Record of Charitable Assignments).

Again, by the guidance of God, I was led to repair and rebuild the edifices and structures of former kings and ancient nobles, which had fallen into decay from lapse of time; giving the restoration of these buildings the priority over my own building works. The **Masjid-i-Jami** of Old Delhi (*i.e.* the Kuwat-ul-Islam Mosque) which was built by Sultan Mu'izz-ud-din-Sam, had fallen into decay from old age, and needed repair and restoration. I so repaired it that it was quite renovated.

The western wall of the tomb of Sultan Mu'izz-ud-din-Sam,[1] and the planks of the door, had become old and rotten. I restored this, and, in the place of the balcony, I furnished it with doors, arches, and ornaments of sandal-wood.

The **Minara** of Sultan Mu'izz-ud-din-Sam (*i.e.* the Kutab Minar) had been struck by lightning. I repaired it, and raised it higher than it was before.

The **Hauz-i-Shamsi**, or tank of Altamsh (p. 284) had been deprived of water by some graceless men,

[1] It is not easy to understand this reference to the tomb of Muizz-ud-din-Sam or Shahab-ud-din Ghori who was buried at Ghazni. Abul Fazl also refers to his grave in Old Delhi, but perhaps he merely followed Firoz Shah's record in doing so.

who stopped up the channels of supply. I punished these incorrigible men severely, and re-opened the closed channels.

The **Hauz-i'Alai**, or tank of 'Ala-ud-din (p. 252) had no water in it, and was filled up. People carried on cultivation in it, and had dug wells, of which they sold the water. After a generation had passed I cleaned it out, so that this great tank might again be filled from year to year.

The **Madrasa** (college) of Sultan Shams-ud-din Altamsh had been destroyed. I rebuilt it, and furnished it with sandal-wood doors. The columns of the tomb, which had fallen down, I restored better than they had been before. When the tomb was built its court,[1] had not been made curved (? with arched arcades) but I now made it so. I enlarged the hewn-stone staircase of the dome, and I re-erected the fallen piers of the four towers.

Tomb of Sultan Mu'izzud-ud-din, son of Sultan Shams-ud-din, which is situated in **Malikpur**. This had fallen into such ruin that the sepulchres were undistinguishable. I re-erected the dome, the terrace, and the enclosure wall.

Tomb of Sultan Rukn-ud-din, son of Shams-ud-din, in Malikpur. I repaired the enclosure wall, built a new dome, and erected a monastery (*Khangah*), (p. 285).

Tomb of Sultan Jalal-ud-din (Khilji — it has disappeared.) This I repaired, and I supplied it with new doors.

Tomb of Sultan Ala-ud-din. I repaired this, and furnished it with sandal-wood doors. I repaired the wall of the *abdarkhana*, and the west wall of the

[1] This is not intelligible with reference to the existing tomb of this Emperor. It might be held to be applicable to the mausoleum of Sultan Ghari (p. 284), which has columns in the grave chamber, corner towers to the enclosure, and steps up to the domed gate leading to this, and this mausoleum has all the appearance of having been restored in the middle Pathan style of the severer type.

mosque, which is within the college, and I also made good the tessellated pavement.

Tomb of Sultan Kutab-ud-din and the (other) sons of Sultan Ala-ud-din, viz., Khizr Khan, Shadi Khan, Farid Khan, Sultan Shahab-ud-din, Sikandar Khan, Muhammad Khan, Usman Khan, and his grandsons, and the sons of his grandsons. The tombs of these I repaired and renovated. (All these have disappeared.)

I also repaired the doors of the dome, and the lattice-work of the tomb of **Shekh-ul-Islam Nizam-ul-hak-wa-ud-din**, which were made of sandal-wood. I hung up the golden chandeliers with chains of gold in the four recesses of the dome, and I built a meeting-room, for before this there was none.

Tomb of Malik Taj-ul-Mulk Káfur, the great *wazir* of Sultan Ala-ud-din. He was a most wise and intelligent minister, and acquired many countries, on which the horses of former sovereigns had never placed their hoofs, and he caused the *Khutba* of Sultan Ala-ud-din to be repeated there. He had 52,000 horsemen. His grave had been levelled with the ground, and his tomb laid low. I caused his tomb to be entirely renewed, for he was a devoted and faithful subject.[1]

The **Dar-ul-aman**, or House of Refuge.—This is the bed and resting-place of great men (*i.e.* the Sultan Balban and his son, the Khan-i-Shahid (p. 278). I had new sandal-wood doors made for it, and over the tombs of these distinguished men I had curtains and hangings suspended.

The expense of repairing and renewing these tombs and colleges was provided from their ancient endowments. In those cases where no income had been settled on these foundations in former times for

[1] It would seem certain from this that the tales of Muhammadan annalists to the effect that Malik Kafar poisoned his master Ala-ud-din, and set himself up as king and was murdered, cannot be true. It is incredible that Firoz Shah could have written thus of him if they were. The grave has disappeared again.

providing carpets, lights, and furniture for the use of travellers and pilgrims in the least of these places, I had villages assigned to them, the revenues of which would suffice for their expenditure in perpetuity.

Jahan-panah.—This foundation of the late Sultan Muhammad Shah, my kind patron, by whose bounty I was reared and educated, I restored.

All the fortifications which had been built by former sovereigns at Delhi I repaired.

For the benefit of travellers and pilgrims resorting to the tombs of illustrious kings and celebrated saints, and for providing the things necessary in these holy places, I confirmed and gave effect to the grants of villages, lands, and other endowments which had been conferred upon them in olden times. In those cases where no endowment or provision had been settled, I made an endowment, so that these establishments might for ever be secure of an income, to afford comfort to travellers and wayfarers, to holy men and learned men. May they remember those ancient benefactors and me in their prayers.

I was enabled by God's help to build a *Dăr-ush-shafa*, or Hospital, for the benefit of every one of high or low degree, who was suddenly attacked by illness and overcome by suffering. Physicians attend there to ascertain the disease, to look after the cure, to regulate the diet, and to administer medicine. The cost of the medicines and the food is defrayed from my endowments. All sick persons, residents and travellers, gentle and simple, bond and free, resort thither; their maladies are treated, and, under God's blessing, they are cured.

Under the guidance of the Almighty I arranged that the heirs of those persons who had been slain in the reign of my late lord and patron, Sultan Muhammad Shah, and those who had been deprived of a limb, nose, eye, hand, or foot, should be reconciled to the late Sultan and be appeased with gifts, so that they executed deeds declaring their satisfaction, duly attested by witnesses. These deeds were put into a chest, which was placed in the *Dar-ul-aman* (*i.e.* the tomb at Tughlakabad, not that of the Sultan Balban), at the head of the grave of the late Sultan, in the hope that God, in His great clemency, would show mercy to my late friend and patron, and make those persons feel reconciled to him.

It may be noted here that, like Timur, the Emperor Baber visited the principal buildings round Delhi after his victory at Panipat, whence he made three marches to Nizam-ud-din. "I circumambulated," he writes, "the tomb of Khwaja Kutab-ud-din, and visited the tomb and palaces of Gheias-ud-din Balban,[1] of Ala-ud-din Khilji and his minaret (the Kutab Minar), the Shamsi Tank, the Royal Tank (Hauz Alai) and the tombs and gardens of Sultan Bahlol and Sultan Sikandar; after which I returned to camp and went on board a boat where we drunk arak (!)" The next day the Emperor marched to Tughlakabad, and so on to Agra.

A number of interesting buildings surround the enclosure of the Kutab Minar, but probably few visitors will have time to examine them. The Jamáli Mosque, and for the sake of the memory of a great man, the ruined tomb of the Sultan Gheias-ud-din Balban near it, and the Dargah of the Kutab Sahib should, however, certainly be visited. The first two are reached by the road running south from the east side of the enclosure past a converted tomb known as Metcalfe House. This stands on the wall of the Lal Kot, and was the resting-place of one Muhammad

[1] It would seem probable that this was the tomb of Shams-ud-din Altamsh, and that the Emperor was misinformed or forgot. It seems hardly possible that if Balban's tomb was complete in 1526, it should now be the utter ruin that it is,

Kuli Khan, brother of Adham Khan, and therefore foster-brother of the Emperor Akbar (pp. 228 and 242), and must once have been brilliantly decorated with painting. **The Jamali Mosque,** which lies five hundred yards south of this, is a fine and pleasing structure of the date of 1528 A.D.: it forms an intermediate stage between the Moth-ki Masjid (p. 245) and that of Sher Shah in the Purana Kila (p. 228), and has been well restored by Government. The picturesque grave chamber of Jamali, Shekh Fazlullah, stands on the north side of the courtyard of the mosque. Rising high up amid ruins, 200 yards east of the two, are the massive walls which once carried the **tomb of the Sultan Balban,** who died in 1287 A.D. (p. 296). This was a square building, like the tomb of Altamsh and the Alai Darwazah, but was larger than either of these: on each side of it is a spacious room, which may have formed the Dar-ul-aman, or Haven of Refuge, established by this king. He was buried in that place — Ibn Batuta says he visited his grave in it—where his son Sher Khan, the Khan-i-Shahid, was interred only two years before him. This prince was slain at Lahore fighting against "Sámar, the bravest dog of all the dogs of Chengiz Khan," and the father never recovered from the loss of the son.

The Dargah of the Kutab Sahib is most conveniently approached from the west side, but can also be entered from the north. The high road from the Kutab Minar enclosure leads to it past the **Tomb of Adham Khan,** which, owing to its being placed on the wall of the Lal Kot citadel, is so conspicuous a feature in all distant views of the Kutab. The tomb, though of so late a date as 1566 A.D., is built entirely in the severe middle Pathan style, and the materials of it were quite possibly taken bodily from some Pathan tomb; the domed interior is very fine, and many beautiful views of the Kutab Minar may be enjoyed from the arcade round the exterior, in which the stone over the grave of Adham Khan has been placed. That of his mother, who is said to have died of grief forty days after the righteous execution of her son, has disappeared. Sympathy with either would be wholly wasted. The story of Adham Khan has been already told (p. 242), and no one who has visited the beautiful old fortress of Mandu and entered the charming pavilion of Rupmati, on the edge of the sheer side of the table-land which overlooks the broad Nerbuddah, will feel anything but satisfaction that such a fate as his was should have overtaken him. Adham Khan had wrested Mandu from the last of the Gujerat kings, and having obtained possession of his beautiful mistress, sought to compel her to yield to his desires, upon which, Lucretia-like, she killed herself. When the Emperor Akbar heard of this he recalled and disgraced Adham Khan, though he was his half-brother as well as his foster-brother, and demanded the surrender of two ladies of the family of the defeated king, whom also Adham Khan had captured. They were accordingly sent to the royal court, and there they were poisoned by Maham Anagah, the mother of Adham Khan, to prevent their making any complaint to the emperor.

A hundred yards to the south-east of this tomb is a fine baoli, known as the Gandak Baoli, in which old Jain columns have been used. Divers jump into this tank also. Three hundred yards further east of it, and among the ruins of many graveyards, is a still finer baoli of the date of 1516 A.D., known as the Rajon-ki-Báin, with a picturesque tomb and mosque on the west side of it. The details here show again how considerable a reversion to the Hindu style took place in the Lodi period.

The **Shrine of Khwaja Kutab-ud-din Bakhtiar Kaki,** known also as Kutab-ul-Aktúb, once the most famous at Delhi, now occupies only the second place, a circumstance doubtless due to the fact that the Dargah of Nizam-ud-din-Aulia was more conveniently situated for resort from the various cities which succeeded and superseded the original Delhi. This saint was born at Ush, not the once famous place in Sind, but a still older one in Farghana (Turkestan), and came to Delhi with the earliest Muhammadan conquerors — perhaps even before them—and died there in 1235 A.D., in the reign of the Sultan Altamsh. His title of Káki is derived from the tradition that during his fits of abstraction (chihal, or forty days—the traditional scene of the fasts of St John the Baptist, near Jericho, is still called Quarantina), he was fed by the saint known as the Khizr, with small cakes, termed kák.[1]

[1] Local pride in the saint converts this into a story that on one occasion these cakes were lowered from Heaven amid an assembly of holy men, at the Aulia Mosque (p. 284), but that only Kutab-ud-din was permitted to take them.

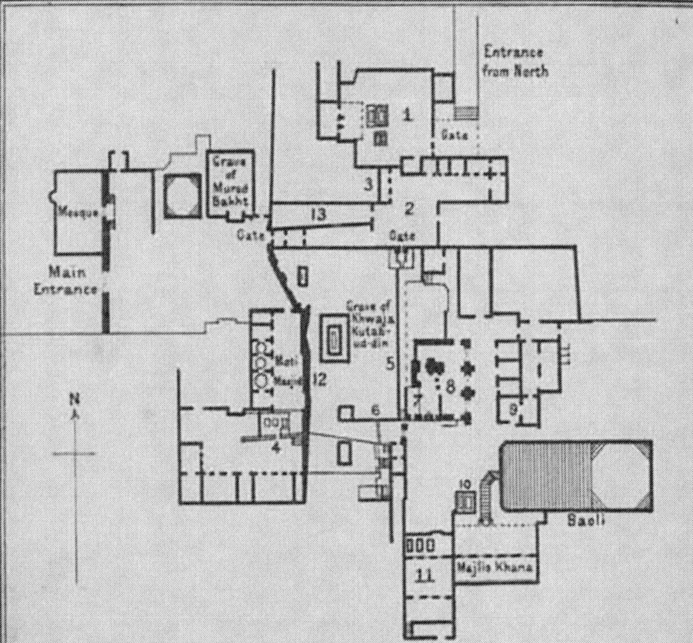

Plan of Dargah (shrine) of

KHWAJA KUTAB-UD-DIN BAKHTIAR KÁKI AT MAHRAULI

1. Grave enclosure of Nawabs of Jhajjar.
2. Main Courtyard
3. Mosque
4. Tombs of Akbar Shah II, Shah Alam & Bahadur Shah.
5. Pierced marble enclosure.
6. Gate
7. Grave of Maulana Fakhr-ud-din.
8. Mosque of Khwaja Sahib.
9. Grave of Dai Ji.
10. ,, ,, Zabita Khan.
11. ,, enclosure of Nawabs of Loharu.
12. Shrine wall with encaustic work.
13. Graveyard of Mohtamid Khan.

Scale of Feet

50 0 100 200

[*To face p.* 281.

In Ferishta's time these cakes were still cooked and given to the poor; now they are prepared and presented to wealthy visitors to the shrine in return for their offerings. They are small, thick, round cakes, made of flour, sugar, and sonf (anise seed).

Outside the Dargah, on the approach from the west, is a mansion and high-standing mosque belonging to the well-known physician Ahsanulla Khan, who was chief adviser of the last king of Delhi, Bahadur Shah, and whose evidence at the king's trial is extremely interesting. Beyond it is a fine gateway leading to the building, known as the Mahal Sarai, which was occupied as a summer residence by several of the latest kings of Delhi, a circumstance which no doubt led to their being buried at the shrine of the Mahrauli saint. Passing through the outer gate of the western enclosure of the Dargah, of which a plan accompanies, we enter a courtyard with a mosque and the grave of Murad Bakht, a lady of Shah Alam II., on the left side, and the Moti Masjid, and the tombs of the last kings of Delhi on the right side. The mosque was built by Shah Alam Bahadur Shah, successor of Aurangzeb, in 1709, and is pretty but feeble. At the corners of the wall facing it are two detached minarets. The three royal graves in the little court to the south side of the mosque lie within a simple marble enclosure—that on the east is the resting-place of **Akbar Shah II.** (died 1837 A.D.), the next to it is that of **Shah Alam II.** (died 1806), then beyond an empty space, intended for the grave of Bahadur Shah, buried at Rangoon, comes the tomb of **Shah Alam Bahadur**

Shah, a plain stone with grass on it. The furthest grave to the west is that of Mirza Fakhru, heir apparent of the Bahadur Shah, whose murder led in part to the palace intrigues which added one more cause to the many others that led to the mutiny of 1857. An inner gate now conducts to the courtyard on the north side of the shrine, with the grave of Mohtamid Khan, Annalist of Aurangzeb, and a mosque on the left; while on the right a paved way with marble walls and a marble gate at the end leads past the enclosure of the saint's grave to the south-eastern court. Visitors entering the grave enclosure by the marble gateway on the south side of it are expected to take off their shoes. As a matter of fact, all that is of interest in it can be seen through the handsome pierced marble screens of the east and south wall, erected by the Emperor Farukhsiyar. The grave is a plain earthen mound, covered by a cloth and surrounded by a low marble railing. A canopy is suspended over it from four marble columns in the court. A number of other graves lie round it. "Many other servants of God," writes Abul Fazl, "instructed in divine knowledge, in this spot repose in their last sleep." The west wall of the enclosure is decorated by tiles of green and yellow in alternate rows. This work is indifferently ascribed to Shekh Farid-ud-din Shakarganj who came to Delhi upon the death of his master, and to Aurangzeb. Probably the former built the wall as a place for prayer, and the latter added the decoration. Outside the south-east corner of the enclosure is the mosque of the Khwaja Kutabuddin, much renovated and added to since his time. Under the shadow of it is the grave of Maulana Fakhruddin, who built the gate at the end of the marble way, and in front of it is the grave of a lady known as the Daiji, on the edge of the tank. (A tank seems to have been a special feature of the Chisti shrines. Visitors to Ajmir will remember the very deep one excavated in the rock under the face of the mountain at the Dargah of Muin-ud-din Chisti, and that of Nizam-ud-din Aulia has already been specially mentioned). This is a fine structure, but unfortunately does not retain the water which comes into it. At the head of the tank is the grave of Zabita Khan, the Rohilla, in front of an assembly hall built by him. The second grave alongside of it is declared by the Khadims of the shrine to be that of Ghulam Kadir Khan. This is not impossible—the tombstone is that of a woman, but there are various instances of such stones being used for the grave of a man—but is not very probable, as Ghulam Kadir was put to death by the gradual amputation of limb after limb, and his body remained exposed for some time before it was secretly removed, and it is likely therefore to have been buried both secretly and hurriedly. The superstitious chronicler of the day records that while the corpse hung from a tree head downwards,

"a black dog with white round the eyes came and licked up the blood as it dropped. The spectators threw clods and stones at it, but it still kept there. On the third day the corpse disappeared, and the dog also vanished."

From the head of the tank is obtained a very effective view of the Kutab Minar. In the north-west corner of this southern court is the graveyard of the

Nawabs of Loharu, and outside the north court and gate is that of the Nawabs of Jhajjar, two ruling families created by Lord Lake after 1803, of which the latter disappeared after the events of 1857. Some distance beyond the inner gate on the north side is another outer gate with Hindu details, built in the time of Sher Shah, who, with Salim Shah, was a special patron of this shrine. The unfinished large Music Gallery or Naubat Khana, on this side also belongs to that period.

The little town of Mahrauli is situated on the east side of the **Hauz Shamsi**, constructed by the Emperor Altamsh. This must once have been a very fine reservoir, but it seldom contains much water now. The view of the tank with buildings and gardens round it is, however, very picturesque. Among those on the east side are a fine structure of red sandstone, known as the Jehaz, or Ship, consisting of a courtyard of much later date added to an earlier mosque, and the **Aulia Masjid**, a simple enclosure marked by a very fine bor tree, where, according to tradition, prayers of thanksgiving for the capture of Delhi were offered up in 1191 A.D. Near this, on the opposite side of the road, the water of an escape channel from the tank falls picturesquely down to the Jhirna Garden with some very fine trees, and passes on towards Tughlakabad. Mahrauli is much resorted to by the people of Delhi after the summer rains have set in, and the Pankah Mela, or Fan Fair, held there, is one of the principal popular festivals of the country-side. Near the north-west angle of the bazar, where there is a tomb of a third brother of Adham Khan, a country road leads to the village of Malakpur, three miles west of Mahrauli and the tomb known as **Sultan Ghari**. This is the resting-place of Nasr-ud-din Mahmud Shah, known as Abul Fatah Muhammad, eldest son of Sultan Altamsh, who, like the sons of Sultan Balban and Firoz Shah Tughlak, died before his father in 1228 A.D., and well deserves a visit. It is situated in the centre of a stone enclosure raised high above the ground, which, with its sloping corner towers, seems to have been a forerunner of the mosques in the severe Pathan style, if indeed it was not restored in that style (see note, p. 274). The picturesque gateway is constructed in the same manner as the screen arches at the Kutab Mosque. The marble tomb chamber itself is mainly underground, only the roof and the walls which support it appearing above the level of the platform, and is approached by a steep flight of narrow steps. From this peculiar arrangement the name of the mausoleum (Ghár=cave) is derived. The roof is borne by stone beams arranged as in mosques made up from Jain materials. The inscription on the gate gives to the son the title of Malik-i-Maluk-ush-Sharak, Lord of the Eastern countries, as he died while Governor of Lakhnauti, the modern Dacca. At the south-east angle of the enclosure on the outside were two fine domed canopies over the graves of Sultans Rukn-ud-din and Muiz-ud-din, also sons and short-lived successors of Altamsh ; but one of these has fallen, and the other will fall unless it is speedily secured. In front of the mausoleum are various buildings of the severe middle Pathan style, including a fine mosque.

Five miles due east of the Kutab stand the grand ruins of the **Fortress and City of Tughlakabad** and the noble tomb in which Tughlak Shah and his son and murderer lie buried.[1] The road descends almost at once from the wall of Lal Kot, and in less than a mile passes through the long earthen mounds which mark the eastern defences of Kila Rai Pithora.

[1] Every one who possibly can, should see these. There are few great ruins or buildings in the world which I have not seen, and I recommend a visit to these advisedly.—H. C. F.

Near this point on the north side of the road are the ruins of an old bridge which led to the Budaon Gate of the city, frequently mentioned in the annals of the time, and half a mile away on the same side are the grove which marks the Hauz Rani, or Queen's Tank, and the village of Khirki, the dark walls of whose mosque can be seen in the trees.

The mosque of **Khirki** is the most interesting of all the old Pathan mosques, and like that of Gulbargah, not far removed from it in date, and the much earlier one of Cordova built in the last quarter of the ninth century, is a covered mosque, which is a rare arrangement, broken in this instance by four open quadrangles in the middle of the arcades. It was built by Jahan Khan in 1380, much about the same time as the Kalan and Begampur mosques (pp. 65 and 251), and some years subsequently to that of Nizam-ud-din (p. 235), which it resembles most. The exterior measurement of the mosque give a dimension of 192 feet each way. (The Gulbargah mosque is 216 by 176 feet). The sides of the quadrangles are thirty-two feet square, and have three arches: each quadrangle is surrounded by pillared spaces of the same area as itself, and the total number of arches from front to back and from side to side being fifteen. The plain square columns which carry them are fourfold at the corners of the courts, and twofold round the courts; the columns of the arcades in line with the former are double, and with the latter single, and the effect of the play of light and shade looking down the vistas of them and across the courts is very picturesque. A separate recess projects in the centre of the west wall, forming a mihrab. After 1857 the mosque was cleared of the villagers who had settled in it.

Two hundred yards north of the Khirki mosque is an extremely pretty sandstone pavilion, with pierced screens over the grave of Yusaf Katál, and half a mile north of this, and 500 yards east of the Begampur mosque, is a handsome tomb of red sandstone, sloping walls raised on a high base and surmounted by a white marble dome, very similar in general appearance to that of Tughlak Shah. This, which is known as the **Lal Gumbaz,** is the grave of Kabir-ud-din Aulia, son of Yusaf Katal, and grandson of Shekh Farid-ud-din Shakarganj of Pakpattan. The tomb was built by Sultan Muhammad Tughlak, and is considerably smaller than that of his father—the internal measurements being twenty-nine feet, and the external forty-five, as compared with thirty-eight and sixty-one feet. The interior of the dome is of red sandstone, and from the centre hang nine chains for lamps over the graves on the floor; at the head of that of the Aulia, is an elaborate lamp pillar. The pierced red sandstone grilles in the north and south walls of the tomb are very fine. East of the village of Khirki in the line of the defences of Jahan Panah is a fine work of masonry forming a sluice for the stream which enters here, known as the **Sat Palah**, or Seven Arches, built by Muhammad Tughlak Shah, in 1326 A.D. Half a mile to the north of this is the shrine of Nasr-ud-din Muhammad, known as **Chiragh Delhi** (the Lamp of Delhi), the disciple of Nizam-ud-din Aulia, and last saint of renown at Delhi, who died in 1356 A.D. The walls which enclose the shrine and village, and a huge untenanted area were built by the Emperor Muhammad Shah in 1729, and rise finely above the banks of the depression, which has worn under them a deep bed, once spanned by a bridge, as also by another lower down its course. A picturesque gate in the west wall leads to the shrine between the tomb of Bahlol Lodi and a mosque. The Dargah is entered from the east by a gate built by Firoz Shah in 1373 A.D. The tomb chamber is surmounted by a dome of red sandstone surrounded by a broad dripstone: it has been much modernised at various times. A gold cup hangs over the grave, as in the Khizri mosque at Nizam-ud-din. In the north-west corner of the enclosure is a fine Assembly Hall. The tomb of **Sultan Bahlol Lodi** (died 1488 A.D.) is occupied by the attendants of the Dargah, so that only its exterior can be seen. It is of unusual shape for a tomb, having five domes over it; the details of the sandstone decoration are all Hindu. To the front of it on the south side is a grave enclosure surrounded by a very beautiful pierced screen of red sandstone, which contrasts happily with the green shade above it.

A fine view of the western portion of the citadel of **Tughlakabad** is obtained from the point where the road makes a sudden turn towards it from the south, about three-quarters of a mile on the Kutab side of the tomb of Tughlak Shah. The ruins of this wall and of its immense splayed bastions, picked out with bushes and grass, are extremely effective everywhere, but are finest along the south side of the upper citadel; this is entered from the lower fortress which is reached by a gate nearly opposite the bridge that connected the mausoleum with the latter. The city and fort were built between the years 1321 and 1323 A.D., were deserted by Muhammad Tughlak Shah in favour of Daulatabad, and were finally superseded by Firozabad; but the real cause of its permanent abandonment was no doubt the badness of the water and general insalubrity of the site, as in the case of Fatahpur Sikri. The curse of the saint (p. 236).

"Ya base Gujar;
Ya rahe ujar."

("Be it the home of the Gujar, or rest it deserted"), is doubly fulfilled; for while most of the area inside the walls lies utterly desolate and covered with masses of ruins, there are also two small Gujar villages inside

Ruined Walls of Tughlakabad. [*To face p.* 288.

it. The great size of the stones used in the wall—the triple storeyed towers—the high parapet, backed inside by terraces with rooms—and the lofty gates, are all very imposing—perhaps the most impressive bit of all is the south-east bastion of the citadel and the east wall above it. The path through the gate abovementioned leads past a large reservoir hewn in the rock: beyond it to the north-west are ruins of the palace and stables and of a fine mosque. From the tank the track ascends to an outwork below the principal gate of the citadel, which must have been a very fine and strong portal, and then winds through ruins to the highest point of all, upon which some royal building no doubt stood. Below this, on the west, was a very deep (baoli) tank for the use of the defenders of the citadel, and all round are underground passages, off which the servants and slaves of the king had quarters. These should not be lightly entered, as they still occasionally harbour leopards and hyænas, and a tiger has within the last twenty years been known to take refuge in them. An extremely fine view to the north is obtained from the top of the citadel—on clear days it includes the domes of the Jama Masjid of Delhi—and to the east are seen many blue curves of the Jumna stream.

The **Tomb of Tughlak Shah**, rising above the fortress walls which surround it, is perhaps one of the most picturesque buildings outside modern Delhi; and when it stood reflected on all sides in the lake below, it must have presented a spectacle of unusual beauty. It is impossible to improve on Mr Fergusson's description of it:

"When the stern old warrior, Tughlak Shah, founded the new Delhi, which still bears his name, he built a tomb, not in a garden as was usually the case, but in a strongly fortified citadel in the middle of an artificial lake.[1] The sloping walls and almost Egyptian solidity of this mausoleum, combined with the bold and massive towers of the fortifications that surround it, form a picture of a warrior's tomb unrivalled anywhere, and a singular contrast with the elegant and luxuriant garden tombs of the more settled and peaceful dynasties that succeeded."

The red sandstone gateway, with its sloping face and jambs and head in the earlier Pathan style, contrasts finely with the dark walls and rounded towers in which it stands, and the trees which overshadow it. The interior of the fortress is much smaller than one would suppose from the outside, and, except for the pointed corner to the east, is almost filled by the tomb. This is the earliest building of which the walls have a very decided slope. They are of red sandstone, relieved in the upper portion by a very sparing use of white marble. The marble slabs of the dome are not well fitted. This may be due to the fact that the dome was the first attempt of its kind in India, but the people of the west village in the fort, who were removed there from the tomb, have a dreadful tale, that the slabs were stripped off after

[1] It is worthy of note that another Pathan king, greater and sterner perhaps than Tughlak Shah, the Sultan Sher Khan Sur, built his tomb at Sassaram, in the middle of a magnificent tank. This tomb depended for its effect upon the brilliantly painted decoration of its exterior, of which the outlines are still quite distinct, and must have presented a most gorgeous spectacle when fresh from the artists' hands, shining against the blue sky and mirrored in the blue water.

Tomb of the Emperor Tughlak Shah, Tughlakabad. [*To face p.* 290.

1857 and were ordered to be sold, but were finally replaced. The interior of the tomb, which is rather larger than that of the Sultan Balban, is very plain, but decidedly effective. It contains three graves, the centre one being that of Tughlak Shah, and one of the others it is believed that of his son, the Khuni Sultan, at the head of which Firoz Shah placed the propitiatory chest (p. 277). In the north-west corner of the enclosure is a small tomb-chamber, with an arcade round it, containing a number of graves. The city, like the ἑκατόμπυλοι Θῆβαι, was designated from the vastness of its defences as that of the Fifty-two Gates, and, as we have already seen (p. 233), Mr Finch refers to it under this description.

Corresponding to the mausoleum at the east end of the lake, and connected with the south-east corner of the defences of Tughlakabad city by an immense embankment, is the ruined fortress of Adilabad, or Muhammadabad. This is entered by a fine gate on the west face, and affords a very charming view from above; it was possibly a water palace, like the splendid buildings at Mandu known by that name. The east face of the embankment is forty feet high; between it and the walls of Tughlakabad city is a fine sluice cut in the solid rock. A mile beyond this is an isolated fortified little hill, known as the Nai's (or Barber's) Fort. This was apparently a College (Madrasa), or the retreat of some holy personage, and was probably fortified as such against a possible Moghal attack.

About two and a half miles south-east of Adilabad is a fine masonry tank, and near it a very fine masonry "band," known as the Surajkund and Arrangpur Band. These date from the eighth century, and are therefore among the oldest Hindu works near Old Delhi. Both are extremely picturesque, and well worth visiting. A long flight of steps led down to the tank from a temple on the west side. The band is nearly three hundred feet long, and more than sixty feet high in the centre, where a small spring (Jhir) rises from under it.

Less than three miles east of this point the road reaches that from Delhi to Muttra, at Badarpur, built inside the enclosure of an old Imperial Sarai. This place is about eight miles distant from Nizam-ud-din and the mausoleum of Humayun; and visitors spending the night at the Kutab, and proceeding to Tughlakabad in the morning, can arrange to return to Delhi by this way.

CHAPTER VI

BRIEF HISTORY OF THE KINGS OF DELHI, WITH PARTICULAR REFERENCE TO THEIR CONNECTION WITH THAT PLACE, TO WHICH IS ADDED AN HISTORICAL TABLE OF THE MOGHAL RULE.

THE early history of Delhi is fairly summarised in the words of the popular distich :—

> "Pahle Dilli Tuwar, piche Chauhan,
> Aur pichle Moghal Pathan."

("First the Tuwar held Delhi, then the Chauhan, and then the Pathan and Moghal.") Of the Tuwars or Tunwars, only the **Kings Anangpal the First and Second** are specially connected with Delhi. The city is believed to have been originally colonised from Kanauj in the sixth century of our era, to which the Iron Pillar belongs, and was refounded by the former king in 730 A.D., and repeopled by the latter in 1052 (p. 264). To Anangpal I., and to a son of his, are ascribed the Arrangpur band and Suraj Kund (p. 292), and to his later successor, the Anang Tal, in the Lal Kot. A hundred years after the second refounding by the Tunwars, a king of that line was defeated by the Chauhans, and the last prince of this dynasty, the **Prithvi Raja,** known popularly as Rai Pithora, built or fortified the city now called by his name, and probably about 1180 A.D. constructed the

Lal Kot as a defence against the Muhammadan invaders from the north, who had recently reappeared in India under the famous Muhammad-bin-Sam, known as **Shahab-ud-din Ghori.**

This Pathan chief had met with a severe defeat in 1191 A.D. at the hands of the Prithvi Raja on the banks of the Ghaggar, near Thanesar, then a very important city, which Sultan Mahmud of Ghazni had already captured 180 years previously; but returning two years later he crushed the Chauhan prince near the same place, the Indian chief falling in the battle, or perhaps being put to death after it. Following up this victory, his general, Kutab-ud-din Aibak,[1] captured Delhi, and later Ajmir and Kanauj. Soon afterwards Shahab-ud-din, who up to this date had been associated with a brother, became sole ruler of Ghor and Ghazni, and assumed the title of Abul Muzaffar Muiz-ud-din-Sam, but was still generally known as Muhammad-bin-Sam, by which designation he is mentioned in the inscriptions on the Kutab Minar.

During the next years the Muhammadan conquest of India was extended as far as Gwalior, Kalinjar, and Benares; and in 1196 Kutab-ud-din visited his master in Ghazni, and on his return erected the great screen of arches in the Kuwat-ul-Islam Mosque. A revolt of the Ghakkars, due to the Sultan's disastrous defeat in Kharizm and their invasion of the Lahore country,[2] called both master

[1] Aibak probably means Moon Lord, the latter syllable representing Beg.

[2] At the time that the Muhammadan Pathans were engaged in wresting India from the Hindus, Richard Cœur de Lion was engaged in trying to wrest the Holy Land from the Muhammadan Saracens.

and lieutenant to that place, and on his way back from there to Ghazni, the king was slain in a night attack on his camp. Thereupon **Kutab-ud-din Aibak** declared himself Ruler of India, and thus in 1206 A.D. founded the Muizzi Dynasty, so-called from the title of the king, known generally as the Slave Kings, three of the principal rulers among them having originally been Turki slaves. Four years later, during which period Muhammadan arms were extended to Bengal, the first emperor of India died from injuries caused by the pommel of his saddle upon a fall with his horse while playing polo at Lahore, and after a year's interval was succeeded by Altamsh (1211-1236), who took the titles of **Shams-ud-dun-ya-wa-ud-din Abul Muzaffar Altamsh.** This prince consolidated the Muhammadan power in India, and was acknowledged as an independent king by the Khalif of Bagdad, whereupon he called himself Násir-i-Amir-ul-Mumenín, or Ally of the Prince of the Faithful. Among his conquests special mention is made of that of Bhilsa, and of the famous Buddhist tope there. He enlarged the great Kuwat-ul-Islam Mosque, completed the Kutab Minar, and built the tomb of his son, known as Sultan Ghári (p. 284). Altamsh was succeeded by his son Muizz-ud-din, who was shortly afterwards murdered by his brother Rukn-ud-din. When the latter sought to seize his sister, the Princess **Raziyah,** whom her father had declared more fit to rule after him than any of his sons, she, according to Ibn Batuta, assumed the coloured dress of a suppliant prescribed by her father, and addressed the people from the palace terrace, upon which the troops deserted her brother, and brought him captive to her from the mosque, and she ordered him to be executed, saying, "The slayer must be slain." For three years she maintained her position, but she was then defeated by the rebellious Turki Governor of Lahore, who compelled her to marry him, and was shortly afterwards murdered in her flight after a second defeat in a battle, by which her husband sought to replace her on the throne. Her grave has been described at p. 66. The chronicler of the time describes the Sultan Raziyah as follows:—

"She was wise, just, and generous, a benefactor of her kingdom, and dispenser of justice, the protector of her subjects, and a leader of her armies. She was endowed with all the qualities befitting a king, but she was not born of the right sex, and so, in the estimation of men, all these virtues were worthless. May God have mercy on her."

Another brother, **Nasir-ud-din,** finally succeeded her, and reigned under the auspices of his minister and brother-in-law, Balban, for twenty years, during which the Moghals repeatedly invaded India. Chenghiz Khan had penetrated as far as the Indus in the reign of Altamsh, and the ambassador of Huluku Khan, who destroyed the Caliphate of Baghdad, and was perhaps the fiercest of all the scourges of God in Asia, was received in Delhi in 1259 A.D.

Nasir-ud-din was succeeded by his minister, the last of the great slave kings, who took the titles of **Sultan Abul-Muzaffar-Gheias-ud-din-Balban,** and reigned from 1265 to 1287. His original name was Ulugh Khan, and he was one of a leading band of the Shamsi slaves of Altamsh, known as the Forty. His court was the refuge of many princes and learned men flying before the Moghal invaders, and it was his son, the Khan-i-Shahid (p. 278), who invited the Persian poet, Sádi, to India. Of him the chronicler of his time wrote:—

"The dignity and authority of the Government were restored, and his stringent rules and resolute determination caused all men, high and low, throughout his dominions, to submit to his authority. He was inflexible in the administration of justice, showing no favour to his brethren, or children, or associates, or servants."

He was succeeded by his grandson, Kaikubad, whose father, Bughra Khan, was practically king of Bengal, and the historians record a touching and dramatic meeting of the son with his father who refused to seek the Imperial dignity. Unhappily, Kaikubad gave himself up to evil courses, and after two years was murdered, whereupon the nobles elected an old and experienced General, **Jelal-ud-din Khilji**, as emperor, and the first Pathan dynasty in India succeeded to the line of Turks in 1290. The latter were naturally opposed to his elevation, and he did not obtain possession of Old Delhi for some time, during which he resided at Kilokhri, about two miles south of the Mausoleum of Humayun. The poet, Amir Khusrau, was one of his close friends, and the keeper of the Kuran. His nephew and son-in-law, Ala-ud-din, while Governor of Karrah (then and long afterwards an important place, which was finally superseded by Allahahabad), penetrated further south than Muhammadan arms had ever reached hitherto, and captured Deogir, now Daulatabad, then one of the greatest cities in the north of the Deccan. On his return to Karrah, mischief was made between him and the king, and in order to remove this, the latter proceeded to the governorship of his nephew. The treachery and murder which were thereupon enacted are thus narrated :—

"When he (Ala-ud-din) met the Sultan, he fell at his feet. The Sultan took his hand, and, treating him as a son, kissed his eyes and cheeks and stroked his beard, and said : 'I have brought thee up from infancy. Why art thou afraid of me?' At that moment the stony-hearted traitor gave the fatal signal, and Muhammad Salim of Samana—an evil man of an evil family—struck at the Sultan with a sword, but the blow fell short and wounded his own hand. He again struck and wounded the Sultan, who ran towards the river crying, 'Ah thou villain, Ala-ud-din! What hast thou done?' Ikhtiyar-ud-din, who had run after the betrayed monarch, threw him down, and cut off his head, and bore it dripping with blood to Ala-ud-din. . . . The hell-hound, Salim, who struck the first blow, was, a year or two afterwards, eaten up by leprosy. Ikhtiyar-ud-din, who cut off his head, very soon went mad, and in his dying ravings cried that Sultan Jelal-ud-din stood over him with a drawn sword, ready to cut off his head."

Parracide as he was, **Ala-ud-din,** who took the title of Sikandar Sani — the second Alexander —was a strong ruler,[1] a great fighter, and, as has been seen (p. 257), a notable builder. He con-

[1] Among other acts of this prince was one which had a far-reaching effect—the imposition of the religious poll-tax, or Jaziyah, upon all non-Muhammadans. This was removed by Akbar in the ninth year of his reign (1565 A.D.), but was re-enacted by Aurangzeb in 1680. It was finally repealed, at the request of Raja Jai Singh, by the Emperor Muhammad Shah.

quered Guzerat, Chitor, and Malwa, while his general, Malik Kafur, invaded Telingana a second time, captured Warangal, and penetrated as far south as the Karnatic coast, and he defeated the Moghals in several pitched battles outside Delhi. On the occasion of their invasion in 1299, under Kutlugh Khan, he fortified his camp at **Siri,** and this place afterwards became **New Delhi,** and was joined to Old Delhi by the defences of **Jahanpanah** (p. 253). The repulse of the Moghals on this occasion was due mainly to the extraordinary gallantry of a general of the king's, named Zafar Khan, and according to the chroniclers, the Moghals for many years afterwards would say to their horses when they refused to drink: "Why are you afraid—do you see Zafar Khan?" Pyramids of the skulls of the slain Moghals used to be erected before the gates of the city. Ala-ud-din died in 1315 of dropsy—"his days did not help him"—and it is recorded that his body was brought out of the Red Palace and buried in a tomb in front of the Jama Masjid (p. 272). Shortly afterwards Malik Kafur was murdered by unruly mercenaries, and when during the next four years repeated murders had practically extinguished the Khilji family, **Ghias-ud-din Tughlak**, Governor of the Punjab, and the bulwark of India, against the Moghals, moved on to Delhi, and, after gaining an easy victory (p. 250) was elected emperor, the nobles declaring, "All who are present here know no one besides thee who is worthy of royalty and fit to rule." This election re-introduced a Ruling House of mixed Turki blood. The Sultan devoted his energies principally to the construction of the city and citadel of Tughlakabad, possibly because he considered the widely extended position of the three cities of Delhi was not capable of defence against the Moghals, and on returning from an expedition to Bengal, in 1324, was murdered by his son, Juna Khan, subsequently Muhammad Shah, who contrived that a pavilion in which he was entertaining his father at Aghwanpur near Tilpat should fall upon him. The story of his quarrel with Shekh Nizam-ud-din Aulia has been narrated above (p. 236).

Muhammad Shah Tughlak, who bore the title of Sultan Abul Mujahid Abul Fatah, is remembered chiefly for his attempts to regulate prices, and introduce a debased currency,[1] for his cruelties, and for the insane persistence with which he sought to transfer the capital of India from Delhi to Deogir, which would inevitably have resulted in the Moghals assuming possession of the whole of the north of the continent. The desolation produced in Old Delhi, a city "which for 170 or 180 years had grown in prosperity, and rivalled Baghdad and Cairo," is thus described: "The city and its serais and suburbs and villages, spread over four or five kos, were all destroyed. So complete was the desolation that not a cat or a dog was left among the ruins." A fearful famine completed the misery of the capital and many of the provinces, and the people and governors rose in rebellion on all sides. While engaged in putting down one of these in Sind, and seeking to capture Thatta, the Sultan died in

[1] It is on record that piles of his coinage tokens lay for many years among the ruins of Tughlakabad, and possibly excavation might yet lead to the discovery of some of them.

1351, and his cousin, Firoz Shah, was forcibly placed on the throne, and proceeded with the army to Delhi, where he ruled till 1388, as **Sultan Firoz Shah Tughlak.** The public works of his reign, and his joys and sorrows, have been already noticed (pp. 273 and 57). He was, further, a great constructor of canals, gardens, and bands—the first canals in India were made by him for his palaces, and they still partially survive in the Western Jumna and Eastern Jumna canals—and he was a mighty hunter; he waged many campaigns, and lost his army and nearly lost his own life twice in the deserts between Sind and Guzerat. Besides his own name, he had the name of nine of his predecessors, Muiz-ud-din-bin-Sam, Altamsh, Nasir-ud-din, Balban, Jelal-ud-din Khilji, Ala-ud-din, Kutab-ud-din, Gheias-ud-din Tughlak Shah, and Muhammad Shah, recited in the public prayers. Towards the end of his life he was apparently deposed by his son, Nasir-ud-din, but he recovered his position before his death. "Since the days of Nasir-ud-din, son of Shams-ud-din Altamsh," writes the author of the Tarikh-i-Mubarik Shah, "there has been no king in Delhi so just and merciful, so kind and religious, or such a builder." The same chronicle tells us that when the Sultan went out in state, "the slaves accompanied him in distinct corps; first the archers fully armed; next the swordsmen, thousands upon thousands, then the fighting men riding upon male buffaloes, and the slaves from Hazarah, mounted on Arab or Turki horses, bearing standards and axes," a warlike state of things denoting very different conditions from those of the reign of Aurangzeb, noticed by Bernier (p. 45). He was succeeded first by a grandson, the son of Fatah Khan (p. 56), who was killed soon afterwards, and ultimately, after much fighting, which extended to the very streets of Firozabad, by the son who had deposed him, and who shortly left the throne to a minor child, **Mahmud Shah Tughlak.** This was the Sultan who suffered utter defeat at the hands of **Sultan Timur** in 1398 (p. 250). For the time he fled to Mandu, Khizr Khan, Governor of the Punjab, being placed in power by Timur, as Shah Alam was by Ahmad Shah, nearly four centuries later; but he afterwards returned and ruled nominally till 1414, when **Syad Khizr Khan,** who had several times failed to drive him out, succeeded him, and founded the Syad dynasty. This lasted till 1450, and was succeeded by the second pure Pathan dynasty, the Lodis, whose first chief re-united the Punjab to Delhi, and from whose last scion, **Ibrahim Lodi,**[1] the Moghal **Baber,** won the empire of India at the battle of Panipat, on 21st April 1526. Nothing in the record of these two dynasties calls for mention in connection with Delhi, beyond the buildings which they erected, and which have been noticed in their place (pp. 244, 245). The last Lodi princes resided at Agra, and here Baber, whose visit to Nizam-ud-din and the Kutab has been noted (p. 277), and, for the most part, his son Humayun, dwelt. **Sher Shah** was too much engaged in fighting throughout his brief reign to reside long in his new city of Delhi (p. 228). His son and successor built the Salimgarh (p. 40), but his second son,

[1] When the dead body of this prince was brought before Baber, he raised the head and said: "Honour to your bravery."

Adil Shah, on whose behalf Hemu contested the empire with Bairam Khan at Panipat, removed again to Agra. The previous battle of Sirhind was won against a revolted brother, Sikandar Shah, whom Bairam Khan and Akbar were endeavouring to intercept when the **Emperor Humayun** met with his death at Delhi. The inception of the Purana Kila by this king, his death at that place, and his mausoleum to the south of it, are the principal events of Moghal rule connected with Delhi previous to the reign of Shahjahan. The interrex Sher Shah, and his successors in the third Pathan dynasty on the throne of India, were naturally attracted to Delhi in preference to Agra (pp. 228 and 40), but the seat of power had been moved again to the southern capital when Humayun returned in 1556 A.D., and Agra and Fatahpur Sikri were the capitals of **Akbar** (1556-1605), as Agra and Lahore were of **Jahangir** (1605-1627). The principal events of the reigns of the five great Moghal emperors and their successors will be found in the tables at the end of this chapter, taken from the "Imperial Gazetteer of India," edited by Sir W. W. Hunter. Modern Delhi, or Shahjahanabad, was founded in 1638 by the **Emperor Shahjahan** (1627-1658), the palace being first built, then the walls of the city, and then the Jama Masjid; the materials needed were largely taken from the half-deserted cities of Firozabad and the Delhi of Sher Shah. Many of the works were no doubt still in progress when the emperor fell ill and was carried off to Agra by his eldest son, Dara Shekoh, and was there deposed by his youngest son,

Aurangzeb, in 1658. Bernier tells a pathetic story of how, in his captivity, the ex-emperor longed to see the last of his building creations once more, but indignantly refused to view them merely from a war vessel on the river, as stipulated by his successor. A native chronicle, translated by Dr Hoey, C.S., states that the father forgave his son when on his deathbed, at the instance of two holy men who lived with him during his latter days. It may be recorded here to the credit of human nature that the Kazi of Delhi refused to recognise Aurangzeb as emperor, so long as his father should live, and was, in consequence, deposed from his post. The title of Delhi Shahjahanabad, to be called an Imperial City, has been briefly noticed on pages 4 and 5. The **Emperor Aurangzeb** resided at Delhi in the early years of his reign, and it was his court which was visited there by Bernier and Tavernier. Much about the same time, viz. in the *Annus Mirabilis* of 1666, it was visited by one who was destined to be the real destroyer of the Moghal power, the great Mahratta Sivaji. One of the most mournful sights perhaps, which the Chandni Chauk ever saw, was, first, the parade of the living Prince Dara Shekoh after his capture, and the subsequent parade of his lifeless body after his murder.

Upon the death of Aurangzeb at Ahmadnagar in 1707, and of his eldest son at Delhi, in 1712, the capital once more became the centre of Moghal interests, and was soon the scene of the dying throes of the empire, which really ceased to exist by the middle of the century (p. 5). In their lifetimes the emperors after Aurangzeb were the creatures of some powerful minister—first Zulfikar Khan, the captor of Sivaji Fort of Rajgarh, then the Syad[1] brothers, then Ghazi-ud-din, the elder, and so on, down to the time of the Mahrattas; and no one of them after that emperor, who was buried[2] by his own request in a simple grave at the Rozah near Daulatabad, attained, on his death, the honour of a mausoleum, while the resting-place, or the exact spot of the resting-place, of several, is not even known. Of those who reigned from 1712 to 1761 Jahandar Shah, Farukhsiyar and Alagmir II. came to violent deaths, while Ahmad Shah and Shah Alam II. were blinded, the former being also deposed.[3] One only, **Muhammad Shah** (1718-1748), the last to sit upon the Peacock Throne, reached his grave in peace (if an end can be called peaceful, which is ascribed to a broken heart caused by the loss of his minister, Kamar-ud-din Khan, who had been killed at Sirhind, while he and Prince Ahmad were

[1] These belonged to the famous Barah family in the Muzaffarnagar district, which, from the time of Akbar, was noted for its bravery, and in the van of battle, a post which it always held, had done many notable deeds of valour.

[2] The pathetic despairing letters which the Emperor wrote to his sons from his dying bed are well known. The chronicler records that "still in the dread hour of death the force of habit prevailed and the fingers of the dying King continued mechanically to tell the beads of the rosary they held."

[3] This takes no notice of two young princes, Rafi-ud-daulah and Rafi-ud-darjat, both of whom died in 1717 A.D. The Emperor Farukhsiyar, it will be remembered, granted the first special firman to the East India Company in 1715, in gratitude for his cure by Surgeon Hamilton, who lies buried in the churchyard of the Old Cathedral at Calcutta. It was in his reign that the Sikh leader Banda was executed in Delhi, a deed which the Sikhs considered was finally avenged in September 1857.

U

repelling the first invasion of Ahmad Shah Durani and his Pathans), and of him it is recorded that his coffin consisted of an old clock-case, found in the palace, and his pall of a tattered cloth obtained from the Zenanah. The massacre which took place at Delhi, upon the invasion of Nadir[1] Shah (1739 A.D.), has been described at page 51. No more heart-rending picture of agony than the slaughters by the

[1] In the hall at the back of the Chihal Situn Palace at Isfahan, is also a picture of the victory of Nadir[1] Shah over Muhammad Shah on 17th February 1739. As a work of art, it is unfortunately the worst of the whole series, but it probably gives a fairly correct representation of the costume and arms of the time. The Delhi king advances placidly from the left, seated on a pad upon a white elephant without any driver; he wears a low crown, and has a closely clipped beard. On either side of the royal elephant are other dark ones, some with sword blades attached to their trunks, and others seizing Persians with their trunks. In the foreground march Indian matchlock men with shouldered arms, clad in saffron dresses. Behind the Delhi forces, and firing straight into them is the Moghal artillery. On the right side Nadir Shah, represented with a full dark beard, advances on a very sorry roan horse, clad in green over red, and with bracelets on his wrists and a mace in his right hand; on his head he wears a high curiously shaped cap, with indented sides and top, and most of his Kizilbash horsemen wear the same. In the foreground by him, and in the centre of the picture, are a number of slain men and some riderless horses, and among these stands an old white-headed man, intended perhaps for Saadat Ali Khan Nawab Wazir of Oudh, and Prime Minister of the Delhi King, who is believed to have betrayed his master. The picture fails hopelessly to give any real idea of the turmoil of battle, and it was probably well for the artist that it was not painted for Nadir Shah and seen by him. The Jeonits who saw Nadir Shah in Delhi, described him as "upwards of six feet high, and stout in proportion. He was burnt brown from campaigning and exposure to all weathers. . . . His glance was keen and piercing, his voice rough and rude, but which he could soften

[1] Nadir Shah should be of some special interest to Englishmen, in that, like one of the Shogun Mayors of the Palace in Japan, he appointed a countryman of theirs to be his Fleet master, with a less successful result than in the case of his Eastern compeer.

Persian king and Ahmad Shah (1756 A.D.), and the treatment of Shah Alam and his sons and ladies by the brutal Rohilla, Ghulam Kadir Khan, is presented by the most lurid pictures of history; and it is really a matter for wonderment that the Moghal empire survived at all, rather than that it survived for only so long as it did. The causes of the decline and fall were many—decay of the original stock (which is what Timur's Amirs wisely objected to when he proposed to make a permanent conquest of India), failure of the influx of fresh Muhammadan military blood, after Kabul and Kandahar were lost to the Empire—internecine fratricidal wars upon each succession (it was always Takht or Takhta, the Throne or the Bier, with every son of the Emperor), which emptied the treasury and taught the great nobles and the Hindu chiefs how to use their power—the awful carnages of Nadir Shah and Ahmad Shah, the never-ending blood sucking of Jat, Mahratta and Rohilla—the greed and treachery of ministers and royal eunuchs; and it is no matter for surprise that seventy years of these should have reduced the emperor of Delhi to the condition in which Lord Lake rescued Shah Alam II. in 1803 (p. 73). It has already been narrated that when Nawab Safdar Jang, in the time of Ahmad Shah (p. 246) called in the Jats to his

at pleasure. It was a face of power, on which was stamped courage and resolution, but his slightly projecting under lip gave an air of sinister fierceness and even cruelty to this great Captain." When Nadir Shah and Muhammad Shah entered Delhi together, they were similarly mounted on a horse and on an elephant. The Persian forces remained in Delhi from the beginning of March till early in June.

aid, his rival, Ghazi-ud-din, the younger, son of the elder Wazir of that name, summoned the **Mahrattas** to his side; the latter proved successful with the help of his allies, who had first appeared at Delhi thirty years previously in support of the Syad king-makers, and deposed and blinded the king. This brought **Ahmad Shah Durani**, now in possession of the West Punjab, again on the scene in 1756, and resulted in the sack of Delhi by the Pathans, but the Wazir managed to make terms with him, and remained in office with his support. Four years later, upon the murder of Alamgir II., the Durani chief once more appeared at Delhi, and Ghazi-ud-din fled to the Jats, with whom he was present at Panipat previous to the battle. (It is a circumstance deserving note that this once powerful minister remained in hiding for some twenty years, and was then discovered at Surat, and enabled to proceed to Mecca by the assistance of the British East India Company.) On this occasion Ahmad Shah remained near Delhi for a considerable time, and having finally crushed the Mahrattas at **Panipat**,[1] in a battle fought on 7th January 1761, placed Ali Gauhar, the eldest son of the late king, and a refugee from Ghazi-ud-din, on the throne as **Shah Alam II.**, under the Wazirship of Shuja-ud-daulah, Nawab of Oudh. The Jats re-appeared at Delhi as soon as the Pathans withdrew, and Suraj Mal was killed at Shahdera in 1764, and the Mahrattas, re-gathering power, presented

[1] Well might Panipat say with Ariminum:
"Quoties Romam Fortuna lacessit,
Hac iter est bellis."

themselves once more only a year after Shah Alam returned to Delhi in 1771. Scindiah, himself, visited the capital in 1784; and, three years later, while the Mahratta prince was too deeply engaged in wars in Rajputanah to interfere immediately, the climax of the Moghal agony was reached on the capture of Delhi by Ghulam Kadir Khan and his Rohillas, after they had been once compelled by the Begam Samru to withdraw. There is no more pathetic incident in the long history of the misery of this time than the reply of Shah Alam, when asked by the fiend who had blinded him whether he could still see: "I see only the Holy Koran between you and me." Three months afterwards the Rohillas were expelled by the Mahrattas, and not much later their leader met with his merited end (p. 283). For sixteen years the Imperial Court remained entirely subject to the Mahrattas, whose power and influence in North India was at last broken by the **Battle of Delhi, on 11th September 1803** (p. 71), as their power in South India was broken at the **Battle of Assaye** twelve days later. Shah Alam survived till 1806, and was then succeeded by his son **Akbar II.**, who in his turn was followed in 1837—the year of the accession of Queen Victoria, first Empress of, and second Empress in, India—by the last King of Delhi, **Bahadur Shah.**

The British Government had sought by all means in its power to secure a peaceful evening of life to the Imperial Dynasty which preceded it. But this was not to be, and its disappearance from the scene, fifty years later, was marked by one of the most blood-red sunsets ever painted on the canvas of history.

Historical tables of the Moghal Dynasty of India, adapted from the "Imperial Gazetteer of India," prepared under the direction of Sir W. W. Hunter:

A.H.	A.D.	ZAHUR-UD-DIN MUHAMMAD BABAR BADSHAH HAZRAT GETI SITANI, 1526–30:
932	1526	Defeat and death of Ibráhim Lodí at Pánipat, and victorious entry of Bábar into Delhi and Agra.
„	„	Capture of Jaunpur by Humáyún, son of Bábar.
„	„	Surrender of Biána, Gwalior, and Múltán to his troops.
933	1527	DefeatsRáná Sanga at Fatehpur Síkri and assumes the title of Gházi.
„	„	Occupation of Lucknow by Bábar's army.
935	1529	Behar subdued.
„	„	Final defeat of the troops of the Afghán coalition by Bábar's army; treaty with Nasrat Sháh of Bengal.
937	1530	Bábar's death at Agra.

NASIR-UD-DIN MUHAMMAD HUMAYUN BADSHAH HAZRAT JAHANBANI, 1830–1556:

A.D.

1530. Accession to the throne. Capture of Lahore and occupation of the Punjab by his rival brother Kámrán. Final defeat of the Lodís under Mahmúd Lodí, and acquisition of Jaunpur by Humáyún.

1532. Humáyún's campaigns in Málwá and Guzerat.

1539. Humáyún defeated by Sher Sháh, the Afghan ruler of Bengal, at Chapar Ghát, near Baxár. Retreats to Agra.

1540. Humáyún finally defeated by Sher Shah near Kanauj, and escapes to Persia as an exile. Sher Sháh ascends the Delhi throne.

1556. Humáyún's return to India, and defeat of the Afgháns at Pánipat by Bairám Khán and his young son Akbar. Remounts the throne, but dies in a few months, and is succeeded by Akbar.

JELAL-UD-DIN MUHAMMAD ABUL MUZAFFAR AKBAR SHAH, 1556–1605:

1542. Born at Umarkot in Sind.
1555–56. Succeeds his father after a few months in 1556, under the regency of Bairám Khán.
1560. Akbar assumes the direct management of the kingdom. Revolt of Bairám, who is defeated and pardoned.
1566. Invasion of the Punjab by Akbar's rival brother Hákim Askari, who is defeated.
1561–68. Akbar subjugates the Rájput kingdoms to the Moghal Empire.
1572–73. Akbar's campaign in Guzerat, and its re-annexation to the Empire.
1576. Akbar's reconquest of Bengal, its final annexation to the Moghal Empire.
1581–93. Insurrection in Guzerat. The Province finally subjugated in 1593 to the Moghal Empire.
1586. Akbar's conquest of Kashmír; its final revolt quelled in 1592.
1592. Akbar's conquest and annexation of Sind to the Moghal Empire.
1594. His subjugation of Kandahár, and consolidation of the Moghal Empire over all India north of the Vindhyás as far as Kábul and Kandahár.
1595. Unsuccessful expedition of Akbar's army to the Deccan against Ahmadnagar under his son Prince Murád.
1599. Second expedition against Ahmadnagar by Akbar in person. Captures the town, but fails to establish Moghal rule.
1601. Annexation of Khándesh, and return of Akbar to Northern India.
1605. His death at Agra.

NURUDDIN JAHANGIR BADSHAH, 1605-27:

1605. Accession of Jahángír.
1606. Flight, rebellion, and imprisonment of his eldest son, Prince Khusrú.
1610. Malik Ambar recovers Ahmadnagar from the Moghals, and reasserts independence of the Deccan dynasty, with its new capital at Aurangábád.
1611. Jahángír's marriage with Núr Jahán.
1612. Jahángír again defeated by Malik Ambar in an attempt to

recover Ahmadnagar. First settlement of the English at Surat.

1613-14. Defeat of the Udáipur Rájá by Jahángír's son Prince Sháh Jahán. Unsuccessful revolt in Kábul against Jahángír.

1615. Embassy of Sir T. Roe to the Court of Jahángír.

1616-17. Temporary reconquest of Ahmadnagar by Jahángír's son Sháh Jahán.

1621. Renewed disturbances in the Deccan, ending in treaty by Sháh Jahán. Capture of Kandahár from Jahángír's troops by the Persians.

1623-25. Rebellion against Jahángír by his son Sháh Jahán, who, after defeating the Governor of Bengal at Rájmahál, seized that Province and Behar, but was himself overthrown by Mahábat Khán, his father's general, and sought refuge in the Deccan, where he unites with his old opponent Malik Ambar.

1626. The successful general Mahábat Khán seizes the person of the Emperor Jahángír. Intrigues of the Empress Núr Jahán.

1627. Jahángír recovers his liberty, and sends Mahábat Khán against Prince Sháh Jahán in the Deccan. Mahábat joins the rebel prince against the Emperor Jahángír.

1627. Death of Jahángír.

ABUL MUZAFFAR, MUHAMMAD SHAHAB-UD-DIN, SHAH JAHÁN, BADSHAH, SAHIB-I-KIRAIN SANI, 1628-58:

1627. Imprisonment of Núr Jahán on the death of Jahángír, by Asaf Khán on behalf of Sháh Jahán.

1628. Sháh Jahán returns from the Deccan and ascends the throne (January). He murders his brother and kinsmen.

1628-30. Afghán uprisings against Sháh Jahán in Northern India and in the Deccan.

1629-35. Sháh Jahán's wars in the Deccan with Ahmadnagar, and Bijápur; unsuccessful siege of Bijápur.

1634. Sháji Bhonslá, grandfather of Sivají, the founder of the Mahrattá power, attempts to restore the independent King of Ahmadnagar, but fails, and in 1636 makes peace with the Emperor Sháh Jahán.

1636. Bijápur and Golconda agree to pay tribute to Sháh Jahán. Final submission of Ahmadnagar to the Moghal Empire.

1637. Reconquest of Kandahár by Sháh Jahán from the Persians.

1640. English settle at Madras.

1645. Invasion and temporary conquest of Balkh by Sháh Jahán. Balkh was abandoned by Sháh Jahán's army two years later.

1647-53. Kandahár again taken by the Persians, and three unsuccessful attempts were made by the Emperor's sons Aurangzeb and Dárá Shekoh to recapture it. Kandahár finally lost to the Moghal Empire, 1653.

1655-56. Renewal of the war in the Deccan under Prince Aurangzeb. His attack on Haidarábád, and temporary submission of the Golconda king to the Moghal Empire.

1656. Renewed campaign of Sháh Jahán's armies against Bijápur.

1657-58. Dispute as to the succession between the Emperor's sons. Aurangzeb defeats Dárá Shekoh; imprisons Murád, his other brother; deposes his father by confining him in his palace, and openly assumes the government. Sháh Jahán dies, practically a State prisoner, in the fort of Agra, in 1666.

ABUL MUZAFFAR AURANGZEB, BAHADUR ALAMGIR, 1658-1707:

1658. Deposition of Sháh Jahán, and usurpation of Aurangzeb.

1659. Aurangzeb defeats his brothers Shujá and Dárá Shekoh. Dárá Shekoh, in his flight being betrayed by a chief with whom he sought refuge, is put to death by order of Aurangzeb.

1660. Continued struggle of Aurangzeb with his brother Shujá, who ultimately fled to Arakan, and there perished miserably.

1661. Aurangzeb executes his youngest brother, Murád, in prison.

1662. Unsuccessful invasion of Assam by Aurangzeb's general Mir Jumlá. Disturbances in the Deccan. War between Bijápur and the Mahrattás under Sivají. After various changes of fortune, Sivají, the founder of the Mahrattá power, retains a considerable territory.

1662-65. English settle at Bombay. Sivají in rebellion against the Moghal Empire. In 1664, he assumed the title of Rájá, and asserted his independence; but in 1665, on a large army being sent against him, he made submission, and proceeded to Delhi, where he was placed under restraint, but soon afterwards escaped.

1666. Death of the deposed Emperor, Sháh Jahán. War in the Deccan, and defeat of the Moghals by the King of Bijápur.

1667. Sivají makes peace on favourable terms with Aurangzeb, and obtains an extension of territory. Sivají levies tribute from Bijápur and Golconda.

1670. Sivají ravages Khándesh and the Deccan, and there levies for the first time *chauth*, or a contribution of one-fourth of the revenue.

1672. Defeat of the Moghals by Sivají.

1677. Aurangzeb revives the *jaziah* or poll-tax on non-Muhammadans.

1679. Aurangzeb at war with the Rájputs. Rebellion of Prince Akbar, Aurangzeb's youngest son, who joins the Rájputs, but whose army deserts him. Prince Akbar is forced to fly to the Mahrattás.

1672-80. Mahrattá progress in the Deccan. Sivají crowns himself an independent sovereign at Ráigarh in 1674. His wars with Bijápur and the Moghals. Sivají dies in 1680, and is succeeded by his son, Sambahjí.

1681. Aurangzeb has to continue the war with the Rájputs.

1683. Aurangzeb invades the Deccan in person, at the head of his Grand Army.

1686-88. Aurangzeb conquers Bijápur and Golconda, and annexes them to the Empire (1688).

1689. Aurangzeb captures Sambahjí, and barbarously puts him to death.

1692. Guerilla war with the Mahrattás under independent leaders.

1698. Aurangzeb captures Jinjí from the Mahrattás.

1698. English purchase Calcutta.

1699-1701. The Mahrattá war. Capture of Sátára and Mahrattá forts by the Moghals under Aurangzeb. Apparent ruin of Mahrattás.

1702-05. Successes of the Mahrattás.

1706. Aurangzeb retreats to Ahmadnagar, and

1707. Dies there (February).

THE DECLINE AND FALL OF THE MOGHAL EMPIRE,
From death of Aurangzeb to that of Muhammad Bahádur Sháh.
1707-1862.

1707. Succession contest between Muázzim and Alam, two sons of Aurangzeb; victory of the former, and his accession under the title of Bahádur Sháh. Revolt of Prince Kambaksh; his defeat and death.

1710. Expedition against the Sikhs.

1712 Death of Bahádur Sháh, and accession of his eldest son,

Jahándar Sháh, after a struggle for the succession; an incapable monarch. Revolt of his nephew, Farukhsiyar; defeat of the Imperial Army, and execution of the Emperor.

1713. Accession of Farukhsiyar, under the auspices and control of Husáin Alí, Governor of Behar, and Abdullá, Governor of Allahábád.

1716. Invasion by the Síkhs; their defeat, and cruel persecution.

1719. Deposition and murder of Farukhsiyar by the Sayad chiefs Husáin Alí and Abdullá. They nominate in succession three boy Emperors, the first two of whom died within a few months after their accession. The third, Muhammad Sháh, commenced his reign in September 1719.

1720. Murder of Husáin Alí, and overthrow of the Sayad "kingmakers."

1720-48. The Governor of the Deccan, or Nizám-ul-mulk, establishes his independence, and severs the Haidarábád Provinces from the Moghal Empire.

1732-43. The Governor of Oudh, who was also *Wazír* of the Empire, becomes practically independent of Delhi.

1735-51. General decline of the Empire; revolts within, and invasion of Nádír Sháh from Persia (1739). The Mahrattás obtain Málwá (1743), followed by the cession of Southern Orissa and tribute from Bengal (1751). First invasion of India by Ahmad Sháh Duráni, who had obtained the throne of Kandahár (1747); his defeat in Sirhind (1748).

1748. Death of Muhammad Sháh.

1748-50. Accession of Ahmad Sháh, his son; disturbances by the Rohillá Afgháns in Oudh, and defeat of the Imperial troops.

1751. The Rohillá insurrection crushed with the aid of the Mahrattás.

1751. Second invasion of India by Ahmad Sháh Duráni, and cession of the Punjab to him. Siege of Arcot.

1754. Deposition of the Emperor, and accession of Alamgír II.

1756. Third invasion of India by Ahmad Sháh Duráni, and sack of Delhi.

1757. Battle of Plassy.

1759. Fourth invasion of India by Ahmad Sháh Duráni, and murder of the Emperor Alamgír II. by his *wazír*, Ghází-ud-din. The Mahrattá conquests in Northern India. Their organization for the conquest of Hindustán, and their capture of Delhi.

1761-1805. The third battle of Pánipat, between the Afgháns

under Ahmad Sháh and the Mahrattás; the defeat of the latter. From this time the Moghal Empire ceased to exist, except in name. The nominal Emperor on the death of Alamgír II. was Sháh Alam II., an exile who granted the Diwani of Bengal to the East India Company in 1765, and resided till 1771 in Allahábád, a pensioner of the British. In the latter year, he threw in his fortunes with the Mahrattás, who restored him to a fragment of his hereditary dominions. The Emperor was blinded and imprisoned by Rohilla rebels. He was afterwards rescued by the Mahrattás, but was virtually a prisoner in their hands till 1803, when the Mahrattá power was overthrown by Lord Lake. Sháh Alam died in 1806, and was succeeded by his son.

1806-1837. Akbar II., who succeeded only to the nominal dignity, and lived till 1837; when he was followed by

1837-1862. Muhammad Bahádur Sháh, the seventeenth Moghal Emperor, and last of the race of Timúr. For his complicity in the Mutiny of 1857, he was deposed and banished for life to Rangoon, where he died, a British State prisoner, in 1862.

Later Events.

1859. Assumption of the direct Government of India by the Crown.

1876. Visit of His Imperial Majesty King Edward VII., as Prince of Wales, to Delhi.

1877. 1st January. Proclamation of the Imperial title at Delhi.

CHAPTER VII

LIST OF THE OBJECTS OF ARCHÆOLOGICAL INTEREST IN AND ROUND DELHI, WITH A BRIEF NOTE ON THE GENERAL CHARACTERISTICS OF THEIR ARCHITECTURE.

THE Muhammadan architecture of Delhi is divided by Mr Fergusson into two styles—the Pathan, earlier and later, and the Moghal.

Properly speaking, the earliest buildings at the Kutab are not really the works of Pathan but of Turki princes; but though the inherent genius of these may have had something to do with their architectural achievements, they were probably acquainted only with the palaces and mosques of Ghor and Ghazni, and perhaps some of Western Central Asia, and the existing nomenclature of Pathan may therefore stand unchanged. The various structures which survive are, however, capable of being further classified than was done by Mr Fergusson, and this subdivision may be made as follows :—

(*A*) *The Earliest Pathan Style*, 1193-1320 A.D., a style marked in the commencement by the use of both Hindu materials and Hindu construction, and by the adaptation of much beautiful surface ornament, and culminating in works of pure Muhammadan construction, with true arches, but still retaining adapted Hindu ornament. Material used is chiefly pale sandstone, white marble also being used in the last example, the Alai Darwazah.

This class includes the Kuwat-ul-Islam Mosque, the Kutab Minar, the tombs of Sultan Ghári and Altamsh, and ends in the Alai Darwazah, in which white marble is first used, and the Khizri Mosque at Nizam-ud-din. The tombs of the Emperors Balban and Ala-ud-din are too ruined to allow of their being specially mentioned in this class.

Among the architectural achievements of Europe during the same period may be mentioned the Cathedrals of Notre Dame of Paris, Rheims, Lincoln (built between 1186 and 1200, and therefore corresponding almost exactly in date with the original mosque of Kutab-ud-din), Salisbury, Ely, Westminster Abbey, Cologne and Strassburg, and in Italy the great churches of Sienna Orvieto and Florence. Giotto's famous campanile dates from 1324, and is therefore just a hundred years later in date than the Kutab Minar. The mosques of Kalaun (1234 A.D.), and Sultan Hasan (1356) at Cairo, were also built during this period.

(*B*) *The Middle Pathan Style* (1320-1414), of a severer, and latterly, from 1355, of a very severe type. The former comprises the tombs of Tughlak Shah and Kabir-ud-din (p. 287), in which use is still made of red sandstone, and that is even relieved by a sparing use of white marble, the walls having a very considerable slope; and the latter includes the buildings of the time of Firoz Shah, viz., the Jama mosque of that prince in the Kotila of Firazobad, the Kadam Sharif, built by him round the grave of his son; the Kalan mosque of Delhi, and the mosques of Nizam-ud-din village, Begampur and Khirki, the tomb of Firoz Shah at Hauz Khas, and the shrine of Shah Alam at Wazirabad, the walls, which slope at a less acute angle, and the roofs being all constructed of stone and cement, plastered outside with mortar stained black with cocoanut oil, and the mosques, many of which are built on high platforms, and all of which are without minarets, containing inside a court or more courts than one, surrounded by arcades of arches, whose heads rise from a slightly projecting angle, and are borne by plain squared columns of local quartzose rock, relieved above by broad dripstones and parapets of the same. In the earlier works of the period the dome began to take a prominent place, but in the later it again became entirely a subordinate feature in the general effect, though more prominent in the case of the latest of all, the tomb of Firoz Shah himself.

In point of date of construction, we may compare with the buildings of this period the Cathedrals of Lichfield, Antwerp, and Milan, the earlier portions of Winchester as rebuilt, Westminster Hall (1292-1348), and the beautiful church of St Ouen at Rouen (1318-1339).

(*C*) *The Later Pathan Style* (1414-1556), which may be held to extend to the buildings of Sher Shah, and really includes several sub-classes of buildings. In these the buildings began to be raised on high plinths, and the dome assumed a prominent place, as did external arcades in the case of tombs at least; and while sombre plaster was discarded for cut stone and even red sandstone, the ornamentation first used consisted principally of encaustic tiles on the exterior, and plaster mouldings in the interior—in one notable instance (p. 244), on the exterior also—and not till towards the end of the style of decoration by means of white or other marble. The specimens of this style in order of date will be found in the table annexed to this chapter. The following famous buildings in Europe may be referred to as cœval with them—Seville Cathedral (1410-1560), the Doge's Palace, Venice (1486-1550), and St Peter's, Rome (1506-1564).

(*D*) *The Moghal Style in its development and full strength*, 1556-1660. This commences with the reign of Akbar, and the mausoleum of his father, the Emperor Humayun, the tomb of Isa Khan (1547 A.D.) being the last work in the old style, to the middle period of which, however, the tomb of Adham Khan (1566) again reverted. The earlier works are of red sandstone, and the latter of red sandstone and marble, and culminate in the splendid structures of the Delhi Fort and Palace, and the Jama Masjid; in the last, black marble was first used upon domes, which in this style assumed the most prominent place in tombs and mosques, while graceful arcades of columns and piers, bearing engrailed arches, were introduced in covered buildings, secular and religious, and in the first decoration of extreme beauty in the forms of panels carved with flowers, and pillars and panels inlaid with precious stones, known as pietra-dura work, was finally adopted.

These, and many other buildings at Delhi, were

all constructed during the brief, glorious space of twenty years, from 1638 to 1658; and as most of the beautiful buildings of Agra, too, were built during the same period, it must be considered one of the most brilliant epochs in the architectural history of the world. There is nothing in Europe which corresponds exactly with the buildings of these two decades in point of time, Inigo Jones' great design for Whitehall being of earlier date, and Wren's St Paul's of later date. The Palace of Versailles, and Louis XIV.'s additions to the Louvre, are not, however, far removed from them in time, and the Escurial corresponds with some of the earlier buildings of this period, and more closely with those of Fatahpur Sikri.

(*E*) *The Moghal Style in its decadence*, 1660-1760. In this style the bold effects of sandstone and marble, and the bold contrasts of colours in these materials were abandoned, and mere prettiness was sought for in decorative effect, and particularly by the use of fawn-coloured sandstone and pale gray marble. Tapering round columns also came into use. (It may be that this was partly caused by the loss to Delhi of her former supplies of red sandstone and white marble from the quarries near Agra and Jeypur.) Finally, art degenerated wholly into mere decoration, as on the marble doors and panels of the tombs at Nizam-ud-din and of Ghazi-ud-din. Lack of money, fortunately, prevented the creation at Delhi of the architectural monstrosities which disfigure Lucknow.

The palaces of the Delhi nobles, which must no

doubt have contained fine courtyards, have almost entirely disappeared. This is due partly to the custom by which, in the earlier days, the property of each noble passed on his death to the emperor, and partly to the circumstance that many had naturally been built as near as possible to the Royal Palace, and were removed in the clearances made in front of that, after 1857. The annexed tables will serve as an index of all objects of special archæological and architectural interest in and around Delhi.

LIST OF OBJECTS OF ARCHÆOLOGICAL INTEREST AT AND AROUND DELHI.

I.—HINDU PERIOD, PREVIOUS TO 1193 A.D.[1]

No.	Situation.	Name of Building or other Object.	Date.	Page to which reference should be made.
1	The Kutab	The Iron Lat or Pillar	550 A.D.	264
2 & 3	Three miles south-east of Tughlakabad	The Band of Arrangpur and Tank of Suraj-Rund	730 A.D.	292
4 & 5	Surrounding the Kutab	Kila Rai Pithora and Lal Kot	1180 A.D.	255-6

II.—MUHAMMADAN PERIOD, SUBSEQUENT TO 1193 A.D.

A.—Earliest Pathan Style, 1193-1320.

No.	Situation.	Name of Building or other Object.	Date.	Page to which reference should be made.
6	The Kutab	The Mosque of Kuwat-ul-Islam. Additions by Ala-ud-din, 1310 C.	1193-1230	258
7	The Kutab	The Kutab Minar. Two top storeys rebuilt by Firoz Shah	1193-1230	265
8	Mahrauli	Hauz Shamsi	1220 C.	284
9	Malakpur, three miles west of the Kutab	The Tomb of Sultan Ghari	1231	284
10	Mahrauli	Grave of Khwaja Kutab-ud-din Bakhtiari Kaki	1235	280
11	The Kutab	Tomb of Emperor Altamsh	1236 C.	269
12	Malakpur (see No. 9)	Tombs of Sultan Rukn-ud-din and Muizz-ud-din	1238 C.	285
13	Delhi, near the Kalan Masjid	Grave of Sultan Raziyah	1242	66
14	Mahrauli, east of Jamali Mosque (No. 47)	Ruined Tomb of the Emperor Balban	1280 C.	278
15	Siri	Walls of Citadel built by Ala-ud-din Khilji	1303	253
16	Nizam-ud-din	Lal Mahal	1305 C.	235
16A	Two and a half miles south-west of Safdar Jang	Hauz Khas or Alai	1305 C.	252
17	The Kutab	The Alai Darwazah of Ala-ud-din	1310	270
18	The Kutab	Ruined Tomb of Ala-ud-din Khilji, died 1315	1312 C.	272

[1] The Lats of Asoka, which were brought to Delhi from outside, are omitted from this list.

B.—Middle Pathan Style, 1320-1414.

19	Tughlakabad, five miles east of the Kutab	Fort of Tughlakabad	1320	288
20	Tughlakabad, five miles east of the Kutab	Tomb of Tughlak Shah	1320	289
21	Tughlakabad, five miles east of the Kutab	Fort of Adilabad	1330 C.	291
22	Near Begampur Mosque (see No. 33)	Tomb of Kabir-ud-din	1330 C.	287
23	Nizam-ud-din	Mosque and Grave of Shekh Nizam-ud-din Aulia	1325	238
24				
25	Nizam-ud-din	Tomb of Amir Khusrau	1325	241
25A	Khirki (see No. 34)	Sat Palah Sluice of Muhammad Tughlak Shah	1326	287
26	South of Delhi Gate of city	Kotila, Firoz Shah	1354-70	222
27	South of Delhi Gate of city	Firozabad		225
28	One mile east of Begampur (No. 33)	Gate of Chiragh Delhi Dargah	1373	287
29	Outside city to south-west of Lahore Gate	Kadam Sharif	1374	63
30	On Delhi Ridge	Kushk-i-Shikar or Jahannuma	1375	56
		Mosques known as—		
31	In Delhi, near Turkman Gate	Kalan Masjid	1365-1390	65
32	Nizam-ud-din	Sanjar Masjid		235
33	One mile east of road to Kutab, two miles south of Safdar Jang.	Begampur Masjid		251
34	One and half miles south-east of No. 33, and one and a half miles north of road from Kutab to Tughlakabad.	Khirki Masjid		286
		Tombs and Mosque known as—		
35	West of Delhi Jail.	Chausath Khambhe	1365-1390	243
36	Wazirabad at end of Ridge, three miles north of Delhi.	Shah Alam		59
37	Hauz Khas, two and a half miles south-west of Safdar Jang (see No. 16A).	Tomb of Firoz Shah	1380 C.	252
38	West of Siri.	Makhdum Sabzawar	1400 C.	245

No.	Situation.	Name of Building or other Object.	Date.	Page to which reference should be made.
	C.—Later Pathan Style, 1414-1556.			
39	One and a half miles south of road from Nizam-ud-din to Safdar Jang.	Tomb of Mubarik Shah	1443	244
40	Half a mile north of road from Nizam-ud-din to Safdar Jang	Tomb of Muhammad Shah	1445	244
41	In Chiragh Delhi (see No. 28)	Tomb of Bahlol Lodi	1486	288
42	One mile south of No. 39	Moth-ki Masjid	1488	245
43	Near Dargah of Khwaja Kutab-ud-din Mahrauli	Rajon-ki-Báin—Well with Tomb and Mosque	1516	280
44	North of Khairpur (see No. 45)	Tomb of Sikandar Lodi	1517	244
45	Khairpur, 300 yards north of No. 40	Gate and Mosque	1530	244
46	South of Nos. 26, 27	Purana Kila and two gateways known as Lal Darwazah	1533-1545	228, 226
47	South-east of Kutab enclosure	Jamali Mosque	1536	278
48	Adjoining Alai Darwazah (No. 17)	Tomb of Imam Zámin	1540	272
49, 50	Purana Kila (No. 46)	Mosque and Pavilion (Sher Mandal) of Sher Shah	1541	228
51	At north-east corner of Delhi Fort and Palace	Salimgarth Fort	1546	40
52	Adjoining Arab Sarai (No. 55) on west	Tomb and Mosque of Isa Khan	1547	234
53	Adjoining Arab Sarai (No. 55) on east	Tomb and Mosque of Afsarwalla	1550 C.	234
	D.—The Moghal Style in its Development and Full Strength, 1556-1660. *Reign of Akbar*, 1556-1605.			
54	Four miles south of Delhi, and two miles south of Purana Kila	Mausoleum of the Emperor Humayun	1556-1569	229

	Near Agra	*Fatahpur Sikri*	1570-1580	
55	In front of No. 54	Arab Sarai	1560	230
56	Opposite bend of road to No. 46	Lal Chauk or Khair-ul-Manazil	1561	228
	Agra	*Fort restored*	1565	
57	In front of Arab Sarai (No. 55)	Bu Halimah Garden	1565 c.	230
58	At Kutab, south-west of Kutab enclosure	Tomb of Adham Khan	1566	279
59	Nizam-ud-din	Tomb of Azam Khan	1566	241
		Reign of Jahangir, 1605-1627		
60	Nizam-ud-din	Tomb known as Chausath Khambhe	1610	243
61	Arab Sarai (No. 55)	East gate of place		230
	Sikandra, near Agra	*Mausoleum of Akbar completed*	1613	
62	Shahji Sarai, east of Begampur (No. 33)	Grave-Stone of Farid Khan	1615	227
63	At south-east corner of Garden of Humayun's Mausoleum	Tomb of Fahim Khan	1624	233
64	South of Arab Sarai (No. 55)	Tomb of Khan-i-Khanan	1626	233
		Reign of Shah Jahan, 1627-1658		
65	South of Firozabad (No. 27)	Palace of Mahabat Khan	1630-40 c.	227
	Shahdara, near Lahore	*Mausoleum of Jahangir*	1630-40	
	Agra	*Khas Mahal*		
	Agra	*The Taj Mausoleum*	1632-1654	
66	Delhi, or Shahjahanabad	Walls of Fort of Lal Kila and buildings inside it	1638-1648	20
67	Delhi, or Shahjahanabad	Jama Masjid	1648-1650	44
	Agra	*Moti Masjid*		
68	Delhi, or Shahjahanabad	City Walls	1644-1649	55
69	Delhi, west end of Chandni Chauk	Fatahpur Mosque	1650	53
70	Delhi, Lahore Gate	Sarhandi Mosque	1648-1660	63
71	Delhi, centre Chandni Chauk	Jahanara Garden and Karavan Sarai	1648-1660	52
72	In Sabzi Mandi Quarter, to north-west of city	Roshanara Garden	1648-1660	61

No.	Situation.	Name of Building or other Object.	Date.	Page to which reference should be made.
		Reign of Aurangzeb, 1658-1707		
73	Delhi Palace	Moti Masjid	1659	39
74	Delhi Palace	Outworks of Fort Gates	1665 c.	22
	Agra	*Probably Taj Screen*		
75	Delhi, in Daryaganj, south of the Palace	Zinat-ul-Masajid Mosque	1700	68
		Eighteenth Century		
76	Mahrauli	Moti Masjid of Kutab Dargah	1709	281
77	Mahrauli	Grave of Shah Alam Bahadur Shah	1712	281
78	Delhi	Sonahri Masjid of Roshan-ud-Daulah, in the Chandni Chauk	1721	50
79	Delhi, two miles south of Ajmir Gate	Observatory of Raja Jai Singh	1724	247
80	North-west of Sabzi Mandi	Gate—Tirpulia—and Garden of Mahaldar Khan	1728	61
81	Delhi, inside Kashmir Gate	Fakhr-ul-masajid Mosque	1728	68
82	Chiragh Delhi. (See No. 28)	Enclosure walls of Chiragh Delhi	1729	287
83	Delhi, near Ajmir Gate	College, Mosque, and Tomb of Ghazi-ud-din Khan	1745 c.	64
84	Delhi, Feiz Bazar leading to Delhi Gate	Sonahri Masjid of Roshan-ud-daulah	1745	68
85	Nizam-ud-din	Grave of Muhammad Shah	1748	240
86	Delhi, outside Kashmir Gates	Kudsia Gardens	1750	54
87	Delhi, near Delhi Gate of Fort	Sonahri Masjid of Javed Khan	1751	43
88	Safdar Jang, six miles south-west of Delhi on Kutab Road	Mausoleum of Nawab Safdar Jang	1753	246
89	Three-quarters of a mile south-east of No. 88	Grave of Najaf Khan	1781	249

Nineteenth Century.

90	On right of road from Purana Kila to Humayun's Mausoleum	Lal Bangala	1800 c.	229
91	Mahrauli, Kutab Dargah	Grave of Shah Alam II.	1806	281
92	Delhi	Present walls of city.	1805-1835	55
93	Nizam-ud-din	Grave of Mirza Jehangir	1832	240
94	Mahrauli Kutab Dargah	Grave of Akbar Shah II.	1837	281

ADDENDUM

The inscriptions on the front and rear of the Delhi Telegraph Memorial (p. 18) are as follows :—

FRONT.

Erected on the 19th April 1902, by Members of the Telegraph Department, to commemorate the loyal and devoted services of the Delhi Telegraph Office Staff, on the eventful 11th May 1857. On that day two young Signallers,

WILLIAM BRENDISH AND
J. W. PILKINGTON

remained on duty till ordered to leave, and by telegraphing to Amballa information of what was happening at Delhi, rendered invaluable service to the Punjab Government.

In the words of Sir Robert Montgomery—

"The Electric Telegraph has saved India."

REAR.

The Delhi Telegraph Office Staff on the 11th May 1857 consisted of the following :—

CHARLES TODD, Assistant-in-Charge, killed near Cable House, on left bank river Jumna, on the morning of the above date, while endeavouring to restore telegraphic communication with Meerut.

W. BRENDISH, Signaller, retired 1st September 1896.

J. W. PILKINGTON, Signaller, voluntarily returned to Telegraph Office from Flag Staff Tower, and signalled despatch to Commander-in-Chief, containing full report of Mutiny. Taken prisoner after doing so, but escaped. Died, Roorkee, 24th March 1867.

ERRATUM

Page 202, note 1.—*For* "Marquis of Wellesley," *read* "Marquis of Hastings."

INDEX

NOTE—*The principal reference under each important word is printed in special type. Reference is not made here to the Table of Architectural Remains, attached to Chapter VII., as that is itself an index.*

D

E

F

G

H

I

J

Eighteen Years in the Khyber,

1879-1898.

WITH PERSONAL REMINISCENCES OF SERVICE IN INDIA, AND ESPECIALLY AMONG THE TRIBES ON OUR N.W. FRONTIER.

By Colonel Sir ROBERT WARBURTON, K.C.I.E., C.S.I., etc.

With Map and Illustrations. 8vo. 16s.

". . his excellent book. . . . The sketches of native character and habits with which his book abounds would alone render it invaluable to all who desire to understand the problem of the Gate of India. . . . Warburton's arguments ought to carry great weight with the Indian Government, for no man could have been more successful in managing the Kyber."—*World.*

The Making of a Frontier.

FIVE YEARS' EXPERIENCES AND ADVENTURES IN GILGIT, HUNZA NAGAR, CHITRAL, AND THE EASTERN HINDU-KUSH.

By Colonel ALGERNON DURAND, C.B., C.I.E.,

British Agent at Gilgit, 1889-1894; Military Secretary to the Viceroy of India, 1894-1899.

With Portrait, Map, and Illustrations. 8vo. 16s.

"A work which is full of life and movement, and gives us many quaint glimpses of the life of strange peoples. It is modestly written, as becomes the narration of the author's surprising success in achieving great results for the Empire, and is full of humorous incident . . . it ought to find a place in the library of every young officer who wants instruction in the art of making a reputation for himself and a new province for the Empire. All that is needed is the opportunity, brains, and pluck—and a broken telegraph behind him."—*Pall Mall Gazette.*

Among the Celestials.

NARRATIVE OF TRAVELS IN MANCHURIA, ACROSS THE GOBI DESERT AND THROUGH THE HIMALAYAS TO INDIA.

Abridged from "The Heart of a Continent," with additions.

By Captain FRANCIS YOUNGHUSBAND, C.I.E.,

(Gold Medalist, R.G.S.)

Author of *The Relief of Chitral.*

With Map and Illustrations. Crown 8vo. 7s. 6d.

Haunts and Hobbies of an Indian Official.

By MARK THORNHILL,

Author of "The Adventures of a Magistrate in the Indian Mutiny."

Large Crown 8vo. 6s.

"Worthy of being classed with 'White of Selborne.' . . . Hardly a page or paragraph can be spared."—*Scotsman.*

A Naturalist in Indian Seas;

OR, FOUR YEARS WITH THE ROYAL INDIAN MARINE SURVEY SHIP "INVESTIGATOR."

By A. ALCOCK, M.B., LL.D., F.R.S.,

Superintendent of the Indian Museum and Professor of Zoology in the Medical College of Bengal.

With Illustrations. Demy 8vo. 18s. *net.*

Leaflet of Special Information regarding the Coronation Darbar at Delhi, Christmas, 1902, and New Year, 1903.

Preliminary.—Though the Christmas-tide sun is decidedly hot at Delhi in the middle of the day, and makes the protection of a light sun-hat or umbrella desirable, the evenings and mornings are cold, especially after rain, and may be found very cold by visitors not accustomed to live in tents. Specially warm clothing, such as would be used in November in England, should be invariably worn in the mornings and at night; for the day-time any moderately light tweed suit is suitable, such as would be usually worn in an English summer, except during the very hottest weeks. If a drive or staying out of doors is likely to be prolonged to sunset, a light greatcoat should always be taken with one. Visitors not accustomed to eastern conditions should wear a really broad protecting flannel-belt day and night, and if occupying tents should see that the ground is thickly strewn with straw or grass under the carpets, which should never be trodden with unslippered or unbooted feet. Any little indisposition should be at once attended to, all sight-seeing being given up until it has been got rid of. As far as possible, only soda-water and other manufactured waters should be drunk, and drinking water should be avoided except in private houses. Visitors should remember that they will need bedding for railway journeys, at the camps in Delhi, and in many hotels; this can be most conveniently purchased in Bombay, and all that need be taken from England is an eider-down quilt.

The Central Camp at Delhi, enclosing in its midst that of the Viceroy, is situated on the parade ground of the Old Delhi Cantonment (p. 78[1]), west of the Ridge, and between it and the canal from the Najafgarh Jhil, and lies nearly two miles from the Kashmir Gate of the city (p. 89), and two and a half miles from the Railway Station. It will be connected with all points of interest by a light railway; and it may be expected that all such points will, at all times, be easy of access. At the back of the Viceroy's own camp is the State Guest House, built for the occupation of distinguished visitors to Delhi, and in which the Viceroy will reside during the Darbar proceedings. On the south side of the Viceroy's camp are the camps of the Governor of Bombay, of the Commander-in-Chief in India, and of the Lieutenant-Generals commanding the four

[1] The references are to "Delhi," by Mr H. C. Fanshawe.

Army Corps, with the Press Camps on their flanks; and probably the camp of H.R.H. the Duke of Connaught will be here also. On the north side are the camps of the Governor of Madras and the Lieutenant-Governor of the Punjab, and above the Grand Trunk Road those of the Lieutenant-Governors of the United Provinces, Bengal and Burmah, and of the various Chief Commissioners and Agents to the Governor-General, who will be present. North of all these will be the Visitors' Camp for those who can make their own arrangements for tents and messing. The central Telegraph and Post-Offices will occupy the first camp on the left after passing the Ridge. There will also be a Branch of the Bank of Bengal in the Central Camp. All this will be clear from the accompanying map.

Proceeding north-west across the Najafgarh Canal (p. 78), the military portion of the assemblage and the site of the Coronation Darbar are reached (p. 79). On the north side of the road are the camps of the 1st, 2nd, and 3rd Brigades, of the Staff, and of the Pioneers and the Supply Department, and on the south side are the camps of the Viceroy's escort and the Volunteers. Below the former is the Polo ground in three portions. The Coronation Amphitheatre, over four miles from Delhi, is reached by three roads from the Grand Trunk Road. The State Procession to the Darbar will be along that through the military camps, the first met after crossing the canal. Lying west of the amphitheatre, and reaching up to the Grand Trunk Road at a point nearly five miles from Delhi, is the Review ground, and beyond it and round the site of the battle of Badli-ki-Sarai (pp. 60 and 118) is the camp of the Cavalry Division. The Imperial Service Troops and the great Indian Feudatories who will be present at the Darbar will be encamped for the most part on sites south of the Grand Trunk Road between the Review ground and the Najafgarh Canal. The camps of other chiefs will be situated on the high road which leads westwards from the Lahore Gate of the city (p. 63), and southwards from the Ajmir Gate (p. 64). The location of the various camps as at present (October) fixed, is indicated on the map.

The amphitheatre prepared for the Coronation Darbar on 1st January 1903 is of horseshoe shape. The daïs on which the Viceroy will be seated is situated at the head of the shoe, and is approached by a drive inside. In the centre will be the Imperial Standard, and round the curved sides will be seated the Ruling Chiefs and other distinguished persons, English and Native, present at the Darbar. The amphitheatre will provide sitting room for about 8000 spectators, and standing room for perhaps 4000 more. Among the invited guests will be a group of veterans who fought on the British side at Delhi and Lucknow, 1857-58, and of representatives of natives specially distinguished for their loyalty at that time. On the occasion of the Darbar the British troops will be drawn up in front of the amphitheatre, the Artillery at the sides, and the native troops in the rear. All the principal Ruling Chiefs of India will be present at the Darbar, including the Nizam of Hydrabad, the Gaikwar of Barodah, the Maharajas of Mysore, Travancore, Udaipur, Kashmir, Gwalior, Indore, Jaipur, Bikanir, Bundi, Kotah, Jodhpur, Jaisalmir, Alwar, Rewa, Orchha, Rutlam, Pattiala, the Begum of Bhopal, the Rajas of Nabha, Kapurthalla, Jind, Sirmur, and Kuch Behar, and the Nawabs of Tonk and Bhawalpur. These chiefs rule over territories very much larger in extent than those of the whole German Empire.

The number of troops present at Delhi during the Darbar will be about 40,000. They will be assembled for extensive manœuvres about 15th November in two army corps, under the commands of Major Generals Egerton and Wodehouse. The Commander-in-Chief, Lord Kitchener, will himself be Chief Umpire. The review of the troops on the Review ground by the Viceroy is likely to be held on either the 8th or 9th January 1903. In addition to the Polo Tournament, for which three grounds have been prepared, there will be various displays of tent-pegging, jumping, etc., and doubtless there will also be special military sports.

There will be three visitors' camps, one practically a private camp for the Viceroy's guests at Maiden's Hotel (p. 13), one in the Central Camp as above noticed, and one outside the Kashmir Gate, where visitors will be accommodated and messed for a fixed daily charge. It is perhaps hardly necessary to observe that there are likely to be heavy and early demands upon the accommodation afforded by the last camp.

The Art Exhibition is situated in the Kudsia Garden, outside the Kashmir Gate (p. 54). Large temporary additions are being made to the Diwan-i-Am and Diwan-i-Khas halls, in the Palace (pp. 28 and 34), to enable them to afford due space for the Chapter of the Indian Orders, which will be held in the former, and the State Ball, which will demand the services of both. The processions to the Viceroy's camp upon Lord Curzon's arrival at Delhi, on 29th December, to the Coronation Darbar on 1st January, and to the Chapter of the Orders on 3rd January, will doubtless be exceptionally brilliant pageants, and the review of the troops will be one of the most splendid ever held in India, and will include, for the first time, the Imperial Service troops of the great feudatory States.

Detailed information as to the exact time of all ceremonies and sights will doubtless be available to all visitors upon their arrival in India or at Delhi.

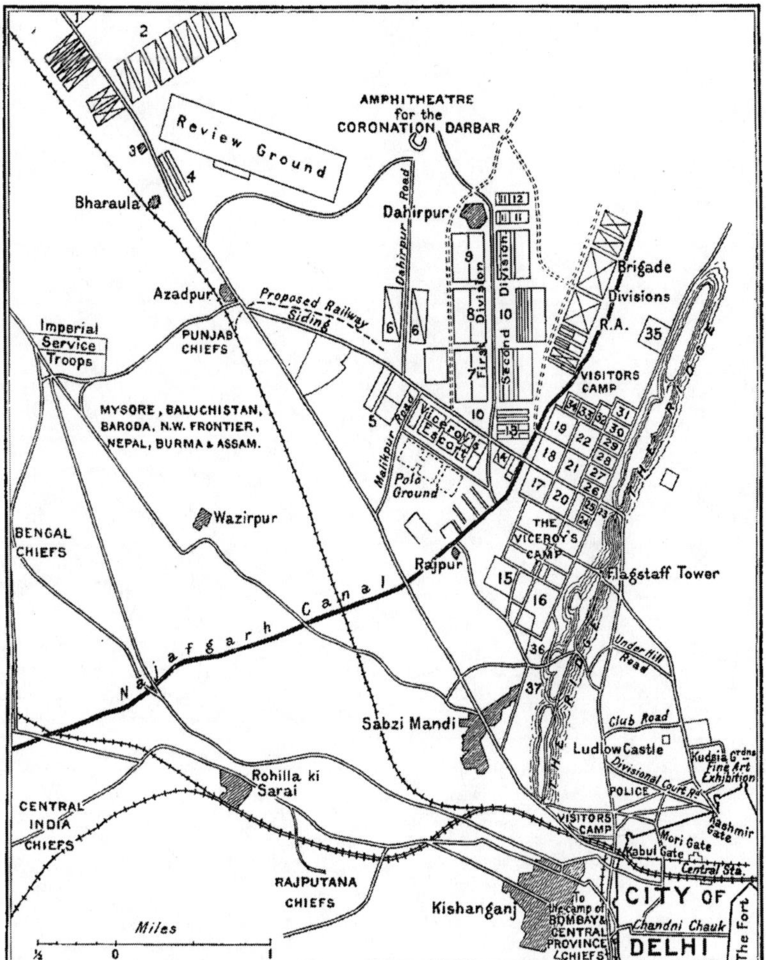

1. Field Hospitals
2. Cavalry Division
3. Badli ki Sarai
4. Royal Field Artillery
5. Volunteers
6. Supply Depot
7. 1st Brigade
8. 2nd Brigade
9. 3rd Brigade
10. Staff
11. Pioneers 2nd Division
12. Pioneers 1st Division
13. Sappers & Miners
14. Executive Committee
15. Governor of Bombay
16. Commander-in-Chief & Lieutenant-Generals
17. Governor of Madras
18. L.G. of Bengal
19. L.G. of United Provinces
20. L.G. of Punjab
21. L.G. of Burma
22. Spare
23. Central Telegraph & Central Post-Offices
24. D.G. Telegraphs
25. D.G Post Office
26. C.C., Assam
27. C.C., Central Provinces
28. Resident, Hyderabad
29. Resident, Mysore
30. A.G.G., Rajputana
31. A.G.G., Central India
32. A.G.G., NorthWest Frontier Prov.
33. A.G.G., Baluchistan
34. Resident at Baroda
35. Hospital
36. British Press
37. Native Press

The official programme, as at present (October) arranged, is as follows:—

1902.		
29*th December*,	Monday	Arrival of the Viceroy, and State Procession to the Vice-regal Camp.
30*th* ,,	Tuesday	Opening of Art Exhibition.
1903.		
1*st January*,	Thursday	Coronation Darbar.
2*nd* ,,	Friday	Illumination of City and Fort.
3*rd* ,,	Saturday	Chapter of the Indian Orders, held in the Diwan-i-Am in the Palace.
4*th* ,,	Sunday	State Church Service.
5*th* ,,	Monday	Probable Review of Troops of Native States.
6*th* ,,	Tuesday	State Ball in the Diwan-i-Khas in the Palace.
8*th* ,, or 9*th* ,,	Thursday or Friday	Review of British and Native Troops.
10*th* ,,	Saturday	State Departure of the Viceroy.